The Sense of an Interior

The Sense of an Interior

FOUR WRITERS AND THE ROOMS
THAT SHAPED THEM

Diana Fuss

Routledge
New York & London

Published in 2004 by
Routledge
29 West 35th Street
New York, NY 10001
www.routledge-ny.com

Published in Great Britain by
Routledge
11 New Fetter Lane
London EC4P 4EE
www.routledge.co.uk

Printed in the United States of America on acid-free paper.

10 9 8 7 6 5 4 3 2 1

Library of Congress Cataloging in Publication Data

Fuss, Diana, [DATE]–
     The sense of an interior : four writers and the rooms that shaped them /
Diana Fuss.
          p. cm.
Includes bibliographical references and index.
     ISBN 0-415-96990-5 (alk. paper)
     1. Literary landmarks. 2. Dickinson, Emily, 1830–1886—Homes and
haunts. 3. Freud, Sigmund, 1856–1939—Homes and haunts. 4. Keller,
Helen, 1880–1968—Homes and haunts. 5. Proust, Marcel, 1871–1922—
Homes and haunts. I. Title.
     PN164.F87   2004
     809—dc22
                                                                    2003022823

ISBN 0–415–96990–5 (hb)

Contents

Acknowledgments

IT IS NOT EVERY DAY that one gets to sit in Emily Dickinson's cupola or to lie on Sigmund Freud's couch. Some research projects are pure wish fulfillment, intellectual enterprises that gratify both mind and fancy. This book was just such a guilty pleasure, the culmination of a persistent desire to occupy, if only for a moment, the private lives of celebrated authors.

I have many people to thank for indulging my passion for all things interior. Curators, archivists, architects, and photographers have participated, in ways both small and large, to the texture and tone of the book. For the Dickinson chapter, I thank Cindy Dickinson, curator of the Dickinson Homestead, for her on-site assistance and her meticulous reading of early drafts. Gregory Farmer, project manager for the Martha Dickinson Bianchi Trust, helped me navigate my way through Austin and Susan Dickinson's house, the Evergreens, before it was restored and opened to the public, and also provided invaluable feedback on an early version of the Dickinson chapter. Frank Ward photographed the Dickinson Homestead, devoting many hours to a careful visual documentation of the space. I also gratefully acknowledge the Amherst College Library, the Jones Library, Inc. of Amherst, the Trustees of Amherst College, and the Houghton Library of Harvard University.

The chapter on Freud's office is a joint venture that in many ways marks the origin of the book proper. I owe my greatest thanks to Joel Sanders, who first commissioned the research on Berggasse 19 for an edited collection of essays on architecture, and who later came on board to help bring the piece to fruition. There are few more gratifying intellectual exercises than collaborative ones, and I consider myself very fortunate indeed to have learned the fundamentals of architectural design from one of New York City's most talented architects. In 1995 we interviewed Edmund Engelman, the photographer responsible for visually preserving Freud's consulting room and study. Mr. Engelman cordially invited us into his home, patiently provided information about Vienna in the 1930s, and kindly granted permission to reproduce some of his photographs (a courtesy later generously extended by his son, Thomas Engelman). Several curators further aided us in our endeavors: Lydia Marinelli of the Freud Haus in Vienna, Erica Davies, J. Keith Davies, and Michael Molnar of the Freud Museum in London, and Christian Witt-Doring of the MAK (Österreichisches Museum für angewandte Kunst) in Vienna. All five provided invaluable assistance on numerous research trips to London and Vienna, facilitating the time-consuming process of documenting the physical space.

Of the four literary houses considered in this book, only one remains a private residence. I thank Daniel and Asami Green for so graciously according me access to Helen Keller's former home in Easton, Connecticut. My time spent with the Greens and their two daughters was one of the highlights of my research; I marvel at their forbearance with a form of academic sleuthing that I am sure, to many, might look more like snooping. The American Foundation for the Blind opened up its library and granted permission to publish a number of photographs from the Helen Keller Archives. In particular I would like to thank Jessica Mathewson, library and information resources manager at the AFB, for her assistance in accessing some of the more obscure materials on the construction and furnishings of Arcan Ridge.

My last chapter, on Marcel Proust's bedroom in Paris, was researched and written during a time of great national and international anxiety. I am grateful to the Banque SNVB, the current occupant of 102 boulevard Haussmann, for granting me open access to the entire Proust apartment, despite heightened security and the closure of *le salon Marcel Proust*. Brigitte Guillaumot, director of communications at the SNVB, was unstinting in her support of this book, opening doors that appeared to be closed, and creating research opportunities that suddenly made the project not only possible but intensely enjoyable. The Réunion des Musées Nationaux and the Bibliothèque nationale de France offered further archival assistance, while Jean-Marie Bruson, curator at the Musée Carnavalet, provided invaluable information along the way, clarifying many of my questions about the Proust family furniture.

For the architectural drawings that accompany this book, I thank Mark Campbell of the School of Architecture at Princeton, Kim Yao, Edowa Shimizu and Ana McDonagh Sá of Joel Sanders, Architect, and Joel Sanders of Yale University for supervising the whole.

Earlier versions of two chapters have been previously published. Chapter One appeared as "Interior Chambers: The Emily Dickinson Homestead" in the journal *differences* 10:3 (Fall 1998): 1–46. Chapter Two appeared as "Berggasse 19: Inside Freud's Office" in a book called *STUD: Architectures of Masculinity*, ed. Joel Sanders (New York: Princeton Architectural Press, 1996), 112–39. My eight years of research were funded by generous fellowship support from the National Endowment for the Humanities, the American Council of Learned Societies, and Princeton University.

If it is true that scholarship is, by definition, the possibility of making errors, then I have many more people to thank for helping me to avoid especially egregious ones. This book could not have received cannier readers reports; Jennifer Fleissner, a literary critic, and Douglas Crimp, an art historian, together helped me strike a balance between the verbal and the visual. My writer's group—Sharon Marcus, Margaret Cohen, Anne Higonnet, and Nancy Ruttenburg—were introduced late to the project but provided such stimulating feedback that the completed book strongly bears the mark of their generous and shrewd interventions. Lee Edelman and Joe Litvak have watched this book unfold from the very beginning, bestowing guidance, inspiration, and conversation to fortify me along the way. Other readers proffered helpful advice on individual chapters, provided timely leads on archival materials, or offered thoughtful feedback on illustrations. I thank Renée Allen, Geoffrey Batchen, Linda Courtney, Susan Buck-Morss, Paul Franklin, Marjorie Garber, Diane Gibbons, William Gleason, Paul Gunther, Khristina Haddad, Fredric Jameson, Alan Kaplan, Thomas Keenan, Dominick LaCapra, Ankhi Mukherjee, John Newall, Julie Newmark, Jacques Rancière, James Richardson, and Naomi Schor. My favorite people to hang out with—Christine Faltum, Patricia Guglielmi, Beth Harrison, Kevin Mensch, Marcia Rosh, Nancy Shillingford, and Marilyn Yates—energize and inspire me everyday. To them a special thanks for their support. Finally, I express my deepest gratitude to my editor, Bill Germano, whose good counsel and good humor have sustained me from the very beginning of my career.

This has been, admittedly, a very difficult book to put aside. I fantasize about writing a sequel one day, adding to my list of writers' houses Edith Wharton's The Mount in Lennox, Massachusetts, Frederick Douglass's Cedar Hill in Washington, D.C., or Charles Darwin's Down House in Down, England. For now I offer the present volume as the first installment in perhaps a series of investigations into the subject of writers and their lairs.

It seems altogether fitting to dedicate this book to the two men who, over the course of my own writing career, have helped to define for me the very meaning of home: Daniel Fuss, who first encouraged me to take up the pen, and James Eatroff, who first encouraged me to put it down.

Diana Fuss
New York City

Introduction

The Sense of an Interior

THIS IS A BOOK ABOUT LITERARY HOUSES: houses that sheltered and shaped the imagination of writers. It is also a book about interiors: of minds, of bodies, and of dwellings. The "interior" of my title is an expansive space, encompassing both the psychological and the architectural meanings of interior life. The unexplored link between inner mind and inner dwelling forms the heart of this exploration of writers' houses, ordinary houses notable less for their architectural distinction than for their powerful guiding influence on the creative lives of their famous inhabitants.

While every act of composition takes place somewhere, many writers are oddly dismissive of the physical staging of their literary exercises. Virginia Woolf articulates the suspicion best: "Let us look at the writer. What do we see—only a person who sits with a pen in his hand in front of a sheet of paper? That tells us little or nothing."[1] In this view, creative genius is idealized as unfettered imagination, transcending base materiality, something cut loose from the mere bodily act of putting pen to paper—a mechanical gesture, Woolf insists, that tells us "little or nothing" about writers. My own book proceeds from the premise that Woolf's little or nothing in fact yields a great deal of something, knowledge not only about writers and their writing rituals but also about texts and their meanings. The theater of composition is not an empty space but a place animated by the artifacts, mementos, machines, books, and furniture that frame any intellectual labor. These material props, and the architectural spaces they define, are weighted

I

with personal significance, inscribed in equal measure by private fantasy and cultural memory. A writer's domestic interior opens a window onto both author and text, reminding us that what we may at first perceive to be the timeless and universal truth of writing cannot be so neatly extricated from the complex particularities of its spatial and material origins.

How do writers inhabit domestic space? How does domestic space inhabit writing? To answer these questions, I want here to bring literature and architecture into closer conversation. Few architectural studies explore how specific individuals creatively dwell in their houses. Architectural criticism focuses attention instead on the overall built environment, evacuating the house of its inhabitants. Social historians like Mark Girouard have criticized the prevailing tendency in architecture to study only the many different ways a habitation might be built, not the many different ways it might be occupied. Girouard's popular histories of private dwellings, most notably *Life in the English Country House* and *Life in the French Country House*, in effect seek to correct the problem by putting the household back in the house. Yet Girouard's household is comprised less of specific historical individuals than of general historical types (the nobility, the servants, the children, the tenants). Like Girouard, other architectural social histories—including two important feminist books, Gwendolyn Wright's *Building the Dream* and Dolores Hayden's *The Grand Domestic Revolution*—also tend to assume that domestic subjects are coextensive with their environments. Such studies take for granted that the cultural and economic realities manifested by various program types—rural cottage, suburban bungalow, or urban apartment—tell us everything we need to know about the individuals who occupy these different domiciles. Of all the architectural studies of the interior, Alice T. Friedman's *Women and the Making of the Modern House* perhaps comes closest to putting the occupant successfully back inside the dwelling. Friedman draws on professional correspondence, finan-

cial records, and personal diaries to document the lives of a handful of twentieth-century women who commissioned their own
houses. But even here, the critical emphasis lies not on the female
client's imaginative relation to her home but rather on her trou-
bled relation to her male architect. Once a house is inhabited and
its interior transformed by the detritus of everyday living, architectural scholars tend to lose interest in the life and activities of
the dwelling, preferring to return to the less metaphoric and mutable ground of program and design.[2]

If architectural historians treat the domestic interior more literally than figuratively, ignoring the metaphorical in favor of the
functional, literary critics, for their part, tend to treat the domestic interior as pure figuration. Literature scholars typically view
houses as metaphors for something else, and rarely as important
constructs in their own right. Judith Fryer's *Felicitous Space: The
Imaginative Structures of Edith Wharton and Willa Cather* approaches literary houses as "physical and spiritual correlatives,"
fictional edifices that complement the moral character of both
persons and nations. Marilyn Chandler's *Dwelling in the Text:
Houses in American Fiction* goes beyond correlation to direct
equivalency, identifying the domestic interior as alternately a
"mask," an "allegory," a "symbol," and a "trope." For Chandler,
"the house is invested with far more than literal significance."
Every house is, in reality, an outer embodiment of the inner life of
its occupant. Far from evacuating the house of subjectivity, as architectural scholars tend to do, literary critics present the house as
nothing other than subjectivity, a self under construction. Ellen
Eve Frank's *Literary Architecture: Essays Toward a Tradition* sees
the relation between literature and architecture in the same terms
as Fryer and Chandler, posing the house as an "analogue" for the
text and emphasizing the "correspondence or equivalence between the two arts." Seeking to establish a perfect equilibrium
between text and dwelling, Frank's premise that "literature is like
architecture" ends up subordinating architecture to literature

through the very power of the literary simile itself. Ultimately literature must incorporate architecture, Frank believes, in order to ground its own insubstantiality in the solidity of built structure. By taking domestic architecture as its analogue, literature claims the shelter and protection of a more concrete and durable aesthetic abode.[3]

My own study of the literary house challenges the too easy bifurcation between literal and figurative space reinforced by the separate disciplines of architecture and literature. To attribute substance and materiality to architecture, and imagination and metaphor to literature, misreads both artistic forms. It is by no means clear that literature is less embodied than architecture, or that architecture is less visionary than literature. Neither the materiality of writing nor the metaphysics of building can be quite so readily elided. My own view on the relation between literature and architecture is one part Martin Heidegger, one part Gaston Bachelard. Whereas Heidegger in "Poetically Man Dwells" argues that a poem is a special kind of building, the "original admission of dwelling," Bachelard in *The Poetics of Space* asserts that a building is a special kind of poetry, "one of the greatest powers of integration for the thoughts, memories and dreams of mankind."[4] A building and a poem are not substitutable, but they are not oppositional either; neither synonyms nor antonyms, architecture and literature work in tandem for the writer to create a rich and evolving sense of the interior. I am struck by how the seemingly intractable distinction between literary metaphor and architectural reality, between figure and ground, quickly falls away. For writers at least, the creative act of composition poses its own physical challenges, while the built environment offers up a store of metaphysical questions.

The following chapters are organized around spaces that I find especially interesting for how they mold the interior lives of the writers who inhabit them. I take as my main case studies four principal sites: Emily Dickinson's homestead in Amherst, Massachusetts, Sigmund Freud's study and consulting room in Vienna, Helen Keller's house in Easton, Connecticut, and Marcel Proust's bedroom in Paris. All four figures have long been subjects of pre-occupation for me, writers whose lives and works are as elusive as they are enthralling. This book is my attempt to encounter these writers where they live, to meet them, to whatever extent possible, on their own ground and on their own terms. At the same time, I am drawn in the first place to these particular writers because of their shared commitment to exploring the deepest recesses of human interiority, whether in the form of a poem, a case history, a memoir, or a novel. Across the divide of genre, gender, generation, and nation, these four very distinct literary figures pursue a common purpose: the exploration and appraisal of inner life. Admittedly, no two writers posed the same archival or theoretical challenge; in fact, from writer to writer, the sense of an interior turned out to be never quite the same. A book on four writers of the interior that appeared to have such strong thematic coherence in the beginning demonstrated to me in the end that there are as many ways to imagine inner life as there are to inhabit domestic space. Yet the sustained interest in interiority, the impassioned investment in life lived internally, links all four authors into a single coterie: writers who have made introspection itself their main subject of literary and cultural inquiry.

For these writers, the architectural dwelling is not merely something we inhabit, but something that inhabits us. They understand interiority itself as built structure, as "imagination merely made."[5] Nowhere is this more the case than in the modern conceptualization of the recesses of human memory, depicted in Emily Dickinson's poetry as the inner rooms of a house:

Remembrance has a Rear and Front.
'Tis something like a House—
It has a Garret also
For Refuse and the Mouse—

Besides the deepest Cellar
That ever Mason laid—
Look to it by it's Fathoms
Ourselves be not pursued—

At the very same historical moment that American architecture privatizes the residential dwelling, Dickinson domesticates the human mind, attributing to memory not only a rear and a front but a garret and a cellar. A private sanctuary where "ourselves be not pursued," memory becomes an interior storage place for personal "Refuse"—an equivocal term connoting both repression and denial. As a container of sublimated thoughts and desires, Dickinson's house of remembrance stands as one of the earliest articulations of what will later become known as the Freudian unconscious.[6]

In a section on "resistance and repression" in the *Introductory Lectures on Psycho-Analysis*, Freud himself depicts the unconscious as a bourgeois interior, with an entrance hall, a drawing-room, and a threshold in between:

> Let us therefore compare the system of the unconscious to a large entrance hall, in which the mental impulses jostle one another like separate individuals. Adjoining this entrance hall there is a second, narrower, room—a kind of drawing-room—in which consciousness, too, resides. But on the threshold between these two rooms a watchman performs his function: he examines the different mental impulses, acts as a censor, and will not admit them into the drawing-room if they displease him.[7]

In this second architectural model for the human interior, the ego in the drawing-room comports itself like a good bourgeois subject, unaware of the superego's vigilant struggles to keep the id from slipping unannounced into the room. In a surprising spatial inversion, the most interior space in the Freudian unconscious— the private drawing-room—turns out, in fact, to be the most conscious space. Sequestered on the inside, the Freudian ego relies on its inner censor to screen out the less refined of the "mental impulses" clamoring at the door for entry into consciousness. For Freud, as for Dickinson, interiority is always something more than just a metaphor. Interiority is also a mental structure constructed over time, with inner chambers and inner walls that exceed in strength and resistance the physical supports of any actual building.

The contemplation of memory as built structure links Proust and Keller as well, two writers for whom remembering is as much a spatial as a temporal drama. Proust, who once described his novel of remembrance as an unfinished Gothic cathedral,[8] pictures memory itself as a more humble country dwelling: "if our memories do indeed belong to us, they do so after the fashion of those country properties which have little hidden gates of which we ourselves are often unaware, and which someone in the neighborhood opens for us, so that from one direction at least which is new to us, we find ourselves back in our own house." Memory may be our most interior property, Proust speculates, but it takes another person outside ourselves to open its gates and to bring us inside. Without external prompting, internal memories eventually become again obscured by consciousness; they remain in our minds "like the furniture placed in the semi-darkness of a gallery which, without being able to see, one avoids knocking into."[9]

Proust's metaphor is more apt than he knows for someone like Keller, for whom furniture functioned as a quite literal guidepost to memory. Relying almost entirely on her sense of touch, Keller negotiated the domestic interior by constructing a mental floor plan, memorizing the placement of domestic objects and producing a cognitive map of her physical surroundings. It was this finely tuned spatial memory that finally unlocked the inner world of language for Keller, whose first words prominently included "door," "open," and "shut."[10] Keller knew full well that every literary figure has a literal base. Always conscious of her immediate environment, she never lost contact with the material ground of language, the touchstone of human interiority.

I proceed in these pages inductively, starting deep inside the space of the literary interior and not so much working my way out of this labyrinth as circling deeper in. My central methodology deploys the fundamentals of architectural design to read both literal and literary space. I rely on site lines, for example, to map the visual and social relations within dwellings, tracking the subject's physical movements through interior rooms and corridors. Drawing on period photographs, site visits to the houses, architectural plans and elevations, as well as the correspondence and writings of the authors themselves, I reconstruct the actual space of the literary interior as the writer experienced it. While no such methodology can capture fully the range of a subject's thoughts and emotions, this somewhat painstaking system of reconstruction does allow me to ask a series of questions about the basics of interior subject formation. How does a body move through space? How does the proximity to people and things shape interior life? How do light, color, texture, and temperature structure our ways of knowing?

The time frame covered in this book stretches from 1830, the year of Emily Dickinson's birth, to 1968, the year of Helen Keller's death. The writers I discuss lived at a time when interiority was taking firm hold on the modern imagination. While I do not purport to offer in these pages a standard design survey of the domestic interior,[11] the emergence of the very notion of interiority in the nineteenth century provides an important unifying backdrop against which to read four very different houses, each with its own unique cultural history. Interiority—along with several other by-products of industrialization like intimacy, privacy, and domesticity—appears on the world stage immediately following the American and French revolutions. The social and political instability of the age of revolution transforms the previously communal house into a personal sanctuary, a place ideologically removed from the turmoil of civic life. The interior, defined in the early modern period as a public space, becomes in the nineteenth century a locus of privacy, a home theater for the production of a new inward-looking subject.

The Arcades Project—Walter Benjamin's own contribution to modernity's fascination with interiority—identifies dwelling as both "age-old, perhaps eternal" *and* "a condition of nineteenth-century existence." Benjamin resolves this apparent contradiction by arguing that, in the nineteenth century, a dwelling signifies more than mere shelter; it becomes coextensive with the person of the dweller, a kind of second skin:

> The nineteenth century, like no other century, was addicted to dwelling. It conceived the residence as a receptacle for the person, and it encased him with all his appurtenances so deeply in the dwelling's interior that one might be reminded of the inside of a compass case, where the instrument with all its accessories lies embedded in deep, usually violet folds of velvet.

The ambiguous image of a compass contained by the sensuous velvet lining of its case (much like a body in its coffin) suggests that the modern subject, surrounded by expensive commodities, has lost its bearings. Yet the deep violet folds of the interior also connote comfort and security, what Benjamin calls "that abode of the human being in the maternal womb."[12] What is new about dwelling in the nineteenth century is the sense of structural encasement, of material containment that, for the dweller, can be as disorienting as it is reassuring, as debilitating as it is intoxicating. "To live in these interiors," Benjamin concludes, "was to have woven a dense fabric about oneself, to have secluded oneself within a spider's web. . . . From this cavern, one does not like to stir."[13]

To a significant degree, changes in domestic architecture account for this evolving notion of human interiority, of life lived outside the public eye. Opportunities for privacy or intimacy were relatively uncommon in pre-bourgeois dwellings. Only as the eighteenth-century multipurpose room gave way in the nineteenth century to specialized rooms, corridors, hallways, closets, and back-stairwells does an interior subject truly begin to emerge.[14] The compartmentalization of the bourgeois interior provides one of the necessary historical conditions for the romantic discovery of the self and for the philosophical exploration of interior life. The architectural privatization of the house also historically coincides with the economic industrialization of work, with previously home-based laborers moving outside the house and into the public workplace.[15] Not all forms of non-domestic labor moved outside the home, however. While other professions followed the general migration into the public sphere, writers remained essentially where they were, seeing no apparent contradiction between the increasingly private act of dwelling and the increasingly public act of writing. The new ideology of the house as a place of solitary retreat perfectly suited the contemplative work of writing, but it also left the profession of writing open to the charge of feminization. Writing became feminized not only because more women were entering its ranks, but also because the labor of writing itself remained within the home, the very heart of domesticity.

But if the place of writing did not change with the cultural shift toward interiorization, both the content and the style of writing did. Houses became themselves literary subjects, as writers discovered the creative potential of the changing face of architecture and design.[16] Writers like Honoré de Balzac, J.K. Huysmans, and Edmond de Goncourt all began to inventory, in exhaustive detail, the newly cluttered interior of the house, frequently offering readers an inside view into their own private abodes. By describing every corner, every object, and every feature of the domestic interior, these writers sought to convey through language what Didier Maleuvre calls "the interior experience of interiority."[17] While not all writers may have agreed with Edmond de Goncourt's 1881 conclusion that "existence is no longer exterior,"[18] most were willing to acknowledge that existence was, in any event, less exterior than it had been before. The bourgeois subject, increasingly invested in the design and decoration of the dwelling place, experienced interiority as a new ontological state, a form of being so novel it required its own social science, and its own narrative strategies, to put it into perspective.

"It is surely subjectivity and interiority which are the notions *latest* acquired by the human mind," William James observes nine years after de Goncourt, revealing the intellectual excitement that compels him to write *The Principles of Psychology*.[19] Captivated by the ebb and flow of human sensory perception, William James coins the phrase "stream of consciousness" to describe the modern experience of unbounded interiority, a notion translated into narrative point of view by Henry James in chapter forty-two of *Portrait of a Lady*, where the reader is invited into Isabel Archer's uncensored private thoughts. Thus while one James brother was laying the groundwork for the scientific study of human behavior, the other was advancing English literature's own commitment to exploring the inner workings of human psychology, an interest that had already culminated in France in the invention of the interior monologue.[20] The well-known preface to *Portrait of a Lady* offers no apology for the cultural ascendancy of interiority and for the narrative turn toward solipsism. James's densely populated "house of fiction," with each interior observer peering through the window of his own consciousness, quite nearly obliterates the exterior altogether, identifying the human scene outside the domain of art "as nothing without the posted presence of the watcher." Himself a privileged occupant of the house of fiction, James focuses self-reflexively on the human agent of perception, placing "individual vision" and "individual will" center stage in a theater of introspection where the main actor is the spectator, and the real drama takes place inside the mind of the observer.[21]

Benjamin had a name for this new cultural spectacle of inner life: "the phantasmagoria of the interior." As the term "phantasmagoria" might suggest, the very concept of the interior is a fantasy construct, a site for the public display of private dreams. "Phantasmagorias of the interior," Benjamin writes in the *Exposé* of 1939, "are constituted by man's imperious need to leave the imprint of his private individual existence on the rooms he inhabits."[22] The modern fantasy that the domestic interior and all its furnishings illuminate the inner personality of its inhabitant is, of course, no less powerful or pervasive for being a fantasy. For Benjamin, the phantasmagoria of the interior defines modernity as such. Modernity is simply another name for the reign of interiority, that moment in history where exteriority is driven indoors by the domesticating passions of the bourgeoisie.

Benjamin turns directly to architecture and design to explain exactly how the interior comes to dominate the exterior. The increasing popularity of mirrors in the nineteenth century offers Benjamin two different models of inner reflection, one based on contraction and the other on expansion. In the contraction model, bourgeois dwellers domesticate the exterior by becoming collectors, drawing inside their private abodes objects that reflect the "remote locales and memories of the past." For the nineteenth-century middle-class subject, intent on outfitting the many rooms of the modern dwelling with artworks and artifacts gathered from other times and cultures, a carefully appointed interior is capable of absorbing the world—or at least a reflection of it.[23] To capture modernity's talent for pulling the whole world inside, Benjamin takes as his central metaphor of contraction the window mirror. A popular feature of nineteenth-century apartments, mirrors set into window casements had a very specific function: "to project the endless row of apartment buildings into the isolated bourgeois living room." A window mirror, Theodor Adorno qualifies, "casts into the apartment only the semblance of things." The interior may seek, through the device of the window mirror, to pull the exterior wholly inside itself, but it ultimately "suffers the street only as a reflection," not as a separate reality.[24]

In the expansion model, interiority subordinates exteriority by overflowing its bounds and subsuming everything in its path. Instead of pulling the outside in so that the external shrinks to a point,[25] interiority pushes the inside out so that the internal expands without limit. Benjamin's favorite figure for this second version of modern interiority is the Paris arcade, an indoor marketplace with mirrors for windows that draw the eye back inside the interior. Attracted by the capacity of the covered arcades to domesticate public space, Benjamin describes these urban galleries explicitly as "rooms" and "dwelling places."[26] Pushing the domestic metaphor even farther, Susan Buck-Morss argues that, in fact, all of modern Paris operates as a phantasmagoria of the interior, "a magic-lantern show of optical illusions."[27] The urban flâneur experiences the city as a magical Proustian chamber in which exterior phenomena appear as mere shadows on a wall. In an updated version of Plato's cave, the exterior is recast as a figment of our imagination, an illusory projection of our own inner thoughts. Adorno puts the spatial inversion best: "the flâneur promenades in his room; the world only appears to him reflected by pure inwardness."[28]

The chapters that follow provide multiple examples of what I have identified here as the contraction and expansion models of interiorization. The increasing cultural value accorded to interiority confronts each writer with the same anxious query: is interiority protective or menacing? liberating or confining? progressive or regressive? The four writers I consider in this book experienced interiority in all of these ways, their evolving reflections on inner life exposing its complexities and contradictions more effectively than either Benjamin or Adorno, who both view interiority exclusively as a bourgeois but generally benign event, a means of sustaining modern subjects in the illusion of an impregnable domesticity. Writers of the interior do frequently subscribe to the ideology of the house as a benevolent, nurturing, and vitalizing presence. Dickinson and Proust, who remained largely housebound, believed that they did not need to step outside the four walls of their dwellings to experience the world in all its dimensions. Keller and Freud, who traveled more frequently, believed that when they left their private dwellings, they carried their homes with them. Yet neither the stationary nor the portable models of interiority were without trial for the subjects who occasionally lost faith in the restorative powers of the interior. Keller, for example, welcomed the opportunity to escape a house she increasingly found oppressive, but in traveling discovered that she could not leave her entourage behind, becoming more dependent than ever upon her personal assistants. Proust, by choosing for long periods not to leave his bedroom, encountered a similar irony, becoming totally reliant in his later years on a burgeoning household staff to support his life as a recluse. Whether contracting or expanding, the interior's assault upon the exterior was capable of creating as many anxieties as it assuaged, frequently confounding a sense of security with a fear of isolation, or a promise of seclusion with a threat of suffocation.

Generally, the most interior space in the writer's domestic dwelling is the space of writing itself, typically a study or a bedroom. While much has recently been written on the material instruments of writing (pen, paper, machine),[29] virtually no attention has been paid to the material space of writing as a whole. This critical neglect is unfortunate, since architecture offers a particularly useful paradigm for understanding literary production, as well as for comprehending modern literature's increasing preoccupation with human interiority.

Each of the following chapters illustrates that interiority is a subjective state formed in relation not only to other subjects but to objects as well. By the nineteenth century, the rise of capitalist production and the spread of commodity culture led to the naturalization and personification of the material object on the one hand, and the mechanization and objectification of the human subject on the other hand. Critical terms like anthropomorphism and alienation signal philosophy's continued discomfort with the mystifications and estrangements that attend the historical conflation of subject and object, another binary yet to be adequately challenged in cultural criticism. In the lexicon of contemporary theory, "to treat a subject like an object is to *reify, objectify*. To treat an object like a subject is to *idolize*, to *fetishize*."[30] But as this book will show, the sudden reversals and intimate exchanges between writers and their possessions are not always experienced in such negative terms. In fact, for all four writers I discuss, the object was a favorite and recurrent subject. Each writer had a different relation to material objects: Freud collected them while Proust recollected them; Dickinson looked through them while Keller conversed with them. In each case, the writer defines subjective identity through a sensory identification with things. By the mid-nineteenth century, when an entire literature on the art of home furnishing began to emerge,[31] subjects had finally learned to live companionably with objects. After more than a century of commodity capitalism, subjects and objects entered the bourgeois Victorian household more friendly cohabitants than violent combatants.

The coexistence of subjects and objects comprises one of the central themes of this book, a critical focus that implicitly challenges the dominant Marxist and psychoanalytic assumptions that to objectify the subject and to fetishize the object necessarily destroys both. If anything, the everyday friction between people and things reminds writers both of the literary potential of objects and the material limits of subjects. As Dickinson, Freud, Keller, and Proust endow their most beloved possessions with human characteristics, they also find themselves tentatively exploring their own status as mute, mortal, and material things. It is for this reason that my book not only resists condemning the twin processes of fetishization and objectification, it incorporates these modes into its own critical methodology. Contemporary inquiry on the subject/object dialectic tends to theorize subjects and to historicize objects. I have elected instead to follow the lead of the writers themselves, treating objects as viable philosophical subjects, and subjects as tenable material objects. Working both ends toward the middle, I locate the emergence of modern interiority in the join between mind and matter, where an interior can refer to either a mental or a physical state, and usually both at once.

A quick look inside the etymological history of the word "interior" illustrates the difficulty of extracting the modern psychological notion of interiority from its pre-modern material roots. From the Latin *interior* (and closely related to *intimus*, the Latin origin of intimacy), the English "interior" makes its earliest recorded appearance in a 1490 allusion to "entraylles Interiores," the body's entrails or internal parts. Cultural references in the early modern period to "interior iye," "interior sense," "interior Grace," "interior worth," and "interior imaginacion" later convert what began as a corporeal term (the inside of a body) into an intellectual or spiritual term (the inside of a mind or a soul). Only in the Enlightenment period, as motivation, character, and feeling become more prominent subjects of cultural concern, does interiority take on the psychological associations it continues to suggest today, connoting individualism, privacy, and secrecy. Yet this apparently linear transition from inner body to inner being is in fact, never a seamless one, for multiple historical discourses continually pull the interior subject back into the object world. The interior appears variously in mathematical books ("interior angles"), mechanical dictionaries ("interior screw"), military encyclopedias ("interior flanking"), sailors' wordbooks ("interior planet"), colonial treatises ("interior trade"), and engineering manuals ("interior rampart"). In 1807 "interior decoration" makes its official debut, designating a profession devoted exclusively to the growing interest in the artistic design of houses. John Lukacs has argued that "the interior furniture of houses appeared together with the interior furniture of minds,"[32] a historical claim amply supported by the etymological history of the interior, which, in its continual mixing of objects and subjects, defies Cartesian dualism.

Still, the question remains: what exactly links the interior furniture of houses to the interior furniture of minds? What connects the objective and subjective meanings of interiority? This book suggests that the most critical bridge between the architectural and the psychological interior is the human sensorium: sight, sound, touch, taste, and smell. All bring the world of objects into the subjective realm. The senses allow the body to register exterior impressions and interiorize them. The senses stand at the border of what is inside and outside consciousness. The senses breach the boundary between literal and figurative space. Currently the least discussed of the senses, the so-called sixth sense actually falls outside the classical grouping of sight, sound, touch, taste, and smell, but offers a useful template for understanding this project as a whole. Defined by biologists not in popular terms, as a paranormal sense of psychical intuition, but in scientific terms, as a normal sense of physical balance, the sixth sense names the inner mechanism that allows a body to orient itself in space and to navigate its way through its surroundings. Dickinson, Freud, Keller, and Proust all demonstrate a strong sixth sense, an intimate awareness of the role distance and proximity, movement and perception, play in the formation of inner life.

Interiority, however, is not shaped by the single sense of spatial orientation alone. These four writers also rely principally, though not exclusively, on one or two of the traditional five senses to set their inner compass. Dickinson and Freud draw mostly on sight and hearing, Keller on touch, and Proust on taste and smell. In each case, sensory knowledge opens a different door onto interiority. For Dickinson the inner dwelling names the space of lyric possibility; for Freud the space of unconscious fantasy; for Keller the space of language formation; and for Proust the space of sensual memory. The sensory experience of dwelling animates the work of all four writers, in ways both intensely physical and deeply philosophical.

To a degree found noteworthy even in her own time, Emily Dickinson embraced the popular view of the domestic interior as a personal and private refuge. Critics have long cited Dickinson's close attachment to the house she rarely left as evidence of the poet's deep-seated agoraphobia, a nervous dread of public spaces. Yet Dickinson's retreat to her home, which may have been motivated in part by episodes of temporary blindness, derived less from a fear of exterior spaces than a fascination with interior ones. Far from incapacitating the poet, the rooms and apertures of the renovated family homestead reoriented Dickinson's vision and provided her with a new way of inhabiting the visual and auditory world of lyric poetry.

If Dickinson's visual impairment shaped her relation to the inner space of house and poem, Freud's deafness in his right ear shaped his own understanding of the theory and practice of psychoanalysis. Initially, in Freud's study, vision established the transferential relation between analyst and analysand, as first-time patients, seeing their images reflected in a strategically placed mirror on the study window, soon had their reflections displaced by the doctor's own imposing visage seated in front of them. In all subsequent sessions in the consulting room, transference operated not optically but aurally; uninterested in studying facial expressions, Freud adjusted his listening ear like a telephone receiver to the more distant messages of the patient's transmitting unconscious. An intimate theater of sight and sound, Freud's study and consulting room were not without their lower sensory appeal. Reclining on an ottoman couch, cushioned by Eastern carpets, and wreathed in the heavy smoke of Freud's cigar, the doctor's patients found themselves at home in a late Victorian fantasy of the opium den.

Unlike Dickinson and Freud, Helen Keller's sense of an interior was neither visual nor aural but principally tactile, her organ of knowledge primarily the hand. Referring to herself as a "vibroscope," Keller derived her knowledge from vibrations everywhere animating the house. The domestic interior was, for Keller, a living text, a medium that conveyed messages through tremors, textures, and temperatures. Of all the writers I consider, Keller's notion of interiority is the most capacious, the least bounded by traditional architectural metaphor. Keller's sense of dwelling extended well beyond the four walls of the house; an interior was, in her mind, any place she felt at home, including the tactile worlds of language and technology.

Perhaps no writer describes better the sense of a room—its sights, sounds, odors, and textures—than Marcel Proust. Driven since childhood ever deeper into the interior of his bedroom by a debilitating battle with asthma, Proust devoted his final years to the production of a novel about lost time. While most critics encourage readers to ignore entirely the conventional image of Proust as an invalid sequestered in a sunless and cork-lined room, my final chapter takes the opposite approach and asks what meanings Proust may have attributed to his recessive domestic interior, and what role the actual space of writing may have played in the materialization of his novel. Creating an interior sensory void in which to write about the phenomenon of sensory memory, Proust's heavily insulated bedroom ironically denied the writer the very perceptual experiences he labored for years to describe in his fiction.

Physical ailments play a decisive role in all four writers' experience of the interior. Freud rearranged his entire consulting room to compensate for the loss of hearing in his right ear. Proust ensconced himself in the farthest corner of the most remote bedroom in the apartment to distance his sensitive nose from the noxious smells of kitchen and courtyard. Dickinson conducted conversations from around corners and behind half-open doors to veil her eye and to magnify her voice. And Keller performed her daily activities as close to the floor as possible to feel the vibrations and to identify the locations of bodies as they circulated

around her. I did not immediately realize when I began research-
ing this book on interiority that I was also, implicitly, writing a
book on disability. But it soon became clear that for each author
whose home I documented, a particular sensory limitation profoundly structured the dwellers' relation to the physical and intellectual worlds they inhabited. While one might expect only Helen
Keller to be featured in the pages of a book on disability, we might
do well to remember that sensory deprivation is a less marginal
condition than typically assumed, and that distinct corporeal
needs and histories structure every subject's relation to the domestic interior.

I take as my four chapter titles the four sensory organs of eye,
ear, hand, and nose precisely to draw attention to the way in
which the body, in all its materiality, shapes even the most theoretical sense of the interior.[33] In focusing so exclusively on the dynamics of the eye, architecture in particular tends to forget the
significant role the other senses play in the production of human
subjectivity. Indeed, disregard of the senses characterizes the field
of architectural criticism as a whole, preoccupied as it is with
studying problems of vision at the expense of investigating fuller,
more multifaceted bodily inhabitations of space. While giving vision its due, this book simultaneously seeks to move beyond the
limits of ocularcentrism by bringing hearing, touch, taste, and
smell back into consideration. Demonstrating how the eye is not
the sole organ of spatial perception, the book calls into question
the assumed priority of this so-called "highest" sense. As writers
of the interior repeatedly document in their private letters and in
their public works, vision is a no more stable or reliable mode of
perception than hearing, touch, taste, or smell.

For each of these writers, interiority begins as a sensory experience. Indeed, without the senses we would have no true idea of
space. And without writing we would have only a partial record
of how individuals experience their own place in the world. It is
not unimportant that writers have conceived the creative act of

writing itself as a sixth sense. "What I would like one to understand about my book," Proust writes in the final months of revising *A la recherche du temps perdu*, "is that it emerged wholly from the application of a special sense . . . that is very difficult to describe (like the sense of sight to a blind man) to those who have never exercised it."[34] For Proust, writing is a sense everyone possesses but few know how to utilize. It is a faculty of perception as natural and transparent to the writer as the sense of vision is to the sighted. Writing operates as a physical medium, a way to register and to process external stimuli. No less importantly, writing also serves to bring the reader directly into the writer's sensory interior. In the final analysis, the greatest achievement of the four writers to whom I now turn is their shared ability to open interiority to public view. In so doing, these authors offer blueprints for the renovation of human subjectivity, models for the reappraisal of the risks and pleasures of living deep inside one's self.

Daguerrotype of Emily Dickinson, approximately seventeen years old, ca. 1847 or 1848. *Courtesy of the Amherst College Library.*

1

Dickinson's Eye

The Dickinson Homestead
Amherst Massachusetts

MORE THAN ANY OTHER WRITER, Emily Dickinson has been intimately associated with her house. Anecdotes from friends, family, neighbors, and the poet herself provide the biographical basis for the reigning view of Dickinson as an eccentric recluse. Considered together, these stories portray a woman acutely aware of her spatial surroundings, whether she is listening to the parlor piano from the shadows of a hallway, lowering baskets of gingerbread from her bedroom window, or conversing with visitors from around corners or behind partially closed doors. Preferring to remain largely unseen within the interior chambers of the family homestead, Dickinson inhabited space in uncommon ways.

Dickinson's retreat into the recesses of her father's house has been the subject of extensive critical commentary. Her love of solitude has been variously pathologized and romanticized, overdramatized and idealized. Critics who pathologize Dickinson interpret her withdrawal as a neurotic response to a range of supposed personal traumas: grief over the loss of a secret lover, guilt over an illicit love for her brother's wife, resignation over the demands of a tyrannical father. John Cody was the first to suggest, in a 1971 study of the Dickinson family romance, that Dickinson was a full-fledged psychotic, experiencing a complete mental breakdown during the crisis years of 1861–63. Armed with the third edition of the American Psychiatric Association's *Diagnostic and Statistical Manual of Mental Disorders*, Cody has since expanded his initial diagnosis of the poet to cover a host of new disorders—avoidant personality disorder, generalized anxiety disorder, major depressive episode, schizotypal personality disorder, and social phobia. Recently an entire book on Dickinson, similarly dependent on historically anachronistic psychiatric categories, cites the poet's comparatively few poems on flight and denial as evidence of Dickinson's "severe agoraphobic syndrome."[1]

Critics who romanticize Dickinson take a less judgmental approach, insisting that she freely chose her seclusion, opting to sequester herself in her father's house in order to assume the life of a professional poet. In this alternate reading, Dickinson spent her life quietly rebelling against patriarchal culture, seeking asylum from the demands of domestic servitude that made writing all but impossible.[2] Yet tributes to the poet's independent spirit notwithstanding, commentators who read Dickinson's withdrawal in a positive vein cannot resist wondering whether her attraction to a solitary life "may have arisen in part from a neurosis, an anxiety about being defenseless when 'seen'." Even the most sympathetic of Dickinson's readers tend to assume that if the poet's need for privacy was chiefly pragmatic, an enabling condition of artistic production, it was also deeply obsessional, and "phobically so."[3]

Ultimately, all of the mythologizations of Dickinson are based on the same twin premise: Dickinson fashioned a radical interior life by shunning a conventional exterior one. In the view of her biographer Thomas H. Johnson, interiority was, for Dickinson, a "living entombment." Jean Mudge, the first curator of the Dickinson Homestead, and the first scholar to link Dickinson's poetry to the domestic interior, also chooses to emphasize the poet's "self-incarceration at home." Some critics combine the burial and prison metaphors, hypothesizing that the poet "immured herself within the magic prison that paradoxically liberated her art."[4] Dickinson's critics all seem to agree that interiority, modeled on the architectural space of tomb or prison, was the necessary prerequisite for her poetry.

But for Dickinson, interiority was not only a matter of physical enclosure. Interiority was a complicated conceptual problem, continually posited and reexamined in a body of writing that relies heavily on spatial metaphors to advance its recurrent themes of joy, despair, death, time, and immortality. Placing Dickinson's poetry of interiority inside the poet's ancestral home has one important historical justification. Dickinson began writing lyric poetry (that most interior of poetic forms) at the very same time the Dickinson family moved back into the family homestead in 1855. All but a handful of Dickinson's poems are, in fact, written in the Homestead, the majority composed in the poet's bedroom, the most private chamber of the antebellum interior.

The rise of interiority in nineteenth-century America was made possible by the growing distinction between public and private space. During Dickinson's lifetime, houses became increasingly privatized as commercial labor moved out of the home and into the town or factory. With her father's law office located several blocks away from the Homestead, Dickinson's family home became a private residence, removed from the world of contract and litigation that comprised the basis of Edward Dickinson's thriving legal practice. No longer the site of professional or economic livelihood, the bourgeois family home becomes in the nineteenth century the stage for an emerging interior life. The domestic interior as private haven, where an individual could withdraw from public view, was a relatively new cultural ideal when Dickinson began writing her poetry. Privacy and publicity were still largely mutable concepts, by-products of a rising American fascination with the domestic interior.[5]

While the classical pairs of interior/exterior and privacy/publicity typically converge in historical investigations of the domestic interior, Dickinson's work is important for the way in which it realigns and rethinks these philosophical tropes. For Dickinson, interiors are public places; exteriors are private retreats. Interestingly, much of the critical disputation surrounding Dickinson's lyrics implicitly invokes the problem of insides and outsides. Jay Leyda, perhaps the most cited of Dickinson scholars, argues that the most notable feature of a Dickinson poem is its "omitted center." Sharon Cameron counters that, just as often, a Dickinson poem has a center but no surrounding context.[6] The confusion over what lies inside or outside the poem, the dislocation of center from periphery, focuses attention on a poetic vision frankly at odds with conventional understandings of space. Even the poet's celebrated notion of Circumference, generally understood by critics as "a symbol for all that is outside,"[7] operates as a sign less of an increasingly elusive exteriority than an infinitely expanding interiority.

In this chapter I offer a cultural history of the Dickinson Homestead, organized around the play of interior/exterior defining the elastic borders of what the poet calls her "Mansion of the Universe" (P 836). Through a reading of Dickinson's poems and letters, as well as the architectural space of the house itself, I explore the idiosyncratic yet highly imaginative ways this most private of American poets negotiated space.

1

Built by Emily Dickinson's grandfather Samuel Fowler Dickinson around 1813, the Dickinson Homestead was most likely the first brick house in Amherst, a two-story Federal-style dwelling with symmetrical windows [figure 1.1]. Originally, the interior followed a standard layout, with a pair of rooms on each side of a large central hallway extending from front door to back. At the time of Dickinson's birth in 1830, the Homestead was a two-family dwelling, with Samuel Fowler Dickinson and his younger children living on the east side of the house and his older son Edward Dickinson and his new family living on the west side. In a common arrangement for the period, as many as thirteen people occupied the two-family homestead, with an invisible property line

FIG. 1.1A. Lithograph of the Dickinson Homestead by Bachelder, ca. 1858. The brick Homestead was originally painted red in the 1830s and then repainted white in the 1840s. At the time this lithograph was made, the Federal-style house was painted yellow, with white trim and green shutters, to mask the extensive structural renovations of 1855. *Courtesy of The Jones Library, Inc., Amherst, Massachusetts.*

bisecting the house down the middle of the hall and staircase. Not until mid-century would the American family dwelling fall into a rigid hierarchy of public and private rooms, organized along a now familiar divide: public downstairs/private upstairs; public front rooms/private back rooms. In all likelihood, the Homestead was initially a more homogeneous public space, with the bedrooms doubling as sitting rooms, and the sitting rooms serving as extra bedrooms. No room was off-limits to visitors, and every room performed more than one function. The relatively straightforward architectural plan of the original Homestead facilitated

FIG. 1.1B The Dickinson Homestead today, with original brick exposed.
Photograph by Frank Ward. Trustees of Amherst College.

communal interaction and mutual cooperation, as the two Dickinson families shared a kitchen during the day and gathered
around a single hearth at night.

After Samuel Fowler Dickinson's financial setbacks led to the
loss of the Homestead in the 1830s, Edward Dickinson relocated
his own family in 1840 to a more spacious home on Pleasant
Street, where Emily Dickinson lived from the ages of nine to
twenty-four.[8] Razed in the 1920s but shown in an 1870 photograph [figure 1.2], the large wood-framed dwelling, organized
around a huge central chimney, is the house that Joseph Lyman, a
frequent visitor of the Dickinson's, once referred to as "that
charming second home of mine."[9] It was here that Emily Dickinson watched funeral processions from a northern window overlooking the gated entrance to the village cemetery adjoining the
Dickinson property. It was here that Dickinson lived her most social years, her correspondence filled with references to sleigh rides,
charades, sugaring parties, country rides, and forest walks. And it

FIG. 1.2 The Pleasant Street house, where the Dickinson family lived from 1840 to 1855. In the Pleasant Street house a huge central chimney drew family members together, while in the Homestead multiple chimneys and numerous Franklin stoves drew family members apart. Photograph ca. 1870. *Courtesy of The Jones Library, Inc., Amherst, Massachusetts.*

was here that Dickinson first met Susan Gilbert, the woman whom, most scholars concede, was the emotional center of Dickinson's life.

It is perhaps not surprising that when Edward Dickinson at last found the financial resources to repurchase the family Homestead on Main Street, Emily Dickinson was reluctant to leave the Pleasant Street house, steeped as it was in memory. The poet's description of the move back to Main Street in November 1855 depicts the relocation not as a triumphant return but as a forced emigration. To Mrs. Holland she confesses:

I cannot tell you how we moved. I had rather not remember. I believe my "effects" were brought in a bandbox, and the "deathless me," on foot, not many moments after. . . . It is a kind of *gone-to-Kansas* feeling, and if I sat in a long wagon, with my family tied

behind, I should suppose without doubt I was a party of emi-
grants! . . . Mother has been an invalid since we came *home*, and
Vinnie and I "regulated," and Vinnie and I "got settled," and still
we keep our father's house, and mother lies upon the lounge, or sits
in her easy chair.[10]

Emily Norcross Dickinson's mysterious invalidism (directly pre-
cipitated by the return to the Homestead) lasted nearly seven
years, during which time Lavinia shouldered the bulk of the
housekeeping duties and Emily assumed the responsibility of
nursing her mother slowly back to health. It was while reacclimat-
ing to life in the Homestead that Dickinson began seriously to
write poetry, composing an entire sequence of lyrics around images of empty, abandoned, or bereaved houses (P 289, 389, 399).

   The Homestead to which Dickinson returns in the mid 1850s
was a substantially different kind of domestic and cultural space
than the one she inhabited for the first ten years of her life. Six
months of architectural renovations—renovations that were as
much ideological as structural—transformed a classic Federal
house into an early Victorian home. Religious revivalism was not
the only social reform movement sweeping America in the 1840s
and 1850s. Housing crusades began investing the American homestead with both nostalgic import and moral value.[11] Architectural
pattern books, along with sermons, advice books, almanacs, and
popular magazines, all idealized the family residence as a refuge
from the outside world, a private domain dedicated to nurturing
the interior life of its newly leisured citizens.

   To meet the new national standard of the republican family
home, Edward Dickinson invested five thousand dollars on improvements for the Homestead, just five hundred dollars less than
what it cost him to build, for his son Austin, a brand new house
on the Homestead's western property.[12] Andrew Jackson Downing's popular 1850 plan book, *The Architecture of Country
Houses*, offered fourteen different designs for "the beautiful,

FIG. 1.3 The Evergreens, home of Austin and Susan Dickinson. Putting a public face on the conflict between generations, the idiosyncratic style of Austin Dickinson's asymmetrical Italianate villa reacts against the authority of his father's more classical Federal-style house next door. Photograph by Charles Prouty, ca. 1870. *Courtesy of The Jones Library, Inc., Amherst, Massachusetts.*

rural, unostentatious, moderate home of the country gentleman."[13] Austin Dickinson and his fiancée Susan Gilbert chose for themselves a modern wood-frame Italian villa the couple named the Evergreens, with asymmetrical dimensions, flat roofs, projecting balconies, and a *campanile* tower to harmonize the whole [figure 1.3]. Edward Dickinson followed a more conservative plan in renovating the forty-two-year-old brick Homestead, considerably expanding the interior living space while largely retaining the structure's classic outline and symmetrical plan. Apparently father and son each selected a building plan that would externally reflect his inner character, taking to heart Downing's central premise that "every thing in architecture . . . can be made a symbol of social and domestic virtues" (23).

Downing's general design plan for the gentleman's country house stands as a near blueprint for the extensive changes made to the Dickinson Homestead. Structurally reinforcing the ideal of the independent, democratic, and self-reliant subject, Downing advocated that family members be given private bedrooms, that servants be assigned separate living quarters, and (most importantly) that rooms in the domestic interior be given specialized functions.

> In every villa of moderate size, we expect to find a separate apartment, devoted to meals, entitled the dining-room; another devoted to social intercourse, or the drawing-room; and a third devoted to intellectual culture, or the library; besides halls, passages, stairways, pantries, and bed-rooms. In what we should call a complete villa, there will be found, in addition to this, a bed-room, or dressing-room, or a lady's boudoir, an office or private room for the master of the house, on the first floor; and bathing-rooms, water-closet, and dressing-rooms, on the second floor. A flight of back stairs, for servants, is indispensable in villas of large size, and, when space can be found for it, adds greatly to the comfort and privacy of even small villas. . . . [The kitchen] is generally provided for in a wing, of less height than the main building, divided into two stories, with sleeping-rooms on the second floor. (272)

Edward Dickinson approximated Downing's masterplan for the new country villa first by adding to the Homestead a two-story east wing [figure 1.4], opening up enough space for a new dining room, pantry, upstairs bedroom, back staircase, and a hallway with five exits that Dickinson called the "Northwest Passage."[14] To the front of the new wing, next to Edward Dickinson's private library, a conservatory was added for an indoor garden, bringing the outdoors into the interior. A two-story rear ell, of moderate height, relocated the kitchen and washroom to the back of the house while creating servant quarters above, accessed by a second back staircase. The only renovation to the Homestead not recommended by the new architectural plan books was the addition of a

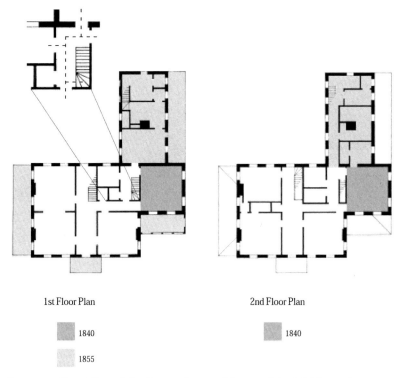

1st Floor Plan   2nd Floor Plan

1840   1840

1855

FIG. 1.4 Floor Plan of the first and second floors of the Dickinson Homestead, based on the 1916 plans by Howe, Manning & Almy Architects.
Darkened areas denote Edward Dickinson's 1855 renovations, which
included a two-story east wing, a two-story rear ell, a conservatory, a west
veranda, and a front portico. The central staircase, originally positioned
on the opposite wall and in the front of the hallway, was moved to the back
of the hallway, physically removing access to the private family quarters
from the public realm of the street.

prominent Greek Revival front entrance and portico, a decorative
classical imitation Downing would have censored for its want of
"local truth."[15]

But perhaps the most interesting renovations to the Homestead
are those that indirectly convey the significant changes in Dickinson family relations during the mid-1850s. Austin Dickinson secured upon his marriage not only a house more grand than the
family Homestead but a law practice of his own. In one of the more

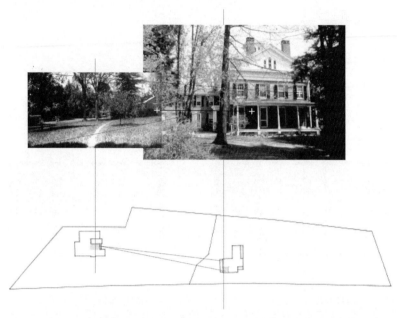

FIG. 1.5 Site plan showing the view from the Homestead's western façade onto the Evergreens. The open lawn between the two houses gave Dickinson a view from her second story room of Austin and Sue's first floor conjugal bedroom, highlighted here.

striking Homestead renovations, Edward Dickinson counters the house's dominant north/south axis by placing a veranda along the west side of the main house facing his son's Italian villa [figure 1.5]. This new frontality reorients the Homestead toward the Evergreens, putting the two houses into close conversation. Whether the Homestead's new eye onto its younger and more fashionable neighbor was protective, competitive, or a little bit of both, the west veranda, with its unobstructed view of the Evergreen's first-floor conjugal bedroom, was as much a site of surveillance as relaxation. The cupola at the top of the Homestead, a popular mid-century renovation, also afforded a clear view of the Evergreens, and may have been added as a final structural feature because Edward Dickinson feared being "out-cupola-ed" by his son.[16]

If, by mid-century, every room in the American country house was to fulfill a single domestic purpose, it is worth noting that the Dickinson family did not, in fact, inhabit the Homestead chambers according to their rigid plan book functions. Over-reliance on advice books, including architectural plan books, can be historically deceptive, since such prescriptive literature failed to mandate completely how people actually lived.[17] In the case of the Dickinsons, the kitchen and the dining room remained multipurpose rooms, resisting the pull toward specialization and privatization. The kitchens in both the Dickinson homes on Main Street and on Pleasant Street were rooms as much for writing and reading as for cooking and eating. Dickinson's mother and sister wrote their formal correspondence in the kitchen, and the Dickinson siblings held their family conferences around the warmth of the kitchen fire. Throughout her life, Emily, who treated architectural spaces as living memorials, associated the domestic interior of the kitchen not with any of the women in the Dickinson household but with her brother Austin. It was in the Pleasant Street kitchen that brother and sister first shared confidences at a table cluttered with books, and it was in the kitchen, with its "empty chairs" and "empty nails," that Emily most deeply mourned Austin's frequent, often prolonged absences (L 109, 118).[18]

The Homestead dining room was even more versatile in function. It contained a writing table by the conservatory window where Emily occasionally wrote, a lounge chair near the fireplace where Emily Norcross Dickinson frequently slept, and a soup tureen most likely on the dining room table where Edward Dickinson stored his law papers.[19] In the typical country villa, formal public rooms could be readily converted into more casual private domains. During the cold New England winters, the Dickinson parlors were closed off, the first floor furniture rearranged, and the dining room converted into a comfortable family sitting room. Throughout the year, the Dickinson dining room was used not only for meals but for writing, reading, sleeping, and even sex.

With its ready front and back exits, it made the perfect trysting place for Austin Dickinson and Mabel Loomis Todd, who first consummated their affair in the Homestead dining room in December 1883 and, with Emily and Lavinia's tacit approval, continued to meet there until Austin's death twelve years later.[20]

Although some furniture from the Homestead remains, mostly in either American Empire or Federal style, very little is known about what kind of furniture the family used, and even less about how these pieces were arranged. Today the rooms of the Dickinson Homestead are displayed to the public almost entirely empty of their original furnishings. The spareness of the chambers draws the viewer's attention to the surfaces of the house and to its most basic architectural dimensions: floors, walls, ceilings, doors, windows. The shift in focus from decoration to design, from ornament to circumference, pays ironic tribute to Dickinson's own spare and uncluttered poetry. Architectural rather than decorative references shape Dickinson's poems. Hers is a vocabulary of plane, beam, and dome, of angle, slant, and degree, of plan, scale, and latitude.

In fact, Dickinson's poetry routinely overlooks the objects within a room in favor of highlighting its spatial perimeters. "Size circumscribes," the poet writes in a poem composed in 1862; "it has no room for petty furniture" (P 641). Twenty years later she expounds on the theme of the unfurnished room in a two-line, eight-word poem remarkable for its economy:

> All things swept sole away
> This—is immensity— (P 1512)

Utilizing the domestic metaphor of sweeping, Dickinson alliteratively sweeps the poem free of internal clutter, exposing in the process the sheer immensity of a minimalist space.

"The Finite—furnished / With the Infinite" (P 906) provides an apt description of Dickinson's own poems, poems that operate as miniature interiors. Dickinson's poems about poetry—"Myself was formed—a Carpenter" (P 488), "The Props assist the House" (P 1142), and "Remembrance has a Rear and Front" (P 1182)—all select the house as a favorite metaphor to describe the work of poetry as both labor and artistry. The poem as interior chamber finds its origins not only in the etymology of "stanza" (Italian for "room" or "capacious dwelling") but in the very definition of lyric, identified in classical lexicons as a type of "musical architecture."[21]

For Dickinson, prose and poetry represent two starkly different kinds of architectural interiors. If prose names a space of confinement and captivity ("They shut me up in Prose— / As when a little Girl / They put me in the Closet— / Because they liked me 'still'—" P 613), poetry offers a more open and expansive interior:

I dwell in Possibility—
A fairer House than Prose—
More numerous of Windows—
Superior—for Doors—

Of Chambers as the Cedars—
Impregnable of Eye—
And for an Everlasting Roof
The Gambrels of the Sky—

Of Visitors—the fairest—
For Occupation—This—
The spreading wide my narrow Hands
To gather Paradise—   (P 657)

On the one hand, a poem constructs private, secret, secure spaces, chambers "impregnable of eye"; on the other hand, a poem's enclosed interior opens onto a limitless expanse, "the gambrels of the sky." The contradiction of solid cedar wall and open everlasting roof to describe the architectonics of poetry suggest that Dickinson aims to reorient our vision by generating new sight lines and creating new views. In this poem, Dickinson directs our eye outward and upward, offering a view of paradise from the fortified vantage point of the inviolable interior.

This chapter addresses not simply the interiors of Dickinson's poems, but the poetry of Dickinson's interiors.[22] Long before Gaston Bachelard began exploring the lyrical recesses of the architectural dwelling, Emily Dickinson was intimately involved in mapping her own "poetics of space." Dickinson occupied the Homestead much as she inhabited a poem, publicizing the private through a discreet retraining of both eye and ear.

I will be focusing here on three of the Dickinson Homestead's most interesting chambers: the parlor, the bedroom, and the cupola. Starting on the first floor and working my way up to the top of the house, I take as my yardstick Dickinson's own philosophy of the interior: "The Outer—from the Inner / Derives its Magnitude / The Inner—paints the Outer" (P 451). But before proceeding directly into the house, I want to pause for a moment at the entranceway, at the place that is neither inner nor outer but somehow both. There is no architectural figure more important, or more weighted, in Dickinson's poetry than the image of the door. The door serves as the central ontological support upon which Dickinson's entire theory of interiority hangs: "The Opening and the Close / Of Being" (P 1047).

2

In Dickinson's letters and poems, the door emerges as a richly layered metaphor for loneliness, loss, and death on the one hand, and memory, secrecy, and safety on the other. The door is the most reversible of Dickinson's images, and the most complex. It dramatizes a tension at the heart of almost all Dickinson's poems, the tension produced by the terror and excitement of the threshold. Doors represent for the poet the possibility of crossing over or passing through. They are the concrete visualization of the tenuous border between the finite and the infinite, the mortal and the immortal, the human and the divine.

In Dickinson's correspondence, the conceit of the door is most often associated with the theme of departure. Dickinson continually portrays herself in her letters as racing to a door or window to catch a final glimpse of a departing loved one.[23] The following letter to Susan Gilbert, written when Dickinson was twenty-three, restages for the "absent One" the effect of her departure on she-who-is-left-behind:

> I ran to the door, dear Susie—I ran out in the rain, with nothing but my slippers on, I called "Susie, Susie," but you didn't look at me; then I ran to the dining room window and rapped with all my might upon the pane, but you rode right on and never heeded me. (L 102)

If the private space of the kitchen memorialized the poet's love for her brother Austin, the public space of the front doorstep commemorates her love for her friend Sue. The doorstep marks the place where the poet first fell in love with Susan Gilbert, the place that continues to remind her of Sue even after her friend has gone "West" to marry Austin:

> I love you as dearly, Susie, as when love first began, on the step at the front door, and under the Evergreens, and it breaks my heart sometimes, because I do not hear from you. . . . I miss you, I mourn you, and walk the Streets alone—often at night, beside, I fall asleep in tears, for your dear face, yet not one word comes back to me from that silent West. (L 177)

Sue, the West, and the Evergreens are all part of the same affective picture for Dickinson.[24] From the "broad stone step" where their lives first "mingled" (L 88),[25] Dickinson need only look to the West to conjure her absent friend:

Dear Susie, I dont forget you a moment of the hour, and when my
work is finished, and I have got the tea, I slip thro' the little entry,
and out at the front door, and stand and watch the West, and remember all of mine . . . . (L 103)

"The Heart has many Doors" (P 1567), Dickinson once
aphorized. The door to the West opened onto Sue.

As she grew older Dickinson was indeed increasingly reluctant
to travel forth beyond the doors of the family homestead. Preferring to be the one left behind, Dickinson writes to Thomas Went-
worth Higginson (after her third refusal to visit him in Boston), "I
do not cross my Father's ground to any House or town" (L 330).
Yet Dickinson's poems are generally not about the fear of *leaving*
interiors but more commonly about the anxiety of *entering* them.
The problem of gaining entry is, for Dickinson, a far greater pre-
occupation.

I Years had been from Home
And now before the Door
I dared not enter, lest a Face
I never saw before

Stare stolid into mine
And ask my Business there—   (P 609)

"Home" may signify for the poet her favorite spiritual locale
(Eden, Paradise, Eternity), or it may refer to the actual house on
Pleasant Street that Dickinson still longed to return to years later.
In either case, the speaker's dilemma is the same: terror in the face
of an unknown presence hidden behind a familiar barrier.

The interior in Dickinson's poetry does not always inspire
fear. Just as often a door may conceal an idealized scene of domestic comfort and plenitude.

A Door just opened on a street—
I—lost—was passing by—

An instant's Width of Warmth disclosed—
And Wealth—and Company.

The Door as instant shut—And I—
I—lost—was passing by—
Lost doubly—but by contrast—most—
Informing—misery—   (P 953)

The misery of Dickinson's anonymous passerby is only deepened
by the momentary glimpse of warmth, wealth, and company revealed by the open door. The repetition of the poem's second line,
"I—lost—was passing by," further underscores the speaker's sense
of exclusion by employing the device of the dash to segregate ty-
pographically the poem's central experience of displacement.
Other Dickinson poems syntactically open and shut on the force
of a dash, but "A Door just opened on a street" makes particularly frequent use of the poet's signature punctuation, both to isolate its speaker internally and to slam the poem shut repeatedly,
end-stopping every line.

The final stanza of Dickinson's longest poem, "I cannot live
with You" (P 640), also relies on the ubiquitous dash to emphasize the state of ontological suspension in which so many of Dickinson's subjects routinely find themselves.

So We must meet apart—
You there—I—here—
With just the Door ajar
That Oceans are—and Prayer—
And that White Sustenance—
Despair—   (P 640)

Although the stanza's second line implies that the You is "there"
and the I is "here," syntactically the speaker is neither here nor
there but hovering somewhere in between, occupying a more liminal space. It is a place Dickinson herself self-consciously occupied
whenever she conducted conversations with visitors from the

FIG. 1.6 A door ajar onto Dickinson's bedroom. *Photograph by Frank Ward.*

other side of a half-open door [figure 1.6]. "I cannot live with You" suggests that close ties can only be maintained by "meeting apart"—an oxymoron that increasingly defined the poet's own interpersonal relations. The door ajar provides the perfect metaphor for conveying the poet's deepest inner conviction that the precondition for all true intimacy is distance.[26]

The door ajar—half open, half closed—evolves over the corpus of Dickinson's poetry into one of her most positive images. For example, in "The Soul should always stand ajar" (P 1055), a soul stands waiting to receive its divine caller, ready at a moment's notice to leave the interior dwelling of the body that has temporarily housed it. The image of the door ajar also animates what may well be Dickinson's most lyrical, tranquil, and perfect poem.

Noon—is the Hinge of Day—
Evening—the Tissue Door—

> Morning—the East compelling the sill
> Till all the World is ajar—   (P 931)

In a single quatrain, Dickinson chronicles the evolution of a day, emphasizing, through precise temporal sequencing, the dawn beyond the dusk, the east beyond the west, the morning beyond the evening. The World is a domestic dwelling, fortified by movement (hinge), mass (door), and foundation (sill). Hinge, door, and sill are all of a piece, forming a translucent "tissue" boundary between spatial and temporal worlds. The East that gently pries open the morning, leaving all the world ajar, illuminates life's most basic movement of opening and closing, the meaning of creation.

Ultimately, the door in Dickinson's poetry is a completely indeterminate figure. A door can symbolize loss or gain, absence or presence, loneliness or reunion, separation or connection, life or death. The very instability of the image is what appeals to Dickinson most, immediately elevating the figure of the door over architecture's other apparently more static forms. Not long after Dickinson's death, the German philosopher Georg Simmel argued (in strikingly Dickinsonian fashion) that the door is far superior to the dead geometric form of the wall. To Simmel, a wall is "mute," but a door "speaks." Moreover, a door more successfully transcends the divide between the inner and the outer; a door is where the finite borders on the infinite; a door marks the plane where separation and connection come together, but still remain apart.[27]

3

In the dynamic interplay of architectural form, such conceptual partitions between door and wall remain more figurative than literal. In the Dickinson drawing-room, for example, folding doors may have functioned as a movable wall, dividing the public front parlor from the private family sitting room behind [figure 1.7]. "If you will stay in the next room, and open the folding doors a few

FIG. 1.7 The Dickinson parlor. Folding doors originally separated the space between the front and back parlors, allowing Dickinson to play the piano, unseen, for visitors. *Photograph by Frank Ward.*

inches, I'll come down and make music for you," Dickinson reportedly instructed her cousin John Graves.[28] Martha Dickinson Bianchi, Austin and Sue's daughter, provides a much fuller description of the Dickinson parlor, its cool interior strangely reminiscent of the poet's famous "alabaster chambers" (P 216).[29]

> The walls were hung with heavily gold-framed engravings: "The Forester's Family," "The Stag at Bay," "Arctic Nights," and other chastely cold subjects. The piano was an old-fashioned square in an elaborately carved mahogany case, and the carpet a fabulous

Brussels, woven in a pattern. It had in the centre a great basket of flowers at the edge. It enjoyed a reputation of its own; and the day of my grandmother's funeral two old ladies came an hour ahead of the service "to get a last look at the carpet before the mourners broke up the pattern."

The wallpaper was white with large figures. The white marble mantels and the marble-topped tables added a chill even on hot midsummer afternoons.[30]

The white marble mantels and tabletops, white wallpaper, and "chastely cold" paintings create a funeral atmosphere in a room Higginson once described as "dark & cool & stiffish" (L 342a). Frequent use of the parlor shutters, closed in the winter to reduce the cold and in the summer to reduce the heat, only added to the room's sepulchral feel. As much mausoleum as salon, the parlor served as the backdrop for Dickinson's own wake.

At least one extant account of the Homestead's most formal room contradicts the dominant view of the parlor as a dark and lifeless crypt. Mabel Loomis Todd, who occasionally played the piano for Dickinson in the years before the poet's death, offers a less somber picture: "although our interviews were chiefly confined to conversations between the brilliantly lighted drawing-room where I sat and the dusky hall just outside where she always remained, I grew very familiar with her voice, its vaguely surprised note dominant." Here Mabel Todd is bathed in the brilliant light of the parlor, while Dickinson is relegated to the dark and shadowy recesses of the hall, the house's main artery and, paradoxically, its most public space [figures 1.8a, 1.8b]. In the spatial allegory of darkness and light that frames so many anecdotes about the poet, Dickinson's place in the shadows by no means eclipses her. Referred to by Todd's daughter as "the invisible voice, the phantom in the enchanted corridor,"[31] Dickinson commands the authority of a stage director, issuing clear directives from the sidelines. Dickinson usually concluded her meetings in

FIG. 1.8A View of the Dickinson hallway and staircase, looking toward the back door. *Photograph by Frank Ward. Trustees of Amherst College.*

ritual fashion, sending a servant into the parlor with a tray containing a glass of sherry, a flower, or a poem.

> Between My Country—And the Others—
> There is a Sea
> But Flowers negotiate between us—
> As Ministry   (P 905)

Like all Dickinson's trysts conducted from around corners or from behind half-closed doors, the encounter with Mabel Todd is a

FIG. 1.8B View of hallway from front door to back. *Photograph by Frank Ward. Trustees of Amherst College.*

carefully choreographed set-piece, one that effectively heightens rather than diminishes the poet's presence.

Dickinson always had a finely tuned sense of the theatrical. Before retiring entirely from view, the poet was known for her memorable entrances. Dickinson's first meeting with Higginson in the Homestead parlor left a vivid impression:

> She had a quaint and nun-like look, as if she might be a German canonness of some religious order whose prescribed garb was white pique. . . . . She came toward me with two day lilies . . . which she put, in a childlike way, into my hand, saying softly under her breath, "These are my introduction."[32]

Of their second meeting, Higginson writes: "She glided in, in white, bearing a Daphne odora for me, & said under her breath 'How long are you going to stay'" (L 405). Dickinson dominated her encounters with Higginson through the very intensity of her recessiveness. "I never was with anyone who drained my nerve power so much," the former Union Army Colonel confessed to his wife; "without touching her she drew from me. I am glad not to live near her" (L 342b).

Joseph Lyman's famous "pen portrait" of the poet also dwells on Dickinson's entrance into a room, this time her father's library:

> A library dimly lighted, three mignonettes on a little stand. Enter a spirit clad in white, figure so draped as to be misty[,] face moist, translucent alabaster, forehead firmer as of statuary marble.[33]

In Lyman's highly romanticized word portrait, Dickinson's face of alabaster and forehead of statuary marble make the poet sound like nothing so much as a classical sculpture. The impression of Dickinson as a piece of art may be only partly Lyman's fancy. Judith Farr has convincingly argued that by wearing white, holding lilies, and sending notes and flowers on a salver, Dickinson was self-consciously quoting an entire iconographic tradition in nineteenth-century painting: the pre-Raphaelite nun in her cloister. Victorian paintings, like Charles Allston Collins's 1850 *Convent Thoughts*, frequently depicted a nun dressed in white, clasping lilies, and sequestered from dejected suitors behind a doorway, a grate, or a garden wall.[34] By adopting the costume and manners of a "Wayward Nun" (P 722), Dickinson celebrated the space of the cloister as the most appropriate setting for the work of the novice writer.

Deprived of such extravagant images of the poet, admirers like Mabel Todd, who never actually saw Dickinson while she was alive, came to know her principally through the sound of her voice. Dickinson's acts of self-concealment forced her interlocutors to apprehend her, not as the "pattering child" (L 342a) Higginson and Lyman perceived her to be, but as the professional bard to which she herself aspired. "Stepping to incorporeal Tunes" (P 1418), Dickinson lay claim to poetic authority by transforming herself entirely into a voice. In so doing, she was enacting the most influential notion of lyric poetry of her time: John Stuart Mill's definition of the lyric as an utterance that is overheard.[35] Emily Dickinson's eccentric relation to space, I would suggest, is not so much *phobic* as *poetic*. Dickinson lyricizes space, recreating in the domestic interior the very condition of poetic address and response. If so many of Dickinson's lyrics resemble miniature domestic interiors, the domestic interior functions for the poet something like a lyre—an instrument of sound.

Sound emerges in Dickinson's intensely musical poetry as a far more reliable organ of perception than sight. Unlike the body's other orifices, the ear is the only organ that cannot close itself. The portals of the ear remain perpetually open, capable at any time of receiving messages from a world beyond the bounds of the strictly visible:

> This World is not Conclusion.
> A species stands beyond—
> Invisible, as Music—
> But positive, as Sound—   (P 501)

The ear's receptivity makes it the most vulnerable of human orifices, and the most finely tuned. It is the ear, not the eye, that offers the most direct route to the human heart:

> An ear can break a human heart
>   As quickly as a spear,
> We wish the ear had not a heart
>   So dangerously near.   (P 1764)

In this poem Dickinson gives the ear the last word, embedding the word "ear" in each of the stanza's concluding images: heart, spear, near. In an 1874 letter to Higginson, the poet explains that the ear is more important than the eye because sound always comes last. Invoking the nineteenth-century belief that hearing is the last of the corporeal senses to fade upon the body's demise, Dickinson notes that "The Ear is the last face. We hear after we see" (L 405). Poems like "I heard a Fly buzz—when I died" reaffirm the transgressive power of the ear, attributing to the voice-from-beyond-the-grave the ability to hear long after "I could not see to see" (P 465).

Mary Loeffelholz cannily identifies the container of the house itself as an ear, "a permeable but protective boundary organ." Loeffelholz reads the Dickinson Homestead as a sensory structure that continually channels and returns sound. As a sensitive medium of sound, this house-lyre embodies for Dickinson "a poetic model of perception and reception."[36] Sound succeeds where sight fails, passing through windows and doors, penetrating walls and floors, infiltrating corners and crannies. Yet the contest between sight and sound is not so simple for the writer whose poems crucially depend upon both bodily senses precisely to work *as poems*. In her 1863 lyric "The Spirit is the Conscious Ear," Dickinson once more plays on the embedded "ear" in "hear," but she adds to this perfect rhyme the homonym "hear" and "here."

> The Spirit is the Conscious Ear.
> We actually Hear
> When We inspect—that's audible—
> That is admitted—Here—
>
> For other Services—as Sound—
> There hangs a smaller Ear
> Outside the Castle—that Contain—
> The other—only—Hear—   (P 733)

Located at the end of four of this poem's eight lines, the ear again appears to have final say. Yet, as Loeffelholz notes, because of the homonym, the central difference in the poem between sight and sound, between "here" and "hear," can only be seen, not heard. The distinction between Romanticism's twin figures of poetic authority, vision and voice, is more visual than auditory (122). The poet must paradoxically rely upon visual understanding to achieve the conceptual elevation of voice over vision, ear over eye.

Dickinson's lack of faith in the sensory power of vision is striking; poem after poem in this poet's expansive corpus stresses the finitude of the human eye, its limitations and imperfections. "Adorned, for a Superior Grace— / Not yet, our eyes can see" (P 575), the poet laments in 1862. A year later the message is even clearer: "I'm finite, I can't see" (P 696). During her most prolific period, Dickinson sees blindness as the precondition of faith, as in this poem from 1864:

> What I see not, I better see—
> Through Faith—my Hazel Eye
> Has periods of shutting—
> But, no lid has Memory— (P 939)

By 1865, after a series of poems challenging the power of vision, the poet concludes, simply, "Best Things dwell out of Sight" (P 998).

The dating of these poems on the failure of vision suggests that Dickinson's distrust of the eye was more than metaphoric. Between 1862 and 1865, Dickinson, fearful that she was going blind, twice sought treatment for inflammation of the eyes from the country's most eminent ophthalmologist, Henry Willard Williams.[37] Famous for his use of the newly patented ophthalmoscope, an optical device powerful enough to illuminate the interior of the human eye, Williams eventually cured Dickinson of her temporary blindness. Unlike the two other great optical inventions that came long before it, the microscope and the telescope, in which the supremacy of the seeing eye remained unchallenged,[38] the ophthalmoscope laid bare the eye's own insufficiencies, radically undermining the traditional authority of the all-knowing human perceiver. Whatever the exact circumstances of Dickinson's visual impairment, the poet lived in a historical period when the reigning classical model of vision was beginning to rupture. The ophthalmoscope reflected in its triple lenses not the traditional all-seeing eye, but a modern eye that could itself be seen, optically penetrated by prosthetic devices infinitely superior to the human organ.

The exposure of the frailties and imperfections of the human eye in the nineteenth century led to the relocation of the organ of vision to the body's interior, where no mere technological instrument could reach it. The poetic eye turned inward, irradiating the private recesses of the soul with all the cognitive power previously expended on the world of empirical phenomena. Thomas Carlyle, speaking in 1852 of "this strange camera obscura of an existence," used the metaphor of "spiritual optics" to describe the new Copernican revolution in vision.[39] Dickinson's spiritual third eye corrects the imperfect sight of the body's two orbs by similarly reversing the gaze, finding more sumptuous quarters inside the body: "Reverse cannot befall / That fine Prosperity / Whose Sources are interior" (P 395). Or again: "The Table is not laid without / Till it is laid within" (P 1223). By 1862, Dickinson had found her subject: "that Campaign inscrutable / Of the Interior" (P 1188).

4

By the time Emily Dickinson had become, in Samuel Bowles's memorable 1863 complaint, a "Queen Recluse,"[40] the American domestic interior had come to represent a place of leisure, a sanctuary for the production of privacy. But for one of Amherst's leading families, the public/private distinction was an exceedingly loose one. The private interior of the Dickinson Homestead was, in fact, a very public place, a hub of Amherst social life even after the center of power shifted in the 1860s to the Evergreens next door. The Homestead was the site not only of teas and dinners associated with Amherst College (where Edward Dickinson was treasurer) but of the college's annual commencement receptions. As a moderator of local town meetings, a twice-elected Massachusetts state senator, and a representative to the Thirty-third United States Congress, Edward Dickinson attracted to his home a steady stream of visitors, among them, newspaper editors, bishops, preachers, judges, lawyers, politicians, academics, writers, generals, and senators.[41] That the Homestead was, for so many travelers to the Connecticut Valley, a final point of destination is pictographically suggested by an 1856 map of Amherst showing the town's new railroad. The Amherst and Belchertown Rail Road, which originated in New London, Connecticut, terminated practically at the Dickinson Homestead's doorstep, just a block away from the only man in town influential enough to build it.

By 1853, two years before moving back to the family homestead, Emily Dickinson was already beginning to feel displaced in her own home: "Our house is crowded daily with the members of this world, the high and the low, the bond and the free, the 'poor in this world's goods,' and the 'almighty dollar'" (L 128). Lavinia's diary of 1851 (the only year in which she kept a daily journal) records hundreds of social engagements. Rarely a day went by when the two Dickinson sisters were not either making or receiving social calls—calls usually associated, as Richard Sewall documents, with college students, tutors, or law clerks from Edward Dickinson's office.[42] Describing to her brother a particularly trying day, as she strove to entertain a series of male callers while her bemused father looked on, Dickinson wryly quipped, "I again crept into the sitting room, more dead than alive, and endeavored to *make conversation*" (L 79). Another time, exasperated by a passerby inquiring at the Homestead for housing, Dickinson claims to have directed the elderly stranger to the nearby cemetery, "to spare expense of moving" (L 427). Even the normally social Lavinia, who for years sought to protect her sister from constant intrusions, could be provoked by a sudden influx of callers to "beat her wings like a maddened Bird, whose Home has been invaded" (L 506).

It was precisely because the Dickinson household was anything but private that Dickinson found it necessary to carve out her own sequestered space within the extended domain of the family living quarters. That the poet was able to retreat to her bedroom at all, at any time of day or year, was to a large extent made possible by the hiring of the Dickinson's first full-time domestic servant in 1855, the year the family moved back into the Homestead. At one point there were as many as eight Irish immigrants on Edward Dickinson's payroll, making Emily officially a daughter of the American leisure class. "God keep me from what they call *households*" (L 36), Dickinson prayed, five years before Margaret O'Brien arrived to fulfill her wish and to save her from the trials of housekeeping, that "prickly art" (L 907). After the return to the Homestead, the bedroom became for Dickinson a space of relative freedom and release—release from domestic labor, family obligation, and social expectation.[43]

Dickinson's retreat to her bedroom can also be attributed to major changes in the domestic interior itself. Greater reliance on relatively inexpensive oil lamps made it possible to light more rooms for longer periods of time. And the addition of two extra chimneys in the Homestead's 1855 renovation facilitated the installation, in all the major rooms of the house, of cast-iron fireplaces. No longer constrained to gather in the evenings around a single fire for warmth and light, family members could disperse themselves through a more evenly heated dwelling. The improved heating arrangements dramatically reconfigured social relations within the home, decentralizing the family and creating new zones of privacy. More than any other revolution of the domestic interior, the Franklin stove made it possible for individual members *within* the family to seek privacy *from* the family.

The newly privatized household had a pronounced effect on Dickinson family relations. After his first visit to the Homestead in 1870, Higginson said of the Dickinsons: "Each member runs his or her own selves" (L 342a). Lavinia, late in her life, admitted that her family lived "like friendly and absolute monarchs, each in his own domain."[44] A letter dating probably from the late 1870s suggests that Emily happily concurred with both assessments, noting "We have no statutes here, but each does as it will, which is the sweetest jurisprudence" (L 545). The compartmentalization of the family into separate spatial domains permitted a new division of family labor. As Lavinia described it, Emily "had to think—she was the only one of us who had that to do. Father believed; and mother loved; and Austin had Amherst; and I had the family to keep track of."[45] Mabel Todd reports that, to the rest of the family, Dickinson's "curious leaving of outer life never seemed unnatural."[46] It was, in Lavinia's words, "only a happen," a logical outcome for the one family member whose main job it was to think.[47] Of all the reasons hypothesized for this nineteenth-century poet's famous withdrawal, one is compelled to wonder whether Dickinson chose to isolate herself within her bedroom for the simple reason that, for the first time in the history of the domestic interior, she could.

Such a view contrasts sharply with the dominant critical portrait of Dickinson as "a helpless agoraphobic, trapped in a room in her father's house."[48] Most Dickinson commentators imagine the poet's bedroom as a claustrophobic space of self-imposed isolation, "a melancholy, even terrifying, sanctuary." The bedroom is the place where the poet "felt herself prematurely fitted to a coffin." It is a "primary Gothic scene" with the heroine "imprisoned on the inside."[49] But the perception of Dickinson's bedroom as a domestic coffin or a Gothic prison is largely a critical projection. The room itself, fifteen-feet-square and ten-feet-high, is spacious and airy [figure 1.9]. Two large southern exposures illumine the white walls of a room further brightened by light straw mat floor-coverings and white linen bedsheets. Situated in the Homestead's southwest corner, Dickinson's bedroom is actually

FIG. 1.9 Dickinson's bedroom writing table and chair, with Franklin stove at right. In her poem "Myself was formed—a Carpenter" (P 488), Dickinson pictures this small writing table, only seventeen-and-a-half-inches-square, as a more expansive surface, the "Plane" upon which she practices "the Art of Boards." *Photograph by Frank Ward.*

the room with the best light, the best ventilation, and the best views.

    If vision was de-emphasized in the parlor, in favor of intensifying sound, it is subtly reinstalled in the bedroom, as if to overcompensate for a failing ear, straining to catch the distant vibrations of household activity below. The place critics routinely identify as removing Dickinson from the domain of the visible in fact invests her with considerable scopic power. More a panoptic center than an enclosed prison cell, Dickinson's bedroom affords its occupant maximum visual control. The poet commands from her corner room a clear view of the Holyoke

FIG. 1.10 Dickinson's mahogany bed. *Photograph by Frank Ward.*
Trustees of Amherst College.

mountains to the South and the Evergreens to the West. As Dickinson surely knew when she perhaps herself selected the room in
1855, she could watch, through the bedroom's western windows,
the sun set (literally) over her beloved Sue. From her single mahogany bed, fashioned in the style of a sleigh [figure 1.10], Dickinson's line of vision also encompassed the street below, where
the voices of pedestrians were close enough to be frequently
overheard. Proximity to the public life of the street thus allowed
Dickinson to continue to indulge her ear for language, or what
she herself called, in reference to the delight she took in overhearing the conversations of passersby, her "vice for voices" (L
prose fragment 19).

The poet's cherry writing table, located in the southwest corner of this southwest corner room, occupies the bedroom's interior within an interior, its *sanctum sanctorum*. Here the poet is
suspended between south and west, between afternoon sun and

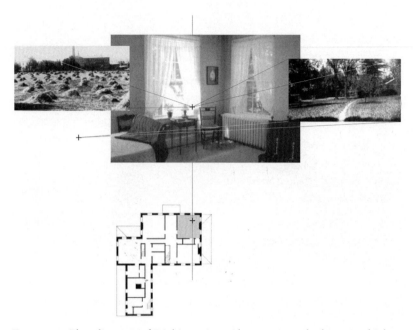

FIG. 1.11 Plan diagram of Dickinson's southwest corner bedroom, which afforded views of the hayfields and mountains to the south and the Evergreens to the west.

evening sunset, between the anonymous world of the street and the intimate world of Austin and Sue. It is a liminal space that is decidedly central, as a conceptual diagram of the Dickinson property demonstrates [figure 1.11]. Three hundred yards east of the Evergreens, but positioned significantly closer to the street, the Homestead's southwest corner bedroom could survey not only the Italian villa next door but the western vista beyond. It presents the viewer with a greater range of views, and with a greater number of opportunities for surveillance. The bedroom's middlemost position further highlights the poet's symbolic role within the family—central but protected, unseen but seeing, a kind of Dickinson family sentinel.

The domain of privacy in which Dickinson is said to have been imprisoned or entombed actually offered the poet ample op-

portunities for intellectual growth; neither a space of confinement nor of death, Dickinson's bedroom proffered ready entry
into the public world of letters. It is one of the great paradoxes of
this poet's interior life that the more she withdrew, the wider her
circle of acquaintances became. The Homestead bedroom was
the place where Dickinson composed the vast majority of her seventeen hundred and seventy-five poems and an estimated ten
thousand letters, of which more than a thousand survive. Here
Dickinson communicated with her "private public,"[50] developing
a public persona *as* a private poet. With pictures of Thomas Carlyle, Elizabeth Barrett Browning, and George Eliot on her walls,
Dickinson elevated her writing into a serious occupation by converting her bedroom into a private study, a more suitable environment for a serious poet. "Sweet hours have perished here, /
This is a timid room" (P 1767), Dickinson wrote of her bedroom-
study.[51]

Images of the mighty in the timid, the great in the small, the
infinite in the finite, recur throughout Dickinson's poems of the
bedroom. Typically, the more limited the space, the more unlim-
ited the speaker:

The Way I read a Letter's—this—
'Tis first—I lock the Door—
And push it with my fingers—next—
For transport it be sure—

And then I go the furthest off
To counteract a knock—
Then draw my little Letter forth
And slowly pick the lock—

Then—glancing narrow, at the Wall—
And narrow at the floor
For firm Conviction of a Mouse
Not exorcised before—

Peruse how infinite I am
To no one that You—know—
And sigh for lack of Heaven—but not
The Heaven God bestow—   (P 636)

This poem about the intensely private, almost furtive act of reading a letter contains within it layers and depths of interiority, the
letter itself functioning as a locked interior within a sealed room.
The experience of reading the letter in the room's farthest corner
enlarges the speaker, expanding the boundaries of "narrow wall"
and "narrow floor" to accommodate her limitlessness. For Dickinson, the most private, hidden, or secret corners of experience leave
one completely vulnerable. In "The Way I read a Letter's—this—"
the speaker presumes, in the poem's final stanza, that her own audience can "peruse" her; through the mimetic act of unlocking the
poem itself, readers are invited to discover their unbounded interiority. The open intimacies of this "poème à clef"[52] immediately call
to mind another famous Dickinson anecdote. Inviting her niece up
to her bedroom one day, and pretending to lock the door with an
invisible key, the poet reportedly declared, "Matty, child, no one
could ever punish a Dickinson by shutting her up alone."[53]

If hiding is a major theme in Dickinson's poetry, so is the thrill
of being found. "Good to hide, and hear 'em hunt! / Better, to be
found" (P 842), Dickinson wrote in 1864, the year she produced
the greatest number of poems on the question of invisibility and
exposure. For Dickinson, there is no place remote enough, or interior enough, to escape God's sight.

The deepest hid is sighted first
And scant to Him the Crowd—
What triple Lenses burn upon
The Escapade from God—   (P 894)

For Dickinson, the most private spaces are the most public, and
hiding is simply the best way to be seen. To be "deepest hid" is to

be, not anonymous, but entirely conspicuous. The one who hides best is the one who is "sighted first," ignited by the "triple Lenses" of God's powerful ophthalmoscope.

5

Nowhere is the image of the exposed hiding place more visible than in the cupola, the Homestead's smallest interior chamber [figure 1.12]. Built in the customary shape of a lantern, the Homestead cupola reestablishes the importance of light and vision in the hierarchy of corporeal senses that so powerfully organizes Dickinson's lyric phenomenology of space. The most intimate space in Dickinson's house is also the most revealing, laid bare on all four sides by a double set of windows. Like four pairs of eyes, the cupola's windows afford panoramic outlooks in every direction, while simultaneously exposing the observer her-

FIG. 1.12 Exterior view of the Homestead cupola, built in the shape of a lantern. *Photograph by Frank Ward.*

self to view. More than any other space within the domestic interior, the cupola conforms to Dickinson's belief that solitary and private interiors are also vulnerable and exposed—places of "polar privacy" (P 1695).

No more than six-and-a-half-feet-square, the cupola is at once the most modest room in the house and the most exalted. From the Latin for "little barrel," the cupola draws the eye upward to the building's greatest point of concentration, much in the manner of a spire on a church. By mid-century, reformers had discovered the symbolic potential of architecture as a vehicle for the consecration of domestic life. The popularity of the cupola, like the sudden design interest in architectural cross-plans, stained glass windows, and parlor pump organs, visibly transformed the American home into a secular place of worship.[54] Accessible by a winding staircase located outside Dickinson's bedroom, the cupola could be approached only by first ascending through a cavernous empty attic, augmenting the feeling of entering a solitary, silent, and sacred space. The cupola's secluded location at the top of the Homestead, removed from the household and buffered by the attic, together with its perimeter of sealed windows in the winter, create an almost soundproof enclosure, where hearing gives way to seeing, and eye displaces ear. As we have traveled upward in the Homestead, from parlor to cupola passing through Dickinson's bedroom situated between, we have moved progressively from the large to the small, from the dark to the light, from the auditory to the visual. At the apex of the house, the cupola promises the advancing subject an all encompassing, God's-eye-view: "His Eye, it is the East and West— / The North and South when He / Do concentrate His Countenance" (P 871). By offering a 360° range of vision, the cupola appears to reinstate a classical all-seeing subject, previously rendered blind by the darkness of the first floor interior.

Yet the view from the cupola is, in fact, a partial view, not a complete panorama [figure 1.13]. Where one expects a conventional central window, offering a more continuous uninterrupted

FIG. 1.13 Plan diagram of the cupola. Instead of presenting the viewer with a panoramic view, the cupola's eight windows create a blind center.

line of vision, the paired windows encasing the cupola instead create a blind center. Vision is limited not only by the structural cross-frame between the windows, blocking the spectator's view, but by the frame of the human body itself, never capable of seeing more than 160° at the same time. Inside the cupola, there is more wall space than window surface. The cupola's cross-frame is broad enough to conceal anyone within it, once again offering Dickinson, if she chose, the privilege of seeing without being seen.[55] The tension between what the mid-century cupola theoretically offers (ideal transparency) and what it actually delivers (real opacity) is neatly reconciled by one of Dickinson's own philosophies: "To disappear enhances" (P 1209).

For Dickinson, transparency is just another form of opacity. The cupola's windows are blank, unseeing eyes, blinded by over-exposure to the very light that makes vision possible.

Before I got my eye put out
I liked as well to see—
As other Creatures, that have Eyes
And know no other way—

But were it told to me—Today—
That I might have the sky
For mine—I tell you that my Heart
Would split, for size of me—

The Meadows—mine—
The Mountains—mine—
All Forests—Stintless Stars—
As much of Noon as I could take
Between my finite eyes—

The Motions of the Dipping Birds—
The Morning's Amber Road—
For mine—to look at when I liked—
The News would strike me dead—

So safer—guess—with just my soul
Upon the Window pane—
Where other Creatures put their eyes—
Incautious—of the Sun—   (P 327)

Not for Dickinson the transcendental powers of Emerson's transparent eyeball, capable of taking in the cosmic world in all its astonishing infinitude. Dickinson shies away from the window pane/pain where "A Vision on the Retina" (P 566) threatens insanity.

> Had we our senses
> But perhaps 'tis well they're not at Home
> So intimate with Madness
> He's liable with them
>
> Had we the eyes within our Head—
> How well that we are Blind—
> We could not look upon the Earth—
> So utterly unmoved—   (P 1284)

The lyric "I" is a blind eye, the lyric seer a sightless visionary. The pun is clear: to see is to be deprived of "our senses," to be addled by what the poet calls elsewhere the "very Lunacy of Light" (P 593). To be blinded by light is a familiar refrain in Dickinson's poetry, a poetry that routinely favors the safer practice of night vision: "I see thee better—in the Dark— / I do not need a Light—" (P 611).

True sightedness, able to pierce the veil of eternity, is achieved not from the ennobling heights of the light-filled cupola but from the ordinary chambers of the dimly lighted interior. Once again, it is a question of access: "Mortality's Ground Floor/Is Immortality" (P 1234). To cross over from the mortal to the immortal, one must progress not upwards but downwards, passing through the subterranean chambers of the grave. Nor does this spiritual journey follow a traditional trajectory from inside to outside. The grave represents simply another interior, a "low Apartment in the Sod" (P 557) that houses "Death's single Privacy" (P 463). In Dickinson's upside-down, inside-out world, direction is radically dislocated and space itself unhinged. The inside subsumes the outside, transforming the exterior into a mirror image of the domestic interior.

6

This is not to say that the poet moves outside exteriority altogether; Dickinson's poetry abounds in natural descriptions—of sunrises and sunsets, mountains and fields, flowers and trees—depicted in every season of the year. Yet, a significant number of Dickinson's landscape poems, including "There's a certain Slant of light" (P 258), "The Angle of a Landscape" (P 375), and "By my Window have I for Scenery" (P 797) are narrated from the perspective of an observer looking out a window. Other famous nature poems by Dickinson, like "I dreaded that first Robin, so" (P 348), "The Malay—took the Pearl" (452), and "I Started early, took my dog" (P 520), are told entirely in the past tense, as if composed retrospectively from the safe distance of house, mansion, or town. Still other poems of the exterior portray nature itself as a domestic interior, lofty as a church cathedral (P 790) or humble as a "Dome of Worm" (P 893).

It is in this latter category that Dickinson's mortuary verse falls. In an era when domestic burial grounds assumed the character of miniature neighborhoods, and family plots imitated private estates,[56] Dickinson analogizes cemeteries to small villages or towns (P 736, 892) and graves to "little dwelling houses" (P 411, 187, 449, 712, 813, 1310, 1489, 1752). Sometimes Dickinson casually figures the grave's interior as a bedroom: "I went to thank Her— / But She Slept— / Her Bed—a funneled Stone— / With Nosegays at the Head and Foot— / That Travellers—had thrown" (P 363). To Mrs. Holland the poet writes in January 1875, six months after her father's death: "Mother is asleep in the Library—Vinnie in the Dining Room—Father—in the Masked Bed—in the Marl House" (L 432). With a gravestone at their head and a footstone at their base, nineteenth-century New England graves, occasionally called "bedbacks," strongly resembled beds, the place where sleep was but a metaphor for death.[57]

At other times Dickinson portrays the grave as a drawing room, a more formal domestic interior whose occupant serves as God's helpmate: "The grave my little cottage is, / Where 'Keeping house' for thee / I make my parlor orderly / And lay the marble tea" (P 1743). The close association of parlors with death is put to ironic use in one of Dickinson's earliest persona poems written in the voice of a corpse, in which the entombed speaker convinces herself "I am alive—because / I am not in a Room— / The Parlor— Commonly—it is— / So Visitors may come—" (P 470). If the grave is indeed a parlor, as the poet suggests in yet another poem on the interior of a coffin, then "No Bald Death—affront their Parlors— / No Bold Sickness come / To deface their Stately Treasures" (P 457). The paradox consoles: in the grave, there is no death.

Dickinson died in her bed on May 15, 1886, after a prolonged battle with what the poet called "Nervous prostration" (L 937) and her death certificate identified as "Bright's Disease."[58] The moment of Dickinson's passing did not go unrecorded. "The day was awful," her brother Austin writes in his diary; "She ceased to breathe that terrible breathing just before the whistles sounded for six."[59] Following a newly popular burial practice that marked the official beginning of the American funeral industry,[60] Dickinson's body was embalmed, transformed in death into the statuary marble figure she had so often been mistaken for in life. Higginson's diary entry for the day of the funeral, which took place in the Homestead parlor, describes the corpse in particular detail:

> a wondrous restoration of youth—she is 54 [55] & looked 30, not a gray hair or wrinkle, & perfect peace on the beautiful brow. There was a little bunch of violets at the neck & one pink cypripedium; the sister Vinnie put in two heliotropes by her hand "to take to Judge Lord."[61]

Dressed in a white flannel robe specially fashioned by Sue, and holding flowers in her hand, Dickinson prepared to enter God's stately chambers in the same formal manner she once greeted visitors to the Homestead, immediately casting all her previous entrances as dress rehearsals for a far more important, and definitive, debut.

Dickinson's funeral procession was exceptionally modest, compared to her father's more elaborate cortege twelve years earlier. While Edward Dickinson's coffin was carried ceremoniously through the Homestead's front door and paraded slowly through the streets of Amherst, Emily Dickinson preferred to exit her life as unobtrusively as she had lived it, slipping quietly out the backdoor.[62] Following her request, the poet's casket was carried on the shoulders of six of the family's Irish men servants, who transported their charge through the open barn and across the fields to the family plot, careful to keep within sight of the house. Inscribed on her tombstone is a simple two-word message Dickinson sent to her cousins in what turned out to be her last piece of correspondence, a personal elegy so condensed it might also be seen as her last poem: "Called back" (L 1046).[63] It is a fitting epitaph for a poet of the interior whose deepest impulse while living was to return to the place she called "Eden—the ancient Homestead" (P 1545), and whose death certificate, under the category "Occupation," bore the equally elliptical yet no less expressive words, "At Home."

Dickinson family plot, Amherst Cemetery. Emily Dickinson's tombstone, second from left, originally bore her initials "EED." It was the poet's niece Martha Dickinson Bianchi who, sometime in the early twentieth century, chose the new tombstone and its eloquent epitaph, "Called Back." *Author Photograph.*

Freud at work in his study. *Courtesy of Edmund Engelman, Photographer.*

2

Freud's Ear

Berggasse 19
Vienna Austria
(with Joel Sanders)

IN MAY OF 1938, ON THE EVE of Sigmund Freud's expulsion from
Vienna and flight to London, Freud's colleague August Aichhorn
met with the photojournalist Edmund Engelman at the Café Museum on Karlsplatz. Would it be possible, Aichhorn wondered, to
take photographs of Freud's office and apartment without drawing
the attention of the Gestapo who, since Hitler's annexation of Austria two months earlier, had been keeping the home of one of
Vienna's most famous Jewish intellectuals under constant surveillance? The purpose of this photographic documentary was to provide an inventory of Berggasse 19 so exact that, as Aichhorn
envisioned it, the home of psychoanalysis might be painstakingly
recreated as a museum after the impending war.[1] Engelman, a mechanical and electrical engineer who ran a local photography shop
on the Karntnerstrasse, agreed to try to provide a pictorial record of
Berggasse 19. In the course of four days and using two cameras (a
Rolleiflex and a Leica), two lenses (a 50mm lens and a 28mm wide-
angle lens), and a light meter, and working without the aid of either
flashes or floodlights, Engelman took approximately one hundred
shots of Berggasse 19, focusing on the consulting room, study, and
family living quarters.[2] These photographs, together with a short
film segment of Freud's office taken by Marie Bonaparte in December 1937, provide the only extant visual record of the place where,
for forty-seven years, Freud treated his patients, met regularly with
his colleagues, and wrote his scientific papers and case histories.

Freud's biographers have written eloquently of his traumatic expulsion from his home in Vienna; cultural historians have studied in fascinating detail the peculiarities of Freud's domestic arrangements and the routine of his office schedule; psychoanalysts have analyzed at length the procedures of Freud's clinical practice; and art historians have recently begun to examine the meaning of Freud's extensive collection of antiquities and the links between psychoanalysis and archaeology. But we have yet to consider the significance of the spatial site that housed these practices and objects. We have yet to fully enter, in other words, Berggasse 19. How might the spatial configuration of Freud's office, and the arrangement of furniture and objects within it, frame our understanding of psychoanalytic theory and practice? What might an architectural study of Berggasse 19 tell us about the play of vision, power, and transference that structures the analytic scene?

Taking as my point of departure Engelman's black-and-white photographs, as well as architectural drawings gathered from site visits to Freud's offices in London and Vienna, I want to examine the porous boundary between the two-dimensional space of photography and the three-dimensional space of architecture. The convergence of these two languages of space highlight the confusion of surface and depth, inside and outside, subject and object that characterize psychoanalysis's own primal scene. Until recently, questions of spectatorship have been theorized largely in terms of a subject's perception of a two-dimensional image (photography, film, television).[3] Like my reading of Dickinson's homestead, my analysis of Freud's office explores the role of both vision and hearing in three-dimensional space. Architecture and psychoanalysis come together here, for both are cultural discourses of the seen and the unseen, of the audible and the inaudible—of public and private space.

My explorations are impelled by the same powerful fantasy that drives Edmund Engelman's photographs—namely, the illusion that one can relive the experience of early psychoanalysis by retracing the footsteps of Freud's patients. But the chambers of Freud's office, no less than the rooms of Dickinson's homestead, are fundamentally irrecoverable. The photographs of Berggasse 19, originally taken for the postwar construction of a Freud museum, have themselves *become* the museum—miniature sites of preservation and display. Today visitors to the consulting room and study in Berggasse 19 will find a space emptied of Freud's possessions (now housed in the Freud Museum in London) but encompassed with enlargements of Engelman's photographs displayed on the walls. This highly unusual mode of museum exhibition insists on the mediating function of the photographs, while preserving the empty rooms of the office as a space of exile and absence: the place Freud was finally forced to flee at the end of his life "to die in freedom."[4] To the extent that this book as a whole is an attempt at recovery, at reconstituting from the fragments of history what has been buried and lost, my reading of Berggasse 19 is inevitably a work of mourning, framed by the same logic of memorialization that so pervasively organized the space of Freud's office.

1

Engelman's photodocumentary opens with three exterior shots of Berggasse 19, motivated, as he was later to write, by a presentiment that the building itself would be destroyed in the war.[5] The façade of this typical late nineteenth-century apartment house comes into focus through a progressive sequence of long, medium, and closeup shots of the entry door. Exerting a kind of centrifugal force, the swastika placed over the door of Berggasse 19 by the building's Aryan owner pulls the camera in, gradually focusing and delimiting the social boundaries of the photodocumentary's visual field.

What kind of space is the urban street space? For the European, the street is the place of chance encounters and accidental dramas. It is also, historically, the site of political uprising and counterrevolution—the birthplace of the modern revolutionary subject. But, as Susan Suleiman notes of the modern wayfare, "after 1933, any attempt to think politically about the street had to grapple with its profound ambiguity."[6] The street, formerly a place of collective resistance to state intervention, becomes, with the rise of fascism in Europe, a public venue for Nazi torchlight parades and other forms of national socialist ideology.

Engelman's three views of the street, taken with a wide-angle lens, capture a near-deserted Berggasse. Far from removing us from the sphere of political action, however, these daytime shots of a scarcely populated urban street illuminate, in visually arresting fashion, the realities of political occupation for the predominantly Jewish residents of Vienna's Ninth District. Most of the Ninth District's Jewish population were located on eleven streets, including the Berggasse, which ran from the fashionable upper –middle-class neighborhood of the University of Vienna at one end, to the junk shops of the Tandelmarkt owned by poor Jewish shopkeepers at the other.[7] Though located just outside the Ringstrasse, the Berggasse was very much at the center of the German occupation. By the time Engelman embarked on his pictorial record of Freud's residence in May 1938, the image of a scarcely populated urban street operated as a potent indexical sign of political danger and social displacement. For Vienna's Jewish residents, occupation meant incarceration; to be "occupied" was to be exiled, driven out of the public space of the street and into the home.

Operating without the use of a flash ordinarily employed for interior shots, and continuing to use a wide-angle lens designed for exterior shots, Engelman transports the codes and conventions of street photography inside Berggasse 19. The building becomes an interior street as the camera's peripatetic gaze traffics through domestic space. Engelman begins his pictorial walking tour by bringing us across the entry threshold and into the lobby, a wide linear space that, with its cobblestone floor and coffered ceiling, resembles a covered arcade. At the end of the entry corridor, a pair of glazed doors, their glass panes etched with antique female figures, provides a view of an aedicule located, on axis, in the rear service courtyard beyond. These symmetrical, semi-transparent doors establish a recurring visual motif that is progressively disrupted and finally displaced as we approach and move through the suite of rooms comprising Freud's office.

Berggasse 19 wears its façade on the inside; those architectural elements normally found on the exterior of a building can be seen on the interior of Freud's apartment house. At the top of the switch-back stair, for example, the visitor encounters a translucent interior window that looks not onto an exterior courtyard but directly into the Freud family's private apartment [figure 2.1]. Illuminated by a light from within, but draped from view by an inside curtain, Freud's interior window troubles the traditional distinction between the private and the public by rendering completely ambiguous whether we might be on the outside looking in or the inside looking out.

The architectural transposition of public and private space chronicled by Engelman's camera captures Freud's own relation to his workplace, for although located at the back of the apartment and insulated from the street, Freud's office nonetheless operated as a busy thoroughfare [figure 2.2]. Patients, colleagues, friends, family, and even pets moved in and out at regular intervals. When he needed privacy, Freud would seek refuge on the Ringstrasse where he would retreat for his daily constitutional, occasionally with a family member or friend to accompany him. For Freud, the interior space of the office and the exterior space of the street were seamless extensions of one another; both were places of movement and conversation, of chance words and surprise meetings, of accident and incident.[8] The commerce of everyday encounters constituted the primary source materials of interior reflection his patients brought to their private sessions with Freud. The transactions of the street quickly became the transferences of the therapeutic scene.

FIG. 2.1 Interior window looking into Freud family apartment. This window reminded patients in their daily climb toward Freud's office that the doctor had a personal life of his own, even if the window's inner curtain blocked any real visual access to this private and forbidden zone. *Author Photograph*.

Inside Freud's consulting room and adjoining study, we are confronted with a confusing assortment of furniture and objects: couch, chair, books, bookcases, cabinets, paintings, photographs, lights, rugs, and Freud's extensive collection of antiquities. Freud displayed in the close space of his office the entirety of his collection, acquired mainly from local antique dealers with earnings set aside from his daily hour of open consultations.[9] The experience of viewing Engelman's photographs of Freud's office is like nothing so much as window shopping, as we are permitted to view, but not

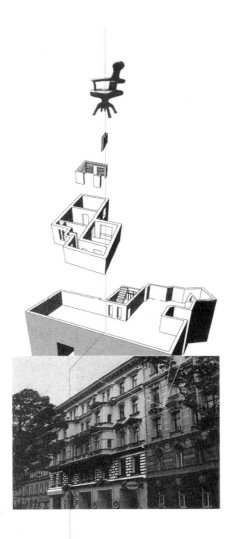

FIG. 2.2 Exploded Axonometric of Berggasse 19. The Freud family apartment occupied the front rooms on the second story. Isolated in the back
rooms and buffered by the apartment, Freud's office was protected from the
disturbances of the street. The double sets of casement windows and double
doors heighten the impression of a sequestered, private, interior space.

touch, the objects before us, many arranged in glass showcases. Ultimately, what Engelman seeks to document in these photographs is not just the objects but their particular sites of display. It is the very specific spatial arrangement of objects within the interior that constitutes the photodocumentary's visual field and that offers a blueprint for the future reconstruction of the office-museum.

The gaze of Engelman's camera is systematic, not random: it documents and surveys, inventories and catalogs. It moves from one corner of the room to the next, from wall to wall, window to window, memorizing the details of the office interior. This archival gaze is also a slightly manic one, obsessively traversing the same spaces, partitioning the office into a series of overlapping but discrete perceptual fields, at once contiguous and enclosed. The prosthetic eye of the camera attempts to take everything in, but finds its efforts frustrated by the very objects it seeks visually to preserve. The visual space becomes a carceral one as Engelman's camera repeatedly tries, and fails, to negotiate the crowded terrain of Freud's office, so cluttered with objects that many of the two thousand antiquities can be seen in these photographs spilling onto the study floor.[10]

Two months after his father's death in October 1896, Freud began assembling the antiquities that would transform his office into a veritable tomb. The debilitating illness and lingering death of Jakob Freud is generally recognized as the emotional crisis that galvanized Freud's compensatory interest in collecting. A father's demise is "the most important event, the most poignant loss, of a man's life," Freud famously opines in *The Interpretation of Dreams* (4: xxvi), a book that has itself been read as Freud's gradual coming to terms with the loss of his father. But it is not just his father whom Freud mourns through his accumulation of reliquary objects; it is also, in some profound sense, himself. Freud's self-described "death deliria"[11] played a central role in shaping the psychical and physical space of his office. Long before his father died, Freud was preoccupied with foretelling the exact time of his own future death. In a letter to Wilhelm Fliess dated June 22, 1894,

Freud insists that although he has no scientific basis for his predictions, he "shall go on suffering from various complaints for another four to five to eight years, with good and bad periods, and then between forty and fifty perish very abruptly from a rupture of the heart."[12] As Freud moved into the period forecast for his "rupture of the heart," it was not his own death that occurred but that of his father, who fell fatally ill and died of heart failure shortly after Freud's fortieth birthday: "All of it happened in my critical period," Freud writes to Fliess a day after his father's funeral, "and I am really quite down because of it."[13] Freud apparently felt that his father died in his place, prompting a labor of self-entombment that exhausted itself only with Freud's own painful and prolonged death almost half a century later.

Like Osiris buried alive in his coffin,[14] Freud began surrounding himself with disinterred objects: Egyptian scarabs, Roman death masks, Etruscan funeral vases, bronze coffins, and mummy portraits.[15] The attempt to chronicle the space of Freud's office for the purposes of erecting a future museum upon its ruins was, by 1938, a touchingly belated act, for Freud's office was a museum long before Engelman arrived to document it. Like all museums, this particular memorial site doubled as a mausoleum, showcasing the self-enshrinement of a collector buried among his funerary objects. "Museum and mausoleum are connected by more than phonetic association," Adorno once commented; "museums are the family sepulchers of works of art."[16] Engelman's photographs dramatically capture what half a century of Freud commentary has overlooked: the location of the analytic scene within the walls of a crypt. When patients arrived at Freud's office, they entered an overdetermined space of loss and absence, grief and memory, elegy and mourning. In short, they entered the exteriorized theater of Freud's own emotional history, where every object newly found memorialized a love-object lost.

We might recall at this juncture that Berggasse 19 was not Freud's first professional office. Freud initially set up his medical practice in a new residential building erected on the ashes of one of Vienna's most famous edifices, the Ring Theater, which burned to the ground in 1881 in a spectacular fire, killing more than six hundred people inside. Austria's Franz Josef commissioned the Viennese architect F.V. Schmidt to construct on the ruins an apartment house for the *haute bourgeoisie*, a portion of whose rent would be allocated to assist the hundreds of children orphaned by the fire. It was here, in an architectural monument to the dead of Vienna's Ring Theater, that psychoanalysis first took up residence. Not even the birth of the Freud's first child, which brought the newly married couple an official letter from the Emperor congratulating them on bringing new life to the site of such tragic loss, could completely erase for Freud the symbolic connotations of treating patients' nervous disorders in a place that came to be known as the *Sühnhaus* (House of Atonement).[17] Freud's psychoanalytic practice, from the very beginning, was closely associated with loss and recovery, the work of mourning.

2

The patient's entry into Freud's office initiates a series of complicated and subtle transactions of power, orchestrated largely by the very precise spatial arrangement of objects and furniture. Freud held initial consultations, between three and four every afternoon, in the study section of his office [figure 2.3]. Preferring a face-to face encounter with prospective patients, Freud seated them approximately four feet away from himself, across the divide of a table adjacent to the writing desk. Located in the center of a square room, at the intersection of two axial lines, the patient would appear to occupy the spatial locus of power. As if to confirm the illusion of his centrality, the patient is immediately presented, when seated, with a reflection of his own image, in a small portrait-sized mirror, framed in gold-filigree and hanging, at eye-level, on a fac-

FIG. 2.3 Freud's Study. For their first consultation with the doctor, patients were seated in the chair at the very center of the study, surveyed not only by Freud but also by the heads and figurines on the surrounding walls and tables. Many of Freud's twenty-five hundred books lined the walls of the study, further cluttered with antiquities. *Courtesy of Edmund Engelman, Photographer.*

ing window [figure 2.4]. As soon as Freud sits down at his desk, however, interposing himself between patient and mirror, the patient's reflection is blocked by Freud's head. Head substitutes for mirror in a metaphorical staging of the clinical role Freud seeks to assume. "The doctor," Freud pronounces in *Papers on Technique*, "should be opaque to his patients and, like a mirror, should show them nothing but what is shown to him" (12: 118).

Freud's clinical assumption of the function of the mirror, and the substitution of other for self that it enacts, sets into motion the transferential dynamics that will structure all future doctor-patient encounters. In preparation for the laborious work of overcoming their unconscious resistances, patients are required to

FIG. 2.4 Study Desk. This view of Freud's work area shows to the left of
the desk the mirror on the casement window and to the right of the desk the
figure of a Chinese sage positioned behind an ashtray; on the desk itself is a
copy of Freud's manuscript *Moses and Monotheism*. During the initial consultation with Freud, the patient, seated at the center of the square-shaped
study, sees his reflection framed within the portrait-sized mirror on the central mullion of the window behind Freud's desk. When Freud sits in his desk
chair, his head blocks and replaces the patient's image in the mirror, initiat-
ing the transferential dynamics governing future therapeutic encounters.
Courtesy of Edmund Engelman, Photographer.

divest themselves of authority while seated in the very center of
power. In a reverse panopticon, the most central location in
Freud's study (the point from which the gaze normally issues)
turns out to be the most vulnerable, as the patient suddenly finds
himself exposed on all sides to a multitude of gazes. Viewed from
both left and right by a phalanx of ancient figurines (all displayed
at eye-level and arranged to face the patient), as well as from behind by a collection of detached antique heads and from in front
by Freud's imposing visage, the patient is surveyed from every direction. Power in this transferential scene is exercised from the
margins. From the protected vantage point of his desk chair,

Freud studies his patient's face, fully illuminated by the afternoon light, while his own face remains barely visible, almost entirely eclipsed by backlighting from the window behind him.

"The process of psychoanalysis," Freud goes on to remark in *Papers on Technique*, "is retarded by the dread felt by the average observer of seeing himself in his own mirror" (12: 210). The analogy of the mirror, used to describe the process of psychoanalytic self-reflection, makes its first appearance in Freud's work in his reading of the memoirs of Daniel Paul Schreber. Mirrors figure prominently in Schreber's transvestic identification: "anyone who should happen to see me before the mirror with the upper portion of my torso bared—especially if the illusion is assisted by my wearing a little feminine finery—would receive an unmistakable impression of a *female bust*" (12: 33). And what did Freud see when, alone in his office amongst his classical heads and ancient figurines, he turned to face his own image in the mirror? Freud, too, saw the unmistakable impression of a bust—head and shoulders severed from the body, torso-less and floating, like the Roman head overlooking his consulting room chair or the death mask displayed in his study. His head decapitated by the frame of the mirror, Freud is visually identified with one of his own classical sculptures, transformed into a statuary fragment.

Looking in the other direction Freud also saw only heads. A wooden statue of a Chinese sage, sitting on the table between Freud and his patient, severs the patient's head in the same way Freud's head is decapitated by the frame of the mirror. From the vantage point of the desk chair, the patient's disembodied head assumes the status of one of Freud's antiquities, homologous not only to the stone heads filling the table directly behind the patient (the only table in the office displaying almost exclusively heads) but also to the framed photographic portraits above them, hanging at the exact same level as the mirror [figure 2.5].

For Freud, every self-reflection reveals a death mask, every mirror image a spectral double. In his meditation on the theme of

FIG. 2.5 Table across from Study Window. The collection of heads displayed on the table included an Egyptian mummy cover, a Chinese Buddha, and a Roman Aphrodite. Above the table Freud hung photographs only of women: the psychoanalyst Marie Bonaparte (who received the honor of two photographs), the psychoanalyst Lou-Andreas Salomé, and the French actress Yvette Guilbert. *Courtesy of Edmund Engelman, Photographer.*

doubling, Freud remarks in "The 'Uncanny'" that while the double first emerges in our psychical lives as a "preservation against extinction," this double (in typically duplicitous fashion) soon reverses itself: "from having been an assurance of immortality, it becomes the uncanny harbinger of death" (17: 235). By captivating our image, immobilizing and framing it, the mirror reveals a picture of our own unthinkable mortality.

Yet, as Freud notes elsewhere, it is finally impossible to visualize our own deaths, for "whenever we attempt to do so we can perceive that we are in fact still present as spectators" (14: 289). The mirror that memorializes also reincarnates, reconstituting us as phantom spectators, witnesses to our own irreplaceability. The mirror thus functions simultaneously like a window, assisting us in passing through the unrepresentable space of our violent eradication, and helping us, in effect, to survive our own deaths. This was indeed the function of Etruscan mirrors (so prominent in Freud's own private collection) on whose polished bronze surfaces mythological scenes were engraved. By differentiating between pictorial space and real space, the frame of the Etruscan mirror offers the illusion of a view onto another world. These mirrors, originally buried in tombs, assisted their owners in passing through their deaths: the Etruscan mirror opened a window onto immortality.

Lacan saw as much in his early reflections on the mirror stage. Radically dislocating the traditional opposition of transparency and reflectivity (window and mirror), Lacan instructs us to "think of the mirror as a pane of glass. You'll see yourself in the glass and you'll see objects beyond it."[18] In Freud's office, the placement of a mirror on a window further complicates this conflation of transparency and reflectivity by frustrating the possibility of opening up the space of looking that both crystalline surfaces appear to offer. Normally, when mirrors are placed against opaque walls, they have the capacity to act as windows; they dematerialize and dissolve architectural edges, creating the illusion of extension and expanding the spatial boundaries of the interior. But in this highly peculiar instance of a mirror superimposed on a window, visual access is obstructed rather than facilitated. Unlike the glass panes on Berggasse 19's rear entry doors, which allow the viewer's gaze to pass easily along a central axis from inside to outside, the composition of Freud's study window, with the mirror occupying the central vanishing point, redirects the gaze inward [figure 2.6]. By forcing the subject of reflection to confront an externalized gaze relayed back upon itself, the mirror on Freud's window interrupts the reassuring classical symmetries of self and other, inside and outside, seeing and being seen.[19]

The architectonics of the Freudian subject instead depends fundamentally upon a spatial dislocation, upon seeing the self ex-

FIG. 2.6 Sections through Entry Vestibule and Study Window. The window in Freud's study possesses certain compositional similarities with the building's rear entry doors. Seen frontally, both sites present us with a rectangular figure (aedicule and mirror) framed by a bifurcated glazed ground (door and window). But Freud's placement of the mirror before the study window inverts the traditional relationship of figure to ground. Disrupting the reassuring trajectory of a sovereign look (embodied by the transparency of the back entry doors), the mirror redirects the patient's gaze inwards, relaying the gaze back upon itself.

teriorized. It is not only that when we look in the mirror we see how others see us, but also that we see ourselves occupying a space where we are not. The statue that confronts us in the mirror permits us to look not just at but through ourselves to the "object who knows himself to be seen."[20] The domain delimited by Lacan's *imago*, "the statue in which man projects himself,"[21] is thus a strangely lifeless one. As Mikkel Borch-Jacobsen pictures it in "The Statue Man," this mirror world is "a sort of immense museum peopled with immobile 'statues,' 'images' of stone, and hieratic 'forms'." It is "the most inhuman of possible worlds, the most *unheimlich*."[22]

What Freud sees in his mirror is a subject who is, first and foremost, an object, a statue, a bust. The "dread" of self-reflection that Freud describes in *Papers on Technique* appears to issue from a fear of castration, of dramatic bodily disfigurement. If, as Freud insists in "Medusa's Head," the terror of castration is always linked to the sight of something, then it is the sight of *seeing oneself seeing* that possesses lethal consequences for the figure in the mirror. Like Medusa, who is slain by the fatal powers of her own gaze reflected back to her by Perseus's shield, Freud's narcissistic gaze makes him "stiff with terror, turns him to stone" (18: 273). Self-reflection petrifies. Perhaps this is the knowledge that so frightened, and so fascinated, Freud: the realization that the subject's "optical erection" could only be achieved at the price of its castration, its instantaneous, fatal transformation into a broken relic.

3

As the clinical treatment moves from the initial consultation in Freud's study to the sessions on the consulting room couch, the distribution of objects in the room produces a new kind of body, and a reconfigured doctor-patient relation [figure 2.7]. In the study, the patient, sitting isolated and exposed at the center of the

FIG. 2.7 Freud's Consulting Room. The arrangement of couch and chair create a warm, protected, intimate corner for the analytic conversation to take place. The silent sitting figures carved out of stone, depicted in the picture of the temple of Ramses II hanging over the couch, may have struck Freud as classical prototypes for the sedentary analyst, required to listen patiently for long hours in a stationary position. *Courtesy of Edmund Engelman, Photographer.*

room, occupied the point of maximum exposure; in the consulting room, the patient finds herself securely situated outside a circuit of visual surveillance. The arrangement of couch and chair, with their occupants facing outward at perpendicular angles, ensures that, once the analysis formally begins, there will never be an unobstructed line of vision between patient and doctor. The most intimate space in the room is thus also the most highly mediated, as if such close physical proximity between patient and doctor can only be sustained by the structural elimination of any direct visual transaction. The placement of articles on and around the consulting room couch—the heavy Persian rug hung vertically from the wall and anchored to the couch by a matching rug, the chenille cushions supporting the patient's head, neck, and upper back, and the blanket and porcelain stove warming the patient's feet—all create the impression of a protected enclave, a room within a room, a private interior space.

The profusion of sensuous Oriental rugs and throw pillows, and the horsehair sofa in the consulting room in Berggasse 19 suggests the subtle encroachment of "female" domestic space into the public sphere of the office. Freud's professional office as a scene of domestic comfort is precisely how the Wolf Man remembers it thirty-eight years after the completion of his formal analysis:

> I can remember, as though I saw them today, his two adjoining studies, with the door open between them and with their windows opening on a little courtyard. There was always a feeling of sacred peace and quiet here. The rooms themselves must have been a surprise to any patient, for they in no way reminded one of a doctor's office. . . . A few potted plants added life to the rooms, and the warm carpet and curtains gave them a homelike note. Everything here contributed to one's feeling of leaving the haste of modern life behind, of being sheltered from one's daily cares.[23]

In her autobiographical work, *Tribute to Freud*, the American poet H.D. recalls Freud's office in similar terms, emphasizing the feelings of safety and security generated by the space encompassing the consulting room couch: "Today, lying on the famous psychoanalytical couch, . . . [w]herever my fantasies may take me now, I have a center, security, aim. I am centralized or reoriented here in this mysterious lion's den or Aladdin's cave of treasures."[24]

H.D. goes on to describe the "smoke of burnt incense" (TF, 23) and the "fumes of the aromatic cigar" (TF, 132) that waft above the couch, emanating from the invisible corner behind her. Freud considered his passion for collecting "an addiction second in intensity only to his nicotine addiction."[25] The air in Freud's treatment room, densely humidified by ceramic water tubes attached to the Viennese stove, hung heavy with the smell of Freud's favorite cigars, which he often smoked during analytic sessions. Reading the visual record of Freud's office alongside these verbal accounts, a carefully staged orientalist scene insistently begins to take shape. Reclining on an ottoman couch, cushioned by Eastern carpets, and wreathed in pungent smoke, patients find themselves at home in a late Victorian fantasy of the opium den.

In Europe's fin-de-siècle fascination with the East, oriental interiors—especially the smoking room—were closely associated with leisure and relaxation. The bright dyes, luxurious textures, and bold designs of increasingly popular Persian carpets were instrumental in importing into the bourgeois Victorian home an aura of Eastern exoticism. In fact, the last decades of the nineteenth century found Europe in the grip of what one German design historian has called "Oriental carpet fever."[26] The first major European exhibition of Oriental carpets took place at the Imperial Austrian Trade Museum in Vienna in 1891, the very year Freud moved his home and office to Berggasse 19. For Freud, these Persian carpets and Oriental fabrics may well have reminded him of his father, by profession a wool merchant who traded in Eastern textiles. For Freud's patients, the enchantment and mystery of these Oriental rugs further sequestered them in the interiorized, reclusive space of the consulting room couch, a place of private fantasy and quixotic danger: a "mysterious lion's den or Aladdin's cave of treasures."

As if in compensation for the risks that must be taken there, Freud envelops the patient on the couch in all the comforts of a private boudoir, ordinarily the most interior and secluded room of the Viennese home. Freud's office, in fact, is located in the back wing of what was originally designed to be part of a domestic residence, in that area of the apartment house typically used as sleeping quarters.[27] It is the sexual overtones of the famous couch—the sofa as bed—that most discomforted Freud's critics and, if Freud himself is to be believed, no small number of his patients.[28] In one of the few essays to take note of the spatial organization of the scene of analysis, Luce Irigaray has pointed out that the sexual connotations of lying supine can vary dramatically, depending on the sex of the patient. A woman reclining on her back with a man seated erect behind her finds her relation to the doctor inevitably eroticized.[29] The same could be said for Freud's male patients, whose daily sessions of private sex talk with their male doctor tacitly homoeroticized the clinical encounter. "Some men," Freud once commented, "scatter small change out of their trouser pockets while they are lying down during treatment and in that way pay whatever fee they think appropriate for the session" (6: 214). The association of lying down with scattered change—in short, of sex with money—invokes the specter of (male) prostitution, a connection that Freud appears to intuit here but not fully register.

What is being staged, or restaged, around the privileged, centralized, over-invested figure of the consulting room couch? "I cannot put up with being stared at by other people for eight hours a day (or more)," Freud acknowledges, defending his mandate that all patients, without exception, assume a reclining position on the couch. But why a couch? The couch turns out to be yet another museum relic—a "remnant," Freud calls it, "of the hypnotic method out of which psycho-analysis was evolved" (12: 133). While Freud abandoned his early hypnotic practice of placing patients into a somnambulistic sleep, he retained the couch as a serviceable memorial to psychoanalysis in its infancy. The couch, given to Freud as a gift by his former patient Madame Benvenisti around 1890, operated as a nostalgic reminder of his professional past.

But there is more to this couch than its store of personal memories for the doctor; the analytic couch served a mnemonic function for the patient as well. The following anecdote, recounted by Freud in *The Psychopathology of Everyday Life*, provocatively suggests a different way of thinking about the prominence of the consulting room couch:

> A young lady suddenly flung open the door of the consulting room though the woman who preceded her had not yet left it. In apologizing she blamed her "thoughtlessness"; it soon turned out that

she had been demonstrating the curiosity that in the past had
caused her to make her way into her parent's bedroom. (6: 214)

What is being subtly replayed here, across the threshold of two
rooms, is nothing less than the spectacle of the primal scene. The
patient in the waiting room, hearing sounds through the consulting room door, bursts into Freud's office, propelled by the same
"curiosity" that drew her, as a child, to cross the threshold of her
parent's private bedchamber. Freud's intruding female hysteric
sees all too clearly the highly eroticized choreography made possible by the very particular configuration of consulting room couch
and chair, so closely juxtaposed that if one were to remove the
arm of the couch and the arm of the chair behind it, the patient's
head (formerly propped at a 35° angle) would fall nearly into
Freud's lap. Shortly after this incident of analysis *interruptus*,
Freud soundproofed his consulting room by adding a second set
of doors lined with red baize. The sound barrier between treatment room and waiting room now insulated the analytic couple,
whose muffled voices previously risked transporting the patient in
the next room back to the trauma of the primal scene, to that interior place of fantasy where "uncanny sounds" are registered but
only belatedly understood.

Freud's own placement in this scene is by no means a simple
one; the question of the analyst's identificatory position is far
more complicated than Irigaray's "orthogonal"[30] pair of prone
patient/erect doctor might suggest. Significantly, Freud chooses to
assume a passive position in his exchange with the patient. Advis-
ing against the taking of notes during treatment sessions, a practice that prohibits the doctor from maintaining a posture of
"evenly suspended attention" (12: 111), Freud recommends that
the analyst "should simply listen, and not bother about whether
he is keeping anything in mind." This passive listening technique
represents the exact correlative to the fundamental rule of analysis
for patients, the injunction to say anything that enters one's head

"without selection or censorship" (12: 112).[31] The analyst must never engage in the work of scientific research while involved in the clinical act of listening. He must instead make himself vulnerable and receptive; he must "lay . . . [himself] open to another person" (12: 116); he must allow himself "to be taken by surprise" (12: 114).

> To put it in a formula: he must turn his own unconscious like a receptive organ towards the transmitting unconscious of the patient. He must adjust himself to the patient as a telephone receiver is adjusted to the transmitting microphone. Just as the receiver converts back into sound waves the electric oscillations in the telephone line which were set up by sound waves, so the doctor's unconscious is able, from the derivatives of the unconscious which are communicated to him, to reconstruct that unconscious, which has determined the patient's free associations. (12: 115–16)

Opening himself to the risk of feminization, Freud assumes the role of an orifice, a listening ear, while the patient becomes a mouth, an oral transmitter. The only telephone in Freud's office was the circuit of communication between analyst and analysand; Freud, as office receptionist, opens a direct line to the patient, adjusting the patient's unconscious to the frequencies of his own psychical interior. This interconnection between patient and doctor, transmitter and receiver, mouth and ear, sets up a technology of oral transmission: transference operates telephonically.[32]

After his surgery for oral cancer in 1923, Freud lost much of the hearing in his right ear. His biographer Peter Gay writes that Freud actually moved the couch from one wall to another so he could listen better with his left ear.[33] The gratification Freud's listening ear derived from the "electric oscillations" of the transferential line suggests that at the center of psychoanalysis's primal scene is a performance of what Neil Hertz has dubbed "oral intercourse in that other sense of the term." Freud's choice of a telephone to describe the intimate exchanges between doctor and patient highlights the "epistemological promiscuity" that characterizes psychoanalysis's therapeutic practice.[34] The very arrangement of couch and chair facilitates an erotics of voice, privileging sound over sight, speech over spectatorship. In the consulting room, telephone replaces mirror as the governing topos of the doctor-patient relation.

However, like the mirror on the window, Freud's imaginary telephone immediately connects us to the place of mourning. This indeed is the lesson of Avital Ronell's *The Telephone Book*, which reminds us that the telephone has always been involved in a hermeneutics of mourning, in a call to an absent other: "like transference, the telephone is given to us as effigy."[35] Invented originally as a device for the hearing and speech impaired, the telephone works as a prosthesis to compensate for radical loss. Freud's ear detected in the electric speech of the telephone the soft reverberations of distant connections, the sound of the unconscious. A powerful transmitter of disembodied presence, Freud's telephone was capable of summoning the very spirits of the dead, modulated voices from beyond the grave.

4

In one respect, the arrangement of bodies in the consulting room bears a certain disquieting resemblance to a wake, with Freud holding vigil over the body of his patient lying immobilized on the couch, most likely enshrouded (mummy-like) in the blanket provided, and surrounded by hundreds of funerary objects. *Eros* and *thanatos* turn out to be comfortable bedfellows as Freud's analytic couch doubles as bed and bier. Occupying the space of an off-screen presence, the analyst's listening ear and ventriloquized speech offer the patient the promise of reestablishing a tenuous connection to the Other who has been lost. By assuming the position of telephone receiver, the one who accepts the call to the Other, Freud thus finds himself addressing the patient from the borderline between presence and absence—the threshold between life and death. In the minds of his patients, Freud was not only healer, prophet, and shaman but gatekeeper to the underworld, "patron of gate-ways and portals" (TF, 106). Like the stone Janus head on his office desk, Freud "faced two ways, as doors and gates opened and shut" (TF, 100).[36] A modern-day Hermes or Thoth, Freud keeps vigilant watch over the dangerous passage across the invisible borders of past and present, memory and forgetting. " 'In analysis,' " Freud once explained to H.D., " 'the person is dead after the analysis is over,' " to which H.D. responded, "which person?" (TF, 141) With characteristic acuity, H.D. troubles the notion of physician as mourner, alluding to the possibility that it is Freud himself who is mourned, Freud who may already find himself on the other side of the portal. In the journey through death staged by the work of analysis, the question of who is the traveler and who the guide remains, at the very least, open.

In one of Freud's most interesting metaphorizations of the scene of treatment, he imagines doctor and patient as fellow passengers on a railway journey. Tutoring the patient on the technique of free association, Freud recommends: "Act as though . . . you were a traveler sitting next to the window of a railway carriage and describing to someone inside the carriage the changing views which you see outside" (12: 135). The train, associated throughout Freud's work with death and departure, carries doctor and patient along the same track, advancing the familiar genre of the travelogue as a model for the talking cure. The picture of easy companionship and leisurely conversation that Freud paints for his patient clearly seeks to domesticate what threatens to be a terrifying venture. Yet what is particularly striking about Freud's scenario of the fellow train travelers is his own severely circumscribed role within it, for Freud is the passenger whose vision is impaired, who can only imagine the view outside the window that his companion is invited to describe. While doctor and patient are located on the same side of the window, the patient alone is visually empowered while Freud is functionally blinded. Freud can listen but he cannot see; hearing must compensate for a radical loss of vision. Once again, then, Freud imagines himself as a passive, responsive organ: "two open ears and one temporal lobe lubricated for reception."[37]

In depriving himself of visual authority, Freud assumes the role of the blind seer, the one who "sacrifices sight . . . with an eye to seeing at last."[38] Through his figurative self-blinding, Freud inserts himself into a long line of blind healers and sightless soothsayers: Oedipus, the guilty son, who achieves wisdom by putting out his own eyes; Tiresias, the prophet of two sexes, who suffers blindness at the hands of the goddess Hera after testifying to women's greater sexual pleasure; and Tobit, the man of last respects, who never stops asking his sons to close his eyes as the time approaches for his own burial. It is impossible to forget the dream Freud had on the night after his own father's funeral, a dream about closing the eyes. Freud dreamt that he was in a place (in one account, a railway station) where a sign was posted that read: "You are requested to close the eyes." Late for his own father's funeral, Freud reads this dream as an expression of guilt for his failure to give his father a proper burial. Freud explains that "the sentence on the sign has a double meaning: one should do one's duty to the dead (an apology as though I had not done it and were in need of leniency), and the actual duty itself. The dream thus stems from the inclination to self-reproach that regularly sets in among survivors."[39]

"You are requested to close the eyes" refers to the literal act of performing a burial rite and to the symbolic necessity of taking one's leave of the dead. As Didier Anzieu perceptively notes, however, the request to "close the eyes" is also one of the instructions Freud habitually gave to his patients when beginning an analytic session.[40] The clinical rehearsal of this particular ritual provides what is perhaps the clearest illustration of the extent to which Freud envisioned the work of psychoanalysis as an elaborate funeral rite. Freud eventually discontinued the practice of enjoining his patients to close their eyes,[41] but vision and blindness continued to define for Freud the core dynamic of the therapeutic relation. Eyes now open, the patient on Freud's consulting room couch encounters the penetrating look of Gradiva, a plaster cast bas-relief hanging on the wall at the foot of the ottoman, carefully positioned to stare directly down at the patient [figure 2.8]. It is Wilhelm Jensen's Gradiva—for Freud the very incarnation of immortality—who offers patient and doctor (eye and ear) a new set of instructions: "look, but not with bodily eyes, and listen, but not with physical ears. And then . . . the dead wakened" (9: 16).

In Freud's theater of inversions, where a healing ritual can lull the living into a nether world of dreams and a funeral rite can waken the dead, subjects and objects are also transposed. When H.D. first enters the office in Berggasse 19, it is the objects, not their owner, that seize her attention: "The statues stare and stare and seem to say, what has happened to you?" (TF, 110) There are more sculptures in Freud's vast collection of antiquities than any other kind of art object, figures with a more immediate and anthropomorphic presence than either painting or photography.[42] These statues are endowed with the vision that Freud himself is denied; the figurines, their faces and their sight animated, stand in obverse relation to Freud, his face composed and his eyes veiled. In one of H.D.'s only physical descriptions of Freud, she describes him as though she were appreciating a piece of statuary, sculpted by an expert craftsman:

His beautiful mouth seemed always slightly smiling, though his eyes, set deep and slightly asymmetrical under the domed forehead (with those furrows cut by a master chisel) were unrevealing. His eyes did not speak to me. (TF, 73)

FIG. 2.8 Plaster Cast of Gradiva. Freud's Gradiva, like the plaster cast that figures so prominently in Wilhelm Jensen's story, is a copy of the original that Freud saw in the Vatican while on a trip to Rome in 1907. Not fully three-dimensional like a sculpture, but not flat like a painting either, this bas-relief at the foot of the couch was more visible to the reclining patient than the copy of Ingres's painting of *Oedipus Interrogating the Sphinx* which hung directly beside it. *Courtesy of Freud Museum, London, UK/Bridgeman Art Library.*

The portals of Freud's eyes are closed to his patients, as if he himself were an inanimate statue. By prohibiting the patient from looking at him during analysis, Freud, ostensibly seeking to ward off the possibility of idolatry, actually lays its foundations. Positioning himself in the place of "the one who must not be looked at," Freud immediately assumes the status of an otherworldly presence, concealed behind the inscrutable exterior of a powerful and mysterious graven image.

Is this why the view from Freud's consulting room chair resists all attempts to reproduce it technologically? And why Engelman's camera, when it attempts to see the space of the office through Freud's eyes, is effectively rendered blind? "I wanted to see things the way Freud saw them, with his own eyes, during the long hours of his treatment sessions and as he sat writing," Engelman concedes in his memoir, but "I couldn't . . . fit my bulky tripod into the tight space between Freud's chair at the head of the couch and the little table covered with an oriental rug on which [were] set a half-dozen fragile looking Egyptian statuettes."[43] Unable to simulate the view from the analyst's chair, Engelman finds that he must redirect his gaze back to the perspective of the patient. The consulting room chair stands as a fundamentally uninhabitable space, a tribute to the imposing figure of the analyst who remains, even to the searching eye of the camera, totally and enigmatically other.

5

"Tucked" away in his "three-sided niche" (TF, 22), Freud once again can be seen to occupy a spatially marginalized position. But while Freud's physical mobility in the consulting room may be more severely restricted than that of his patient, his field of vision is actually far greater. From his treatment chair, Freud can see not only the cabinet of antiquities below the now famous reproduction of Pierre Albert-Brouillet's engraving, *La Leçon clinique du Dr. Charcot*, but also the room's two main apertures (window and door) that frame it on either side. While from this position he is capable of monitoring any movements in or out of the consulting room, Freud's view of the entry door is partially obscured by a set of fully intact antiquities displayed on the table in front of him, a double row of figurines that, like the patient on the couch, are carefully arranged on a Persian rug. Are we to see these unbroken antiquities as visual surrogates for Freud's patients ("there are priceless broken fragments that are meaningless until we find the other broken bits to match them," H.D. writes [TF, 35]; "I was here because I must not be broken" [TF, 16])?[44] Or are we to see Freud's patients as simply another part of his collection, a conjecture reinforced by the photographs of Marie Bonaparte and Lou-Andreas Salomé, two of Freud's former patients, placed on the study bookcases alongside Freud's other antiquities?

It seems likely that the relation between Freud's antiquities and his patients is more complex than either of these two possibilities allows. Notably, the Egyptian statues in front of the consulting room chair are visible to Freud from the side, like the figures in profile found on the Egyptian papyrus hanging on the wall closest to Freud's immediate line of vision. This particular mummy covering, which depicts a scene of embalming,[45] holds a privileged place amongst Freud's antiquities, its location next to the treatment chair permitting hours of careful study. For Freud, interpreting a patient's dream is like deciphering an Egyptian hieroglyph. Pictographic script emblematizes the work of dream interpretation, offering a visual analog to the template of the dream text, the "picture-language" (13: 177) of the unconscious.

From his consulting room chair, Freud also has an unobstructed view of the desk in the adjoining study, where he will adjourn late in the day to take notes on his sessions and to write up his research. "One of the claims of psycho-analysis to distinction is, no doubt, that in its execution research and treatment coincide" (12: 114), Freud remarks, immediately qualifying that it is, in fact, unwise to begin scientific research on a case while treatment is still in progress. The architectural design of the office accordingly splits the interior in two, artificially divorcing the space of listening from the space of reflection. But the strict methodological barrier Freud erects between study and consulting room is nonetheless breached by the two doors that remain, like listening ears, perpetually open between them [figure 2.9]. A single axial line links desk chair to treatment chair, reflection to reception. While Freud listens to the patient from his consulting room chair, he has a clear view of the desk that awaits him, and a vision of the work of analysis towards which the clinical session aspires. Similarly, while Freud composes his scientific notes and theoretical papers at the study desk, consulting room couch and chair stand before him like an empty stage set, a visual reminder of the drama that has recently unfolded there in which Freud himself played a prominent role. The centers of knowledge in these adjoining rooms are thus visually continuous: treatment anticipates research; research rehearses treatment.

The immediate view from Freud's desk chair is no less phantasmatically staged, with many of Freud's favorite figurines lined up in a row on his desktop like so many members of a "silent audience."[46] Freud's desk, the most interior place in the office and the most difficult to access, is also the site of greatest structural fortification. Surrounded on three sides by three wooden tables, Freud's work area marks out yet another protected enclave, more confining yet more secure than the interior room created for the patient on the couch. It is at his desk that Freud makes the perilous transition from listening to writing; it is at his desk that he

FIG. 2.9 View of Study from Consulting Room Entry Door. The doors between Freud's study and consulting room remained open, keeping theory and practice in continual conversation. Freud entered his study through a doorway flanked by pictures of the Egyptian sphinx on the left and the Roman Forum on the right, visually delineating the two poles of mystery and reason that guided Freud's work. *Courtesy of Edmund Engelman, Photographer.*

enters into dialogue with his professional demons; it is at his desk that he struggles to put his own manuscripts to rest. Visible in Engelman's photographs of the study desk are the spectral outlines of Freud's *Moses and Monotheism*, Freud's last completed work, the one that, he confesses, "tormented me like an unlaid ghost" (23: 103).

In what sense might Freud's office, and the clinical encounter that takes place there, be read not just as an elegiac space but as a haunted one? Freud, it appears, was forever exorcising ghosts. A year after moving his office into a wing of his living quarters, Freud writes to Carl Jung of what he calls his "poltergeist," a cracking noise issuing from the two Egyptian steles resting on top of the oak bookcases. Believing at first that these ancient gravemarkers are possessed by spirits whenever Jung is in the room, Freud only reluctantly relinquishes his fanciful superstition when the steles continue to groan in his friend's absence: "I confront the despiritualized furniture," Freud laments, "as the poet confronted undeified Nature after the gods of Greece had passed away."[47]

But the Greek gods are not the only apparitions haunting the furniture and antiquities in Freud's office; for Freud's patients, these possessions operate as spectral doubles for the analyst himself. At least once in every analysis, Freud explains, the patient claims that his free associations have stopped; however, if pressed, he will admit that he is thinking of the objects around him—the wallpaper, the gas-lamp, the sofa: "Then one knows at once that he has gone off into the transference and that he is engaged upon what are still unconscious thoughts relating to the physician" (18: 126).[48] A transferential force emanates from Freud's possessions; these over-invested forms operate, for the patient, as shadowy substitutes for the analyst who must not be seen. Whether or not Freud's patients actually related to their physician's objects in this way is perhaps less interesting than the revelation of Freud's own deeply cathected relation to his things, which his theory of animation implicitly betrays. For this quasi-mystical account of the patient's transference onto the doctor through the medium of surrogate-objects is based on Freud's ready presumption that these inanimate possessions *could* somehow function as versions of himself.

The possibility that Freud may identify with these objects, may actually see himself as a part of the vast collection amassed around him, finds ironic visual confirmation in the last of Engelman's office photographs. In the only office photograph that includes a human figure, Freud's upper torso and head appear behind the study desk like yet another classical sculpture. Captured in a moment of statuary repose, Freud's imperturbable facial features appear to imitate the bust of him sculpted seven years before by the Yugoslavian artist Oscar Némon. This final image of Freud amidst his collection provides eloquent testimony to Jean Baudrillard's claim that, while "a given collection is made up of a succession of terms, . . . the final term must always be the person of the collector," for in the end "it is invariably *oneself* that one collects."[49]

The very medium of the photograph participates in the process of memorialization that so deeply permeates the space of Freud's office. Theorists of photography inevitably return to the camera's technological capacity to objectify the subject, to turn the image of the living into a memorial to the dead. "The home of the photographed is in fact the cemetery," Eduardo Cadava writes; "a small funerary monument, the photograph is a grave for the living dead."[50] Engelman's camera captures that moment, identified by Roland Barthes, when the one who is photographed is neither subject nor object but a subject becoming an object, a subject who is truly becoming a specter.[51] The photograph of Freud amongst his relics mortifies its living subject; it embalms Freud in a tomb he spent over forty years preparing. It is a suitable memorial to the man who seemed to glimpse, more assuredly than anyone, the many elusive ways in which our deaths anticipate us and our lives encrypt us.

Photography might be said to haunt psychoanalysis in another way, for a principle of photographic likenesses, of double exposures and exposed doubles, animates and reanimates the transferential scene. Insofar as the mechanism of transference works precisely by means of a double exposure—a superimposition of one figure onto another—the process of psychoanalysis can be seen to operate as a form of photographic development. Like photography, the technology of transference performs a kind of spirit work in which the phantoms of missing or lost others come back to life in the person of the analyst. In "Introjection and Transference," Sandor Ferenczi refers to the physician as a "revenant" in whom the patient finds again "the vanished figures of childhood."[52] Freud, as object of his patients' transferences, was just such a revenant, the living image of an absent person. Psychoanalysis, in this respect, was never very far from the schools of nineteenth-century spiritualism it so vigorously sought to bury. The ghost of the spirit medium speaks through the psychoanalyst every time the patient, through the agency of transference, communes with the dead.

A year and four months after Engelman took his clandestine photographs of Freud's Vienna office, Freud died of cancer in his new home at 20 Maresfield Gardens in London. He died in his office, a room that had been renovated by his architect son Ernst and arranged by his maid Paula Fichtl to reproduce, as closely as possible, the office at Berggasse 19. In this, the most painful period of his sixteen-year battle with oral cancer, Freud's office became his sickroom. It was here that Freud slipped into a coma after Max Schur, at Freud's request, administered the fatal doses of morphine that would end Freud's life on September 23, 1939. Cremated three days later, Freud's ashes were placed, according to the family's wishes, in a Greek urn, a red-figured bell krater presented to Freud as a gift by Marie Bonaparte. One might say that Freud at last found a resting place amongst his beloved antiquities.

Freud at Study Desk. The only photograph of the office to include Freud himself, this image reveals Freud's close identification with the objects that surround him. The branches behind Freud's shoulder are contained by the same Greek urn (originally intended for use as a burial gift) that will later hold Freud's own ashes, along with the ashes of his wife Martha. *Courtesy of Edmund Engelman, Photographer.*

Helen Keller, photographed directly in front of an open sun-drenched window, bathed in a figurative enlightenment so intense it nearly eclipses her. *Courtesy of the American Foundation for the Blind, Helen Keller Archives.*

3

Keller's Hand

Arcan Ridge
Easton Connecticut

So far I have focused predominantly on how the sensory faculties of sight and sound organize interior life. Dickinson and Freud draw largely on vision and hearing to mediate between inner dwelling and inner mind. These two writers of the interior each depend upon eye and ear to transform the mundane space of living into the contemplative space of writing. Yet interiority is not fashioned by the "higher" senses alone. As Keller and Proust demonstrate, the "lower" senses also play a central role in the production of one's inner thoughts, dreams, and memories. Keller, left blind and deaf from an early childhood fever, did not need vision or hearing either to enter into language or to apprehend her surroundings. She relied primarily on touch, and secondarily on smell, to orient both mind and body. Requiring neither eye nor ear to develop a talent for introspection, Keller instead built a complex inner life around hand and nose, her two dominant organs of sense perception.

For Keller the domestic interior operated as several spatial arenas at once: a classroom of semantic instruction, a theater of scientific invention, and a zone of personal injury. A house was a body and a machine, both a living organism that spoke to her "in unheard but tender accents"[1] and a technological apparatus more akin to Le Corbusier's machine for living. Once Annie Sullivan began using a manual alphabet to describe to Keller every new room they entered,[2] the house and all its furnishings also became a linguistic construct, a text to be read and recommitted to memory with each new structural renovation. Keller, who once referred to the physical world as God's "raised print" (*M* 311), perceived her inner dwelling as a Braille book writ large, a material discourse to be deciphered chiefly through touch.

Keller routinely identified her pre-linguistic self as "a phantom living in a no-world"—an uncanny echo of Millicent Todd Bingham's perception of Emily Dickinson as "the phantom in the enchanted corridor." As with Dickinson, the most common metaphors used to describe Keller's interior life are the two somber figures of prison and tomb. In Keller's case, however, it is not simply a house that is said to confine her; her very mind is figured as a place of internment. In his report on the eight-year-old Keller to the trustees of the Perkins School of the Blind, its Director Michael Anagnos announces Keller's liberation from her dark and silent cell: "As soon as a slight crevice was opened in the outer wall of their twofold imprisonment, her mental faculties emerged full-armed from their living tomb as Pallas Athene from the head of Zeus."[3] Twenty-five years later, the singer Georgette Leblanc, an acquaintance of Keller's, describes her new friend as an animated corpse, "immured upright, enigmatic in her tomb."[4] Keller herself participated in the representation of the deaf-blind as the living dead, imprisoned in the crypt of their own bodies, referring repeatedly in published accounts of her education to the "dungeon of sense" which incarcerates her. While the reference is sometimes to the "double dungeon of soul and body" and other times to the "triple dungeon" of blindness, deafness, and muteness, in every instance Keller's invocation of her body's "prison bars of sense"[5] unwittingly reinforces widespread public perceptions of the deaf and the blind as disturbing figures of darkness and death.

The power of such loaded metaphors to describe the deaf-blind derives exclusively from the privilege accorded sight and sound in the cultural hierarchy of sensory knowledge. Blindness especially is subject to the pull of ocularcentrism, even when the lack of sight would seem to necessitate bringing the other senses more immediately to our attention. Blindness appears in contemporary criticism and theory as a form of visual negation rather than as tactile, auditory, or olfactory sensation.[6] Even the many largely sympathetic cultural commentaries on Helen Keller, which one assumes might foreground the physiological and philosophical importance of hand, skin, or nose, ultimately deemphasize touch and smell in favor of attributing Keller's inner knowledge to a mysterious faculty of "inner sight."

I am interested both in exploring Keller's sensory relation to the world at large and in investigating her more intimate relation to her immediate domestic surroundings. For the last thirty years of her life, Keller lived in a Neo-Colonial home commissioned especially for her by the American Foundation for the Blind. Like Dickinson's New England homestead and Freud's Viennese apartment house, Keller's Connecticut home is notable more for its effects on its famous occupant's creative life than for any originality or distinction in its architectural design. Called Arcan Ridge, the home where Keller lived the longest is also the place where she largely ceased professional writing, after a lifetime devoted to the production of lyric poems, political essays, public addresses, spiritual testimonials, and personal memoirs. Of Keller's thirteen books, only one, her tribute to Annie Sullivan published in 1955, was completed in the home where Keller spent the last third of her life. While there may be many reasons for Keller's apparent writer's block after moving into Arcan Ridge—the death of Annie Sullivan, the increasing demands of a busy travel and philanthropic itinerary, the inevitable infirmities of advancing old age—the home itself provided a decidedly inhospitable place for the intellectual work of writing.

The place of writing and dwelling for Keller depended on the two contact senses of smell and touch; for Keller, interiority was more proximate than distant, more palpable than perspectival. Because seeing and hearing did not shape Keller's sense of the interior, I have chosen in my reading of Arcan Ridge not to employ the architectural site lines and plan diagrams that figure so centrally in the case of Dickinson or Freud. I shift my focus here from visual or auditory perceptions to the oft-neglected sensations of texture, temperature, pressure, and vibration. In particular I am interested in the critical role tactility plays in language and subject formation. To that end, I turn to a consideration of first the semiotics of touch, and second the phenomenology of touch, before proceeding to a reading of the house itself and to Keller's association with the decorative and functional objects within it. This chapter explicitly seeks to recuperate the centrality of the hand in the construction of Keller's interior life, a writer's life which for Keller, no less than for Dickinson and Freud, encompassed both the poetics of space (architecture) and the space of poetics (language).

1

The relation between architecture and language was, from the beginning, more than merely figurative for Keller. Keller learned language *through* architecture, acquiring the building blocks of the spoken and written word from the built environment of her childhood home in Tuscumbia, Alabama. The Keller homestead, named Ivy Green for its luxuriant English vines, included not only a white clapboard house in classic Virginia cottage construction, but also a small annex that served for a time as a schoolroom, the scene of Keller's daily instruction. Composed of just two rooms, the annex was the place where Keller and Sullivan resided full time, their personal and professional liaison evolving largely outside the strictures of conventional family relations. The story of Helen Keller's education is the story, in part, of how Annie Sullivan, a former ward of a state poorhouse and herself visually impaired, came quickly to usurp the place of Keller's immediate family, setting up lifelong domestic housekeeping with her charge. Ivy Green's annex was simply the first of half a dozen rooms, apartments, and houses that Keller and Sullivan would share for the nearly fifty-year duration of a relationship that friends compared to the great romances of Romeo and Juliet, or Orpheus and Eurydice. "It took the pair of you to make a complete and perfect whole," Mark Twain once commented to Keller and her "other half" Annie Sullivan, an assessment neither Keller nor Sullivan ever disputed (*DH 5*, 107).[7]

While the popular literature on Keller's early childhood education accords near-mythic importance to Ivy Green's outdoor water pump, the site where Keller first understood the referential power of words, it was within the more ordinary rooms of the annex that Keller actually learned to put words into sentences. It was here, in the domestic interior, that a six-year-old Keller received her earliest lessons in symbolic language, arranging and rearranging the furniture into what the adult Keller describes as "object sentences." Sullivan taught Keller to read and to write by printing individual words in raised letters on slips of cardboard and attaching these cards to the objects they designated. In her first autobiography, *The Story of My Life* (1902), Keller briefly recounts one of her earliest language lessons:

> I had a frame in which I could arrange the words in little sentences; but before I ever put sentences in the frame I used to make them in objects. I found the slips of paper which represented, for example, "doll," "is," "on," "bed" and placed each name on its object; then I put my doll on the bed with the words *is, on, bed* arranged beside the doll, thus making a sentence of the words, and at the same time carrying out the idea of the sentence with the things themselves. (25)

This short passage describes three different kinds of "sentences": a sentence comprised of objects alone, a sentence comprised of words attached to objects, and a sentence comprised of a mix of objects and words. In the first case, objects, through their spatial placement, convey a grammar all their own. In the second case, words attached to these objects point indexically to their material referents, in classic Saussurean fashion. In the third case, objects and words coexist in the same sentence. The grammatical subject of the sentence is a literal object (doll), while the rest of the sentence (is, on, bed) is comprised of raised words on slips of paper. Keller's tactile linguistics never presupposes the alienation of subject and object that both Saussure and Lacan identify as the central feature of the birth of "the speaking subject."[8] Instead, Keller's subject and object occupy the same epistemological frame, a frame in which the very terms subject and object refer to both the world of matter and the world of grammar.

Consider a second "object sentence" Keller recalls in her autobiography, one which includes Keller herself as an object noun.

> One day, Miss Sullivan tells me, I pinned the word *girl* on my pinafore and stood in the wardrobe. On the shelf I arranged the words, *is, in, wardrobe*. Nothing delighted me so much as this game. My teacher and I played it for hours at a time. Often everything in the room was arranged in object sentences. (*S 25*)

In this second example, Keller is at once the subject of the sentence and an object amongst other objects. Keller perceives her own body as a linguistic sign, analogous to the doll, bed, and wardrobe that comprise the adjacent nouns in her simple object sentences. In the now standard account of subject formation, the act of naming a thing blocks our imaginary identification with that thing, separating subject from object: "in linking names to things, the word kills the thing as immediate presence."[9] But, if Keller's autobiographies are any indication, words do not so much kill as convey the immediate presence of things. For Keller words are not completely opposed to things, precisely to the degree that things are themselves words, variously sequenced syntactical units waiting to be read.

Keller's close identification with objects might account for a quirk in her writing that has long puzzled her biographers:

FIG. 3.1 Keller's delight in conversing with trees and other inanimate objects (so often dismissed as mawkish romanticism) grew out of Keller's early lessons in symbolic language, lessons that suspended rigid subject-object distinctions. *Courtesy of the American Foundation for the Blind, Helen Keller Archives.*

namely, a tendency in her letters and memoirs to refer to herself in the third person, either as "Helen" or as "Phantom." If Keller perceived her material body as a linguistic sign, she also perceived her very subjectivity as a material thing, on par with the objects around her. Keller's affinity with material things goes a long way toward explaining her much ridiculed and little understood "communion" with inanimate and natural objects [figure 3.1]. Keller spent a lifetime, as she describes it, "talking to toys, to stones, trees, birds and dumb animals" (*S* 45). Her relation to the environment she lived in was never entirely predicated on the traditional elevation of subject over object. Keller attributed to the

objects around her subjective qualities, while at the same time re-
fusing to relinquish her own objective status. Keller's symbolic
world achieved an interactive equilibrium of word and thing, an
exchange of properties between the animate and the inanimate,
the active and the passive, the ideal and the material.

If Keller's relation to words offers a new model of the Symbolic, one that denies rigid subject-object distinctions, her relation
to things offers an equally suggestive alternative model of the
Imaginary, one that resists privileging the specular. Keller lost her
sight and hearing at the age of nineteen months, having presum-
ably already passed through the mirror-stage, that developmental
period between the ages of six and eighteen months when the
child first sees itself, in mirror reflection, as a separate entity.
However, while Keller may have passed through the mirror-stage
like other infants, she never experienced the innumerable specular
encounters that subsequently verify the body's newfound unity
and integrity. Mirror reflections held no interest or utility for a
woman with no vision, a point of unending fascination to Keller's
sighted friends.

> I rise absent-mindedly and catch sight of Helen in the glass. A
> strange vision! . . . The blind girl is seated stiff and straight in a
> chair which happens to be opposite a mirror. Her set, unconscious
> face looks like a portrait in its frame. . . . Many times I have asked
> myself what Helen lacks; the mirror tells me: it has not instructed
> her; it has never told her charms and her defects; it has never re-
> vealed her image to her. That image lives and dies in the mirror.

This extraordinary description of Keller by Georgette Leblanc reflects a common tendency amongst the sighted to deny the blind
any self-image at all. What Helen "lacks," Leblanc concludes, is
not only vanity but self-understanding, the self-knowledge that
can only be gained "in the glass of the docile and faithful mirror"
or in "the look of others" (111–2). Deprived of both kinds of visual reflection, Keller, with her two prosthetic glass eyes, becomes

herself the mirror for the sighted subjects around her. Leblanc was not the only observer to find herself exposed by Keller's "too penetrating glance" (29).[10] As Dorothy Herrmann details, Keller's highly reflective glass eyes regularly gave rise to depictions of her as "a sightless high priestess" or a "seer who had penetrated the mysteries of the universe in her dark silence" (193). If Freud figuratively transformed himself into a listening ear in order actively to insert himself into a genealogy of sightless soothsayers, Keller had the role of blind visionary more or less thrust upon her. Keller's "set, unconscious face," as Leblanc coolly describes it, produced the uncanny effect of reflecting her interlocutors' own images directly back to them. Keller became, in short, a cultural cipher for the sighted. The "portrait in its frame" that Leblanc suggests Keller physically resembled was more a screen for the fantasy projections of those around her than a reliable picture of Keller's own self "image."

While Keller seemed to have played a significant if unwanted role in the specular transferences of others, her own imaginary identifications followed a different path; Keller's identity was molded by something entirely other than visual images. Her imaginary world was a rich repository of textures, temperatures, vibrations, odors, and flavors. I do not mean to suggest here that only Keller had access to these particular sensory realms; rather, Keller's unique sensory life reveals something important about interiority in general, namely that it comprises a far more complex, and far more complete, sensory matrix than psychoanalysis has ever acknowledged. Commentators on Lacan's mirror-stage rightly encourage us not to take the figure of the mirror too literally, arguing that the mirror is simply a representative trope for any psychical process of self-reflection, and yet the focus on visual misrecognition and specular identification persists in virtually every Lacanian account of subject formation I know. The ideal images of self that constitute the imaginary are treated as just that: ideal *images*. Psychoanalytic literature includes virtually no discussion of subjectivity's other sensory registers, save perhaps Kaja Silverman's *The Acoustic Mirror*, an important theoretical recuperation of the primacy of sound in the subject's early identifications, yet a study that nonetheless reestablishes the sensory priority of sight in the prominence that the book's very title accords to the central visual metaphor of the mirror.[11]

The near-total exclusion of touch, taste, and smell from Lacanian accounts of subject formation suggests that the theory of the mirror-stage may itself operate as a distorted mirror, an intellectual deflection that conceals the role the other senses play in producing illusions of self-identity. Lacan's mirror-stage model assists us in misrecognizing ourselves as purely specular or auditory subjects, upholding the conventional philosophical association of sight and sound with the "humanizing" power of mind and spirit, while re-securing the obverse association of touch, taste, and smell with the "animalizing" forces of appetite and desire. I want to recover the central roles the three contact senses play in orienting our relation both to ourselves and to the spaces we inhabit. Beginning from the premise that the human subject is an infinitely more complicated sensory being than traditionally acknowledged, I seek here to explore the full range of corporeal experiences that comprise the individual's intimate engagement with self.

2

"The hand is the most highly developed organ of sense," Keller informs her readers in *Midstream: My Later Life,* published in 1929. With its higher concentration of nerves, the hand is more responsive, flexible, and efficient than the body's other sense organs. Covering a "wide field of sensation," the hand operates as a metonym for all corporeal touch:

> I think people do not usually realize what an extensive apparatus
> the sense of touch is. It is apt to be confined in our thoughts to the

finger-tips. In reality, the tactual sense reigns throughout the body, and the skin of every part, under the urge of necessity, becomes extraordinarily discriminating. It is approximately true to say that every particle of the skin is a feeler which touches and is touched, and the contact enables the mind to draw conclusions regarding the qualities revealed by tactual sensation, such as heat, cold, pain, friction, smoothness, and roughness, and the vibrations which play upon the surface of the body. (*M* 256–7)

Unlike the other four senses, localized in the specific body parts of eye, ear, mouth, and nose, touch operates more as a sensory system spread out across the surface of the body.[12] In describing every part of the skin as "a feeler which touches and is touched," Keller highlights a reciprocity in tactility not matched by the other organs of sense. A hand can be the subject or the object of touch; it can be agent or receiver, and often both at once. Unlike vision, which depends upon the spatial distancing of the object from the perceiving subject, touch immediately brings subjects and objects into closer conversation.

This proximity of subject and object produces a notably different kind of subjectivity, a less egocentric sense of self, that situates the body squarely in the material, physical world. The French phenomenologist Maurice Merleau-Ponty summarizes the significance of the tactile subject this way:

In visual experience, which pushes objectification further than does tactile experience, we can, at least at first sight, flatter ourselves that we constitute the world, because it presents us with a spectacle spread out before us at a distance, and gives us the illusion of being immediately present everywhere and being situated nowhere. Tactile experience, on the other hand, adheres to the surface of our body; we cannot unfold it before us, and it never quite becomes an object. Correspondingly, as the subject of touch, I cannot flatter myself that I am everywhere and nowhere; I cannot forget in this case that it is through my body that I go to the world, and tactile experience occurs 'ahead' of me, and is not centered in me. It is not I who touch, it is my body.[13]

I cite Merleau-Ponty at length here, for he is one of the only philosophers of the twentieth century to provide an extended theorization of touch. Merleau-Ponty, who briefly references Keller in his major work *The Phenomenology of Perception* (1962),[14] positions touch as the body's superior sense precisely because of its *lack* of superiority. While vision allows the subject to achieve distance and power over objects, touch weds us to them, reminding us that, insofar as it is the flesh of the human body that both brings us into sensory contact with the world and that underwrites all the senses in the first place, the subject is decidedly an object after all.

While Merleau-Ponty's philosophical demotion of vision in favor of touch recalls Keller's own more personal investigations of the primacy of tactility, Keller's four autobiographies in turn resemble nothing so much as exercises in phenomenology, impassioned defenses of the experiential life of both subjects and objects.[15] In their reverence for things themselves, Keller's books often read as extended catalogues of objects touched and scents smelled. John Macy, who was once briefly a member of the Keller-Sullivan household,[16] claimed that Keller was deeply reluctant to acknowledge her reliance on a sensory organ of such ill repute as the nose, but Keller in fact expended a great deal of ink on rescuing smell from its cultural exile. "There is something of the fallen angel" about smell, Keller laments in *The World I Live In*; "for some inexplicable reason the sense of smell does not hold the high position it deserves."[17] Keller used her own olfactory sense as an example of smell's considerable cognitive powers, revealing that she could not only identify a person's profession by the odors which clung to their garments (W 72), but she could even name from the street the kinds of cosmetics used by a home's occupants, or distinguish through smell whether a church she passed was Protestant or Catholic (M 165). Although unpleasant odors gave her "a nervous tremor" whenever they came between her and "a beloved object," Keller actually singled out smell as the most human, and the most social, of the senses. As she explained to Thomas Edison, everyone has "a particular person odor," an individual scent by which they can be immediately recognized (*M* 291).

Keller's even more extensive comments on the hand indicate that touch was, for her, the most important medium of contact with the world (*M* 256). It was through hand-to-hand contact that Keller believed she could best read people's inner emotional states, since she found hands to be as easily recognizable as faces, and considerably more revealing: "People control their countenances, but the hand is under no such restraint. It relaxes and becomes listless when the spirit is low and dejected; the muscles tighten when the mind is excited or the heart glad" (*W* 27). Keller, by John Macy's account, had a phenomenal tactile memory: "She remembers the grasp of fingers she has held before, all the characteristic tightening of the muscles that makes one person's handshake different from another" (cited in *DH* 153). For Keller, the hand's temperature, pressure, and texture provided subtle clues not only to a person's identity but also to their temperament, personality, and mood. More than any other body part, hands were external signs of internal character, barometers of alterity and difference.

In the twentieth century, two hands touching each other have provided philosophy with perhaps its most powerful model of self-other relations. Merleau-Ponty suggests that a subject's perception of itself as other begins not in narcissistic self-reflection in the mirror but in one hand touching the other, which is itself touching an object. Subjectivity begins when we first become conscious of one part of ourselves grasping another part, or, as Merleau-Ponty more particularly describes it, "when my right hand touches my left hand while it is palpating the things, where the 'touching subject' passes over to the rank of the touched, descends into the things."[18] A hand touching a hand touching an object establishes the reversibility of the sensible object and the sentient subject, confirming our "double belongingness" to the order of both subjects and objects. Objecting to Merleau-Ponty's largely instrumentalist model of subjectivity, in which one hand clearly wields greater power over the other, Luce Irigaray repositions the two grasping hands into a more equal and symmetrical relation. Irigaray's hands are contemplative rather than manipulative: "hands joined, palms together, fingers outstretched." With neither one dominating the other, these two hands, like Irigaray's favorite metaphor of the two lips, brush up against one another without taking hold.[19] Although Irigaray provides a more intimate tactile model of alterity than Merleau-Ponty, her perfectly matched hands remain frozen as if in prayer. Closed gently together, they assume a single position, with little or no movement between them, and no possibility for exploring the world outside their sealed communion.

I would like to suggest here that, in many ways, Helen Keller's hands provide a more suitable and suggestive model for figuring self-other relations than either of these two other pairs of modern hands. For both Merleau-Ponty and Luce Irigaray, hands remain always on the edge of speech, grasping and caressing but never finally communicating. Keller's hands similarly grasp and caress, but they also, crucially, converse. These hands are expressive hands, agents of articulation as well as exploration. They are instruments of conversation and communication, vehicles of transmission between self and other that are neither strictly materialist nor purely idealist.[20]

When manually spelling, Keller's hands are both in motion and at rest, as she patiently explains to her readers in *The Story of My Life*:

> One who reads or talks to me spells with his hand, using the single-hand manual alphabet generally employed by the deaf. I place my hand on the hand of the speaker so lightly as not to impede its movements. The position of the hand is as easy to feel as to see. I

do not feel each letter any more than you see each letter separately when you read. Constant practice makes the fingers very flexible, and some of my friends spell rapidly—about as fast as an expert writes on a typewriter. (46)

In hand-spelling, only one hand can spell into the palm of the other, and yet Keller's manual conversations illustrate that the process is truly a reversible one, with Keller sometimes transmitting words, sometimes receiving words, and sometimes using two hands to do both in unison. When Keller spelled to herself, Michael Anagnos observes, the acts of transmission and reception were one: "So rapid were the movements of her little fingers, that the three processes of reception, transmission, and expression of ideas became simultaneous . . . an electric play of gestures and of features, an unconscious eloquence of the whole body" (cited in *DH* 72). Keller's self-spelling hands demonstrate more palpably than Merleau-Ponty's grasping hands or Irigaray's praying hands the body's dual allegiance to the objective and subjective worlds. In self-spelling, Keller was both speaker and listener, toucher and touched, self and other at once.

As Anagnos's metaphor of "the electric play of gestures" suggests, the coupling of subject and object in hand-spelling carries almost an erotic charge for the speller, an association confirmed by Keller's own recollection of the "quasi-electric touch" of Annie Sullivan's fingers upon her palm (*T* 52). Certainly no act on Keller's part was ever more carefully monitored and vigorously censored than her love of self-spelling. Speaking of herself alternately in the first and third persons, Keller recounts in her published tribute to Sullivan how she and her teacher tried to break Keller of her shameful "habit":

Helen sinned in another way by spelling constantly to herself with her fingers, even after she had learned to speak with her mouth. All teacher's reproaches and entreaties, all her eloquence in holding up

examples of other children were in vain. . . . I determined to stop
spelling to myself before it became a habit I could not break, and so
I asked her to tie my fingers up in paper. . . . For many hours, day
and night, I ached to form the words that kept me in touch with
others. (*T* 50)

Once Keller began lessons in vocal speech, hand-spelling became
an illicit, secretive, and highly pleasurable practice, a kind of linguistic onanism. The punishment for self-spelling was severe:
wrapping paper around the hands of a child who can neither see
nor hear not only broke off all communication with the speaking
world, the paper itself served as an ever-present reminder of the
textual world Keller longed to enter. The sheer degree of sadism
invested in the censoring of Keller's automanualism reflects the far
greater social value modernity accords to the sense of hearing than
to the sense of touch. Even early advocates for the deaf were not
immune to the cultural idealization of voice. As Keller herself pas-
sionately believed, "without a language of some sort one is not a
human being; without speech one is not a complete human being"
(T 61).[21] Releasing Keller's "inner voice" from the material confines of the body required subordinating the "physical" faculty of
touch to the "spiritual" faculty of sound. For Annie Sullivan, who
labored until the end of her life trying to perfect her pupil's inaudible speech, the only proper ending to the narrative of the young
deaf and blind girl's conversion from "wild creature" to "civilized
human" was proficiency in vocal speech.[22] Interestingly, despite
persistent attempts to shift her primary organ of speech from hand
to vocal chord, Keller never fully mastered the mechanics of oral
communication, and she never apparently stopped spelling to herself. At seventy years old Keller was willing to admit that "even
now, in moments of excitement or when I wake from sleep, I occasionally catch myself spelling with my fingers" (*T* 50).

Hand-spelling did not so much sublimate sexuality as give it
an alternate form of expression. For Keller, and perhaps Sullivan

FIG. 3.2 Sullivan spelling into Keller's hand, 1893. Although both Sullivan and Keller were visually impaired, they were often photographed staring into one another's eyes, while their hands met in the center of the image— two conventions of late Victorian romantic portraiture. *Courtesy of the American Foundation for the Blind, Helen Keller Archives.*

as well, language *was* eros, a practice of mutual physical stimulation and response. Sullivan and Keller engaged in their "secret" language for forty-nine years, spelling together for the better part of every day [figure 3.2]. Defending her disinterest in a doctor's courtship, Sullivan once confided to a friend that only Keller's hands touched her deeply:

> My work occupies my mind, heart and body, and there is no room in them for a lover. I feel in every heart beat that I belong to Helen . . . . It is not in the nature of man to love so entirely and dependently as Helen. She does not merely absorb what I give, she returns my love with interest, so that every touch and act seem a caress.[23]

For her part, Keller (again speaking of herself in the third person) explains that "she was drawn to Teacher, not by any sense of obligation but by the natural impulse of receiving from her finger-motion what her word-hunger craved, just as the infant reaches out to his mother's breast for milk" (*T* 43). Theirs was a relationship of uncommon physical intimacy, based on a complex interaction of need, dependency, nurturance, affection, and desire, all expressed through the medium of the hand. Perhaps the most poignant and painful gift Keller received in her lifetime was a cast of Annie Sullivan's hand, presented to Keller shortly after Sullivan's death in 1936.[24] Far from the comforting facsimile it was intended to be, the cold artistic likeness of her teacher's hand stood as an intolerable reminder of everything Keller had lost when Sullivan lapsed into a coma and died, almost half a century after first instructing Keller in the tremendous expressive eloquence of touch.

3

The house Keller occupied in Easton Connecticut from 1939 to 1968 was a living memorial to Annie Sullivan [figure 3.3]. Constructed three years after Sullivan's death, this classic New England Colonial, filled with the furniture and possessions the two women collected over a thirty-year period, was named Arcan Ridge after a cottage in Scotland. There Keller assisted in nursing Sullivan through a debilitating illness while both were on a sabbatical year from the American Foundation for the Blind. The Scottish Highlands farm was also the place where Keller first began to write the last of her memoirs, an encomium to Annie Sullivan that would not be completed for another twenty years. *Teacher* (1955) was delayed by two devastating losses: the death of its subject and the destruction, a decade later, of the home named in her memory. The two losses were closely associated. The fire that burned Keller's

FIG. 3.3 View of Arcan Ridge II, modeled on the first house that was destroyed by fire in 1946. Although it was an improved copy of the original, the second Arcan Ridge never succeeded in compensating Keller for everything she had lost, including the home furnishings that daily sustained her memories of Sullivan. *Author Photograph*.

wood-frame house to the ground in 1946 also destroyed all the furniture, mementos, and books Sullivan had bequeathed to Keller, along with Keller's own literary tribute to Sullivan, three-quarters finished. Keller, at the age of sixty-six, survived the loss of her home surprisingly well, perhaps because, after the death of her life-long companion, she already knew the deep hurt of emotional displacement. Keller's own summation of the fire puts the tragedy in perspective: "this loss is not like parting with Teacher which, as it were, broke my life habitation" (*T* 31).

The house Keller occupied for the last two decades of her life was, in fact, the second Arcan Ridge, built as an almost exact replica of the first. This second Arcan Ridge, like the cast of Annie Sullivan's hand, was a static reproduction of the original, alike in outline and size but, in Keller's opinion, completely devoid of personal warmth. Filled entirely with mass-produced department store furniture, the new Arcan Ridge typified the postwar American fascination with function over form. The simply furnished twelve-room "country home" followed the architectural plan of a Neo-colonial Revival house, traditional on the outside and fully modernized on the inside. By the 1930s, the elaborate hallways and parlors of the nineteenth-century Greek Revival and Gothic Revival houses had long since been replaced by the twentieth-century Colonial Revival's multipurpose living room, with built-in bookcases and buffets, window nooks and seats, and a fireplace at the room's center. With fewer pieces of furniture, made in less heavy materials, the living room of Keller's modern Colonial was a notably less formal space than the front and back parlors of Dickinson's Federal-style home. Indeed, the open floor plan of the modern living room was the first radical change in architectural house design since the eighteenth century, signaling the emergence of a less privatized and more mobile domestic subject.[25] In keeping with the new architectural aesthetic of economy and efficiency, improvements in the second Arcan Ridge were chiefly practical: a dining terrace close to the serving pantry, a more modern kitchen with electrical instead of gas appliances, an outdoor railed sundeck adjoining Keller's second-floor study, and a private bathroom for Polly Thompson, Keller's live-in assistant.

Perhaps the most striking feature of Arcan Ridge is its sheer ordinariness, its strict adherence to programmatic type. Keller and Sullivan may have thought of themselves as "two handicapped women" keeping house (*T* 129), but, interestingly, none of the renovations on their older homes made any structural allowances for the sensory world they lived in. Architecture's apparent indifference to the physical needs of the hearing- and vision-impaired is nowhere more evident than at Arcan Ridge. The only house conceived, designed, and built specially for Keller incorporated no major structural changes to accommodate its well-known occupant. And yet, the conventional layout and standard design of Keller's Connecticut home was precisely the point. The traditional New England Colonial was an advertisement for independent living, proof that the deaf-blind could function self-sufficiently in the most ordinary of domestic environments. Keller's familiar if unexciting dwelling stood as concrete testimony to the enduring value of her personal achievement. As one press release on Keller's new house marvels, "she has so adapted herself to normal living that the house presents no special architectural innovations."[26]

Seeking to lay to rest public perceptions of the deaf-blind as socially backward and helplessly dependent, filmmaker Nancy Hamilton made a visual record of Keller's public and private life in the early 1950s. This short non-fiction film, which won the 1955 Academy Award for Best Feature Documentary, follows Keller through a typical day at Arcan Ridge, performing such normal activities as fetching food from the kitchen, taking a morning constitutional around the yard, having afternoon tea with visitors, and washing dishes after dinner. Devoting the film's beginning, middle, and end to the recording of life at Arcan Ridge, Hamilton's film is clearly more interested in the details of Keller's home life than in her charity work or philanthropic travels, subjects that are all but eclipsed by the novelty of entering directly into the innermost quarters of the most famous woman in America. *The Unconquered* brings its audience across the threshold and inside the privacy of Keller's home, revealing intimate views of Keller eating breakfast at Polly Thompson's bedside, selecting clothes from her dressing room closet, and reading in her bathrobe on the study floor. Each of these scenes underscores Keller's physical autonomy in a world of familiar objects. "Here where every table, every chair, every dish in the cupboard is their intimate friend, Helen can move freely and independently," the narrator intones. This engaging if rather reverential film, which dwells on Keller confidently negotiating stairs and moving easily through interior rooms, aims to convey a clear message: Keller is most remarkable for her normalcy; her extraordinary achievement is to live in a most ordinary fashion, on equal footing with the hearing and the sighted.

And yet, Keller's experience of the domestic interior was undeniably distinctive. Keller knew that she did not need hearing to hear; her oft-repeated claim that she could "hear" with her feet was based on the lived knowledge that there is no such thing as complete deafness, since sound vibrations are registered not only by hearing but by touch. Deriving much of her knowledge from the "jars and jolts" that resonate throughout the house, Keller experienced her spatial environment primarily through vibration. While Dickinson saw her inner dwelling as if through the eye of an ophthalmoscope, and Freud heard the consulting room confessions of his patients as if through the ear of a telephone, Keller filtered her own sensory impressions through the medium of what she called her "vibroscope" (W 49–50). A device for the recording of mechanical vibrations, the vibroscope once again positions Keller on the receiving end of an electrical charge. Keller, it seems, experienced her entire body as a finely tuned seismic machine, not at all unlike the technological gadgets and appliances that animated her newly modernized home.

Most of the information Keller divined from vibrations came from architecture's fundamental design components: walls, windows, doors, stairs, chimneys, and especially floors. To Emily Dickinson the built materials of the house simulated a musical instrument; to Helen Keller they operated as a communication device. "By means of a dot and dash system," Sullivan informs Anagnos, "I can stand at one end of a large room and Helen on the other and by simply tapping my foot upon the floor I can transfer to her any information which I may desire to convey."[27] The floor operated, in effect, as a long distance telegraph, a conductor of coded messages across a spatial divide. Keller favored the enclosed space of interiors over the open space of exteriors for the simple reason that the vibrations she felt in a house, as subtle

as a pencil rolling onto the floor, were imperceptible out of doors
(*W* 46–7). Sitting on the floor Keller could feel through its vibrations whenever someone "kneels, kicks, shakes something, sits
down, or gets up" (*W* 45). She could also identify those who approached her by their tread, since footsteps, she discovered, "vary
tactually according to the age, the sex, and the manner of the
walker" (*W* 43–4). Not surprisingly, Keller's favorite bed was a
Japanese *tatami*, a woven straw mat that allowed her to feel the
vibrations of sliding doors, windows, and footsteps (*T* 229). More
than simple structural supports, floors were vital communication
aids, prosthetic devices for the conveyance of sensory data.

Given Keller's reliance on her "vibroscope" to locate herself in
her surroundings, it is all the more remarkable to find, in the architect's list of alterations for Arcan Ridge II, specific instructions
to "soundproof Helen's study to eliminate vibration."[28] Sound-
proofing Keller's private office might have been intended to remove distractions from her workspace, but this architectural
renovation also muted her chief conduit of outside information.
Amazingly, the whole house was constructed to erase the very vibrations that Keller crucially depended upon to orient herself in
the world. The architectural house plans for the new Arcan Ridge
specify that every staircase and room save the kitchen be laid with
wall-to-wall carpeting, while the building contract further stipu-
lates that the floors on the second floor be laid on sound-deaden-
ing felt. Keller had little control over the construction of her new
home, commissioned and paid for by wealthy benefactors at the
American Foundation for the Blind. The result was a living space
not merely indifferent to her sensory situation but openly hostile
to it.

In general, the interior of Arcan Ridge is notable for its sensory sameness and tactile homogeneity. Its design materials present little variety in grain and texture, with the same clear white
pine timber utilized for the woodwork on the stairs, the fireplace
mantel, and the interior trim. The built-in bookcases with bottom

cupboards were also constructed in white pine, as were the six-pane colonial doors in the interior. Glass top covers for all the wood tables further dulled Keller's tactile environment, while plastic slipcovers for the rest of the furniture made even the texture of fabrics inaccessible to touch.

A similar program of sensory deprivation severely limited Keller's ability to register external information through smell. In the confined quarters of the domestic interior, odors and fragrances ordinarily provided Keller with an immediate read on her housemates' activities and whereabouts; "when a person passes quickly from one place to another," she writes of an earlier house in Wrentham, Massachusetts, "I get a scent impression of where he has been—the kitchen, the garden, or the sick-room" (W 72–3). Smells not only helped Keller to navigate her own way through the labyrinthine spaces of the house, they also assisted her in keeping track of the movements of other bodies around her. But in the newly modernized Arcan Ridge, the addition of a superior ventilation system and a central air conditioning unit made such olfactory identifications more difficult. The new heating system, by keeping the house at a constant temperature, created a neutral thermal environment that reduced both the temperature gradients and the air pressure changes that the deaf-blind typically rely upon to orient themselves spatially. Closely regulating both the natural flow of air and the changes in room temperature, Arcan Ridge's hermetic environment minimized rather than maximized the powers of touch and smell, Keller's two primary organs of sense perception.

The architect for both versions of Arcan Ridge, Cameron Clark, explained in a 1939 letter to Keller that he much preferred structural harmony "to more individualistic and extreme design"—a not so veiled reference to the newly prominent work of modernist architects like Le Corbusier, Mies van der Rohe, and Frank Lloyd Wright.[29] And yet the perfect modern home for

Helen Keller might well have been a house designed by Frank Lloyd Wright. His prairie houses and bungalows, often constructed out of the fragrant timbers of cedar or redwood, presented richly textured living spaces, mixing wood, stone, brick, tile, and terra cotta. Wright's open-floor houses, an inspiration for today's Universal Design Movement, are far more amenable than traditional homes to people with disabilities.[30] By eliminating interior walls and facilitating circulation between rooms, Wright's uncluttered dwellings are easier to navigate than a multi-room, multi-level home like Arcan Ridge. The simple bungalow offered the kind of highly imaginative tactual and olfactory environment so conspicuously missing in Keller's own home, an interior space that might have been immeasurably enriched by more creative variation in program, function, and design.

4

Any artwork that might originally have added greater warmth and personality to Arcan Ridge is little in evidence by the time of Nancy Hamilton's 1955 documentary film. The large medallion of Homer that for years hung low on the study wall so Keller could readily touch the Ionian poet's "sightless eyes" (*S* 96) was destroyed in the fire, as were the Asian paintings, wall hangings, and sculptures that previously made Keller's home resemble a "Japanese museum." Some of these lost objects were replaced through charitable gifts;[31] souvenirs from trips abroad provided the rest of the home's collectibles, which included, most prominently, a fragment of the Parthenon, one of several ancient ruins Keller was visiting in Europe when her own home was reduced to rubble. Once ensconced in the second Arcan Ridge, Keller, perhaps in reaction to her newly barren surroundings, took up sculpture as an avocation, shaping life-sized heads out of warm wax and wet clay (*T*

69). To Keller, sculpture was the highest art form, the only artistic practice that "could be more subtly felt than seen" (*S* 96). Keller was herself frequently perceived by those around her as an *objet d'art*, a cold, silent, and stationary ornament. Georgette Leblanc, who initially compared Keller's mirror-reflection to a portrait in its frame, eventually concluded that a far more apt metaphor to describe her friend's frozen visage was Greek sculpture: "When we study her profile and her rather masculine throat, straight and pure as a column, we are reminded of the Athenian youths on some bas-relief" (30).

The common cultural representation of the blind as classical sculpture informs many of the official photographs of Keller, which often depict her simulating famous works of art. A 1903 studio photograph captures a diaphanous Keller reaching up to stroke a miniature copy of Winged Victory, reproducing in her own dress and posture the flowing lines and elevated pose of the ethereal statue [figure 3.4]. Another photograph, taken almost half a century later, shows Keller in the French studio of sculptor Jo Davidson, feeling the enlarged head of Franklin D. Roosevelt with one hand while receiving hand signals from Polly Thompson with the other [figure 3.5]. This photograph, which both formally and thematically foregrounds touch as the main organ of aesthetic sense perception, reestablishes the priority of vision by including among the studio's artworks an oil painting of Keller herself. The life-sized half portrait of a seated Keller neither hangs on a wall nor leans on an easel but rests squarely on a display table, on a par with the sculptures that surround it. Keller's own face in the photograph, shadowed in profile on the left, is frontally and fully exposed by the competing portrait painting on the right. Visually dismembering both of Keller's hands in the painting, this carefully cropped photographic representation of the blind woman as art connoisseur simultaneously reduces its subject to an object of the viewer's own aesthetic appreciation. Touch is ultimately dwarfed

FIG. 3.4 Keller, aged 23, touching the Winged Victory. The decomposition of this fragile photograph appears to give Keller herself a pair of wings, enhancing the visual identification of woman with statue. *Courtesy of the American Foundation for the Blind, Helen Keller Archives.*

by vision, as an entire wall of masks pronounces the face, not the hand, the over-invested site of subjectivity.[32]

The figuration of Keller as a silent work of art finds its most overt expression in the words of Gutzon Borglum, a sculptor who identifies Annie Sullivan as the couple's true creative genius, a modern-day "Praxiteles, breathing life into [Keller's] sense-shut faculties." Keller agreed, writing in her journal after Sullivan's death that "Teacher hewed my life bit by bit out of formless silent dark as Rodin hewed that mind-genesis out of rock" (*J* 161 and 166).[33] Celebrations of Helen Keller as Annie Sullivan's artistic

FIG. 3.5 Keller and Thompson in the French studio of the artist Jo David-son, admiring a bust of Franklin D. Roosevelt. During a trip to Europe in 1950, the two women sat for a joint portrait painting, which can be seen on the far right of this photograph. While Keller is fully visible, Thompson, as was so often the case, is completely excised from view. *Courtesy of the American Foundation for the Blind, Helen Keller Archives.*

masterpiece led to counter-charges that Keller was actually a mere carbon copy of her mentor. "All her knowledge is hearsay knowl-edge," writes one critic for *The Nation* shortly after the publica-tion of Keller's first autobiography; "her very sensations are for the most part vicarious" (*DH* 136). As often as Keller was praised by admirers as a "miracle," she was dismissed by critics as an "automaton," a walking, talking imitation of her creator.

Repeated portrayals of Keller as an automaton link her more to the world of technology than to the world of sculpture. Public fascination with Keller focused as much on her recurrent associa-tion with the new eyes and ears of modern technology as on her close identification with the unseeing and unhearing icons of classical art. Indeed, Keller's fascination with machines, and her own allegedly mechanical nature, made her something of a national symbol for modern science's artificial reproduction of human sensation. Helen Keller, a woman both blind and deaf, became the chief cultural cipher for the new sight and sound technologies of the late nineteenth and early twentieth centuries.

Born in 1880, the year Friedrich Kittler identifies as the beginning of the modern media revolution, Keller's very public coming-of-age coincided with the invention of not only the storage technologies of "gramophone, film, and typewriter" but also the transmission technologies of telephone, dictaphone, and radio.[34] The large number of photographs in the American Foundation for the Blind's archives that depict Keller "seeing" statues are matched only by the dozens of images that showcase Keller "listening" to a radio, "speaking" into a dictaphone, or "keeping time" with a phonograph. The juxtaposition of these two sets of images place Keller at the contested border of old and new media, poised between a world of man-made artifacts on the one hand and a world of mechanical devices on the other hand. Commenting on the historical reorganization of the senses at the turn of the century, Walter Benjamin attributes the decay of an artifact's aura to the desire of new technologies like photography and film "to get hold of an object at very close range."[35] Working faster than the human hand, these new visual and auditory media, in their strenuous efforts to become one with their objects of perception, ironically labor to emulate touch in its intimate proximity to things, making Keller the ideal personification of the work of art in the age of mechanical reproduction.

Of all the many technologies Keller was associated with in her lifetime, it was the telephone that reached her first, in the person of its inventor, Alexander Graham Bell.[36] It was Bell who took Keller to the electrical building at the 1893 Chicago World's Fair and introduced her to the telephone, autophone, and phonograph, all inventions originally designed as hearing aids for the

FIG. 3.6 Helen Keller, Annie Sullivan, and Alexander Graham Bell at Chautauquay, New York, 1894. The subjects of this photograph, formally composed in a triangle with Sullivan at its apex, demonstrate the mathematics of executing three forms of communication at once: oral speech between Bell and Sullivan, manual spelling between Keller and Bell, and lip-reading between Keller and Sullivan. *Courtesy of the American Foundation for the Blind, Helen Keller Archives.*

deaf. Bell was also the figure responsible for establishing the initial connection between Keller and Sullivan, serving as a long-distance channel of communication between the Keller family and the Perkins School of the Blind where Sullivan was a recent graduate. Figure 3.6 captures the close relationship amongst Keller, Sullivan, and Bell, pictured in this 1894 photograph demonstrating their favorite method of three-way conversation. Keller, whom photographs generally represent as the passive receiver of the manual alphabet, here actively spells into Bell's open hand. Bell, in turn, verbally relays Keller's words to Sullivan, whose own re-

FIG. 3.7 Keller "listening" to the radio at her home in Forest Hills, New York. Keller was herself perceived to be a human radio, a blind medium picking up remote signals from the beyond. *Courtesy of the American Foundation for the Blind, Helen Keller Archives.*

sponse is received by Keller through lip-reading. Using one hand to "speak" and the other hand to "listen," Keller's two hands together operate as a telephonic mouthpiece and ear, a device for the transmission and reception of vibrating messages.[37]

Popular fantasies of Keller as, in dancer Martha Graham's words, "a completely receptive instrument" (*DH* 34) found even stronger corroboration in images of Keller listening to the radio [figure 3.7]. "When the radio is playing it is hard to keep Helen's hands on her work," Hamilton's film documentary confides to its audience, twice capturing Keller interrupting her domestic chores to enjoy the vibrations of Arcan Ridge's two radio consoles. Like its successor the television, one of the few technologies absent from Keller's home and from her writings,[38] the radio brought the sounds of the outside world directly into the private domain of the home, unlocking a putative realm of privacy to the intrusions of the public sphere. Yet unlike the television, which commentators lauded as opening a "window" onto the world, the radio sealed the eyes of its audience, rendering all its listeners functionally blind. Rudolf Arnheim's 1936 characterization of the radio listener as someone who "hears people tramping up and down and doesn't know what they are doing" immediately recalls Keller's own descriptions of her earliest perceptions of remote activity.[39] To her friends and family, Keller, whose internal vibroscope could pick up even the most distant signals, was a human radio, open like all radio receivers to the danger of telepathic suggestion. At least one Keller friend openly suspected Sullivan of practicing mind control over Keller, while virtually all of their acquaintances assumed the two women, rumored to be fascinated by the paranormal, could read each other's minds (*DH* 101, 65). "Who can say that our thoughts are not causing vibrations?" Upton Sinclair wrote in his 1930 essay "Mental Radio." Is not telepathy, Sinclair argued, "some kind of vibration, going out from the brain, like radio broadcasting?"[40]

The figuration of a deaf woman as a finely tuned radio receiver finds its analogue in earlier representations of Keller as a gramophone [figure 3.8]. Edison's talking machine was invented in 1888, just two years before Keller began her own voice experiments in the mechanical reproduction of sound. Like Edison's gramophone, Keller's vibroscope recorded only vibrations. And like the early gramophone, Keller had tremendous difficulty reproducing accent, pitch, and tone. Her struggle to control what she called her throat's "motor, vibrator, and resonator" (*M* 94) reveal that Keller imagined her vocal chords as a technical apparatus for the production of acoustic vibrations. Placing her hands on different objects, she would test her phonetic pronunciation by determining how different materials conducted and returned the

FIG. 3.8 Keller standing by a phonograph cabinet beneath a poster com-
memorating Pearl Harbor, keeping time to Bing Crosby's "Silent Night." Of
all the new sound technologies, Keller found the gramophone to be the most
inanimate and impassive, a judgment reflected in her description of her
Radcliffe College professors as men who were "as impersonal as victrolas"
(M 15). *Courtesy of the American Foundation for the Blind, Helen Keller
Archives.*

vibrations of her voice (*T* 162). Keller could always detect her
own voice on the phonograph by its "discordant vibration" (*J*
177), a less harsh self-description perhaps than Edison's identification of Keller's voice as "very unpleasant, like steam explod-
ing." Edison's chief difficulty with Keller's speech precisely echoed
his main complaint about his own gramophone: he could only understand the consonants, not the vowels (*M* 291). More than any
other feature of her public persona, it was her voice that
most clearly identified Keller with the world of the mechanical.
Described variously by one biographer as "broken," "metallic,"

FIG. 3.9 Keller and Sullivan recording into a Dictaphone, in the living room of their Forest Hills home. Seated squarely between person and machine, Sullivan performs her customary mediating function, translating the language of touch into the language of sound. *Courtesy of the American Foundation for the Blind, Helen Keller Archives.*

"tinny," and "robotic" (*DH* 5, 180), Keller's monotonous speech confirmed public perceptions of her as Sullivan's "automaton, a mouthpiece that echoed her thoughts and sentiments" (*T* 105).

Portrayals of Keller as Sullivan's mechanical mouthpiece actually disguised the far more common scenario in which it was Sullivan who served as Keller's public voice. A photograph taken in the living room of Keller's Forest Hills, New York home depicts Keller spelling into Sullivan's hand while Sullivan verbally relays Keller's words into the mouth of a dictaphone [figure 3.9]. Situated solidly at the center of the image, suspended between person and machine, Sullivan is the figure most closely aligned with the recording apparatus. Mechanically translating the language of touch into the language of sound, Sullivan demonstrates for the camera the same task she performed for years on the lecture circuit and the vaudeville stage: reproducing and recording Keller's thoughts and sentiments for an audience gradually coming to see the teacher as the true prosthetic attachment to her more sibylline, and increasingly more famous, student.

Keller's Easton home had all these new media—telephone, radio, phonograph, dictaphone. Reproducing on a more modest scale the electrical building of the Chicago World's Fair, Arcan Ridge was a domestic showcase for modernity's newest inventions in sound technology. Yet the most important machine in Keller's home, the apparatus that defined her more than any other, was in fact the oldest of the new media, the typewriter [figure 3.10]. Invented in 1865 as a writing instrument for the blind, the typewriter subordinated the individuality of handwriting to the mechanization of machinewriting. Referring both to a typing machine and a human typist, the typewriter eliminated the boundary between person and thing, introducing history's first writing machine subject. That Keller wholly identified with this new form of machine writing is not surprising. Typewriting was a blind activity, a form of writing that concealed from view the actual appearance of the letter at the moment of inscription, and that further relied on touch rather than sight for the location of its keys.[41] Like the radio, the typewriter rendered all its users temporarily blind, immediately equalizing Keller's relation to her sighted peers. No less important, the typewriter allowed Keller to convert the private tactile language of the manual alphabet, understood only by a select few, into the public visual language of standardized type, legible to a much larger audience. It was the typewriter, Keller believed, that finally linked her to the world at large, and the typewriter, no less than hand-spelling, that secured her bond to Sullivan.

Once Sullivan taught Keller to type in 1891, the typewriter was always between them. Keller, who could type on virtually any

FIG. 3.10 Keller using a manual typewriter, with her radio console clearly visible behind her. The typewriter, like the radio, presumed a sightless subject, making Keller feel particularly at home with these two modern machines. *Courtesy of the American Foundation for the Blind, Helen Keller Archives.*

kind of machine, including the Hammond typewriter with its movable type shuttles, typically wrote a dozen letters a day, which Sullivan would send back to her student stenographer for correction and retyping. Keller and Sullivan surely deserve an entry in Friedrich Kittler's long list of modern "desk couples," their typewriter affair analogous to the technological pairings of Henry James and Theodora Bosanquet, or Nietzsche and Lou von Salomé.[42] Unlike these opposite sex couples in which one party alone served as amanuensis, Keller and Sullivan performed alternately as each other's scribes. Early on, Sullivan assumed the tasks of proofreading and editing Keller's letters and overseeing the couple's finances. Later, as Sullivan's eyes began to fail, Keller took over as secretary, assisting Sullivan with her correspondence and typing the household accounts. The typewriter was the real third party in the Keller-Sullivan romance, as an estranged John Macy vaguely seemed to intuit when he bitterly denounced Keller as "more of an institution than a woman" and Sullivan as its "chairman of the board, vice-president, secretary, treasurer, janitor, matron, and office boy."[43]

More than any of modernity's other "intelligent machines," the typewriter perceptibly conjoins subject and object, fusing the manual labor of the hand to the automated reflex of the machine. "The typewriter is not really a machine in the strict sense of machine," Heidegger clarifies in 1943, "but is an 'intermediate' thing, between a tool and a machine."[44] This delicate equilibrium between tool and machine can be seen in photographs of Keller's office desk, where art and technology face off on the same level plane [figure 3.11]. A Remington typewriter to her left and a Braille typewriter to her right, Keller faces at the back of the desk a row of figurines, all positioned within arm's reach. These artistic representations of the human figure, which Keller could run her hands over while working, include a mask of the American poet Walt Whitman by Jo Davidson, a bust of the Spanish social activist Dolores Ibarruri, also by Jo Davidson, and a second bust of the founder of Japan's deaf-blind educational movement, Toshiro Furukawa. Like the classical Greek and Egyptian figures on Freud's desk, Keller's more contemporary international icons serve as her silent audience, a carefully selected coterie of literary muses. The photograph of Keller at her desk, her hands obscured from view by the massive carriage of the typewriter, positions her not only as the extension of an information machine but as the prototype of her own artistic double, a large terra cotta bust created, like the figures on her desk, by the artist Jo Davidson. Seated amongst her artifacts and machines, Keller physically embodies

FIG. 3.11 Art and technology face off on Keller's desk in her study at Arcan Ridge. Less weighted with artifacts than Freud's study, Keller's desk nonetheless includes its own silent audience of figurines, with the additional counterweights of a Braille and a Remington typewriter, her prosthetic right and left hands. *Courtesy of the American Foundation for the Blind, Helen Keller Archives.*

the convergence of two worlds, balancing a culture's attraction to technological prostheses on the one side against its equally strong nostalgia for unmediated touch on the other side. If Keller symbolized the spirit of an age, it was her affinity to objects that made her such a powerful icon, a living sign of the new cultural interface between art and science, hand and machine.

5

The machines that surrounded Keller were not merely objects of décor but conduits of interiority, vital tools for self-expression and communication. Keller was, in many ways, at home with technology. But this is not to say that she was unaware of its limitations, or even its dangers. As Keller grew older and her body began to fail, her fears about mechanical malfunction grew proportionately greater. Beset in her seventies and eighties by chronic and severe bronchial colds (*T* 177), Keller lost much of her olfactory sense, and, along with it, the ability to locate and to identify people and objects by their smells. Equally problematic, one of Keller's toes was amputated, partially reducing her awareness of vibrations. But the most serious loss of all was the decreased sensitivity of her hands, crippled by arthritis and further disabled by chronic eczema. Like sight and hearing, touch ages. Increasingly infirm, Keller found herself unable to use a typewriter and uncomfortable reading Braille. By the time Keller completed *Teacher* in 1954, she needed to warm her hands continually in order to read a book. As her skin condition worsened, requiring twice daily visitations by a nurse, Keller was unable to communicate as easily through the manual language, generally requiring every message to be spelled to her twice (*DH* 317). Keller also experienced considerable difficulty tactilely recognizing familiar objects, objects that crucially defined her subjective sense of self. The dulling of touch and the fading of smell, two common symptoms of aging, imposed on an elderly Keller an unwelcome withdrawal, a return to the physical and social isolation her early training in the cognitive use of these two contact senses had largely dispelled.

As Keller's senses became less responsive to her environment's telltale smells and vibrations, Arcan Ridge became an increasing source of anxiety. The house became not only a site of frequent minor accidents and injuries but a place of death and mourning as well.[45] It was not long after rebuilding Arcan Ridge that Thompson and Keller together stood vigil over the body of their live-in handyman, who lay for many hours on the floor of his room, felled by a cerebral hemorrhage. This scene was nearly repeated when, some years later, Polly Thompson collapsed on the kitchen floor from a stroke. Too emotionally distraught and spatially disoriented to find the special telephone installed for precisely such an emergency, Keller remained by Thompson's side until a postman found them.[46] Keller herself died of a heart attack at Arcan Ridge, confined for the last years of her life to the isolation of her bed, after suffering a series of debilitating strokes (*DH* 334).

In its very design and construction, Keller's second Easton home was, from the beginning, a house in a state of emergency. Its predecessor destroyed by a malfunctioning oil furnace, Arcan Ridge II boasted a separate chimney for the new furnace, an electric rather than a gas stove, a fireproof cellar, and fire resistant walls. If these precautions were not protection enough, this twelve room house was outfitted with as many as twenty-one fire alarm units in addition to thirty-seven fire extinguishers, each installed on a side wall or ceiling, sealed in glass, and designed to release automatically fire-retardant chemicals. Keller's fear of fire was deep-seated. Years earlier Keller had detected the odor of burning tar and wood in the floorboards of her sister's home, the result of a defective flue. Concerned in her later years that her fading sense of smell was no longer an adequate protection against fire, Keller prevailed upon an electrician to adapt the fire alarms at Arcan Ridge to trigger large gongs that could be felt through vibrations anywhere in the house. By 1963, five years before her death, Keller held no less than five principal insurance policies on her home and its possessions, policies that were entirely redundant in light of comprehensive household and fire insurance the American Foundation of the Blind already held on Arcan Ridge.

For Keller, it was the parts of the house she could not smell or touch that posed the greatest threat. By placing its energy sources out of reach, Keller's fully automated home radically undermined her tactile and olfactory knowledge. Relocating the technology of power to the most inaccessible regions of the contemporary dwelling, modernity brings danger into the house where it can be

FIG. 3.12 Real estate ad for Arcan Ridge, following Keller's death in 1968. Realtors advertised Keller's home as "a superbly constructed fireproof dwelling."

less easily detected by the human senses. Constructed upon the ashes of the first Arcan Ridge, Keller's second modern house was built with the most advanced forms of fire prevention and detection. And yet, as Keller knew, the technology that transformed her home into what real estate advertisements later described as "a superbly constructed fireproof dwelling" [figure 3.12] also significantly increased the likelihood of circuit malfunctions and electrical fires.

If for Gaston Bachelard the ancestral house represented chiefly a "material paradise," a maternal womb built for shelter,[47] for Helen Keller the modern house was first and foremost a material inferno, an atomic bomb wired for destruction. *Teacher*, which begins with a narration of Keller's return to the ashes of Arcan Ridge, ends with an account of her trip to another ruined site, the bombed out cities of Nagasaki and Hiroshima. While Keller never presumes to equate these radically different disasters,[48] she ultimately blames the internal combustibility of modernity itself, with its unchecked embrace of scientific technology, for the twentieth-century scourge of sudden violence and catastrophic destruction. As much a space of primal fear as primal fantasy, the house in Keller's experience was anything but a Bachelardian benevolent presence keeping patient vigil like "an eye open to the night."[49] Keller, eschewing the specular metaphor so common to philosophical personifications of the bourgeois dwelling, located the real threat to the security of the modern home inside its walls, hidden in basements and attics and concealed beneath floors. With wires snaking through its infrastructure, electrifying every corner of the house, Arcan Ridge was a modern bulwark fortified not just against the likelihood of external threat but against the possibility of its own internal failure.

Although terrified of fire throughout her life, Keller, like Freud, chose to be cremated after her death. The urn containing her ashes was placed, according to Keller's wishes, next to the urns of Annie Sullivan and Polly Thompson in the Columbarium at Washington's National Cathedral. Echoing Dickinson before her, Keller envisioned the moment of death as "no more than passing from one room to another."[50] The only difference, Keller fervently believed, was that in this other domestic space she would once again be able to see and to hear (*M* 341). Sensory fullness, not sensory deprivation, would animate the interior dwelling of an imagined afterlife free of physical disability and bodily pain. Death signified for Keller not the cessation of all sensory experience but nothing less than the promise of its immediate and complete restoration.

The urn containing Keller's ashes on the altar of the Washington National Cathedral, 1968. Keller, who feared fire more than anything else, chose to be cremated when she died, her ashes interred alongside those of both Annie Sullivan and Polly Thompson in the Cathedral's columbarium. *Courtesy of the American Foundation for the Blind, Helen Keller Archives.*

Proust, around 1905, a year or two before moving to 102 boulevard Haussmann. *Courtesy of Bibliothèque nationale de France.*

4

Proust's Nose

102 boulevard Haussmann
Paris France

MARCEL PROUST'S BEDROOM might at first seem to be a peculiar choice to conclude a book about space. After all, Proust devoted his thirteen years in his apartment on boulevard Haussmann to the single-minded production of a book about time. *A la recherche du temps perdu* is a novel that concerns nothing if not involuntary memory, the sudden sensory reclamation of a time past, or what Proust calls, in *Le temps retrouvé*, "a fragment of time in the pure state."[1] Yet *A la recherche* is as much a book about the search for lost space as the search for lost time. The involuntary memory triggered by the touch of a stiff napkin, the sound of a railwayman's hammer, or the smell and taste of a madeleine soaked in tea evoke not just a past moment but a forgotten place. Involuntary memory, in many ways the inverted mirror image of traumatic memory, effects an immediate temporal and spatial dislocation that suspends not only then and now but also here and there. In Proust's novel, time inhabits space; the one cannot be refound without the other.

Such is precisely the central claim of George Poulet's seminal 1963 phenomenological study, *L'Espace proustien*. "Proustian time is time spatialized," Poulet epigrammatically notes; what rises up like steam from the famous cup of tea is not only a prior instant but an actual room (more often than not, we might add, a bedroom). Poulet was, notably, one of the first critics to insist on the equivalent importance of space in a novel formerly considered to be significant chiefly for its theorization of time.[2] Poulet's investigation of Proustian space, however, remains curiously intangible and indefinite, more interested in plumbing the depths of metaphorical space than in taking the measure of its more literal manifestations. Interestingly, Poulet ignores altogether the space of the domestic interior, both in Proust's furniture-obsessed novel and in his carefully secluded life, preferring to develop a phenomenology of inner space largely abstracted from any actual interiors.

In point of fact, virtually all the commentaries on Proust take pains to distance him from the domestic sphere, perhaps because, like the common representation of Emily Dickinson as an eccentric and phobic introvert, the popular mythologization of Proust as a sickly and neurotic recluse also verges on parody. Yet while Dickinson critics tend to embrace the notion of the female writer as agoraphobe, Proust critics devote their considerable energies to forestalling any perception of the male writer as agoraphobe—a term tellingly never applied to Proust, despite the many hours this famously solitary writer spent in self-imposed confinement. For Proust's critics and biographers, it is specifically the image of the sunless cork-lined bedroom, with its placenta-like inner lining or skin, that summons up all the connotations of effeminacy, passivity, narcissism, and infantilism that together threaten to turn Proust, if not into another Emily Dickinson, then into another Anna-Élisabeth Noailles, a contemporary and friend of Proust who also wrote from her bed and lined her walls with cork.[3]

"Forget the cork-lined room and the dallying aesthete," Roger Shattuck instructs his readers in *Proust's Way: A Field Guide to In Search of Lost Time*; "Proust lived in this world and wrote about it with fervor." William Sansom's *Proust and His World* no less insistently attempts to rescue the male novelist from his spatial isolation, with the book jacket assuring readers that, in this study, "Proust himself is shown to be much more than the familiar invalid sealed in his cork-lined room and chasing with his pen after the phantom of Time." Even the promotional material for Jean-

Yves Tadié's *Marcel Proust: A Life* promises that this magisterial biography will reveal Proust as "a man in time rather than a solipsist in a cork-lined room."[4]

Scholars are united in their recommendation to readers to ignore the "comic-strip picture" of Proust confined in a cork-lined bedroom and to concentrate instead on the writer's "rapid and frequent contact with the world outside."[5] This critical suppression of domestic life comes with a price: the disappearance of Proust himself from the scene of his novel's creation. The insistence on Proust's worldliness speaks more, in the end, to critical preconceptions about the rugged urbanity of the male modernist writer than to Proust's own deep affinity for the culturally feminized space of domestic interiority. While it is certainly true that Proust wrote about the world, he nonetheless chose to do so from the perspective of a very precisely arranged, heavily insulated, and carefully regulated bedroom. If the goal is to bring a measure of humanity to a much caricatured and misunderstood figure, then a better approach to the problem might be not to ignore the cork-lined bedroom but to enter more fully into it. As I have in the previous chapters, I will argue here that a reading of the actual space of writing, infused as it is with the lived experiences of sensation, memory, illness, and intellect, provides a revealing and sometimes surprising context in which to understand the literary work that is so painstakingly produced there.

Proust's novel itself sheds a certain amount of light on its author's sensory experiences, on the sights, sounds, textures, tastes, and smells that comprise Proust's daily existence. How much of this work represents fact and how much fiction remains a matter of genuine critical dispute among biographers, some of whom draw as freely on *A la recherche du temps perdu* as on the more obviously self-referential *Jean Santeuil* to illuminate Proust's life, while others vigilantly resist the tendency to cull any biographical information at all from Proust's literary works.[6] In my own opinion, the imaginatively wide-ranging *A la recherche du temps perdu* does not, strictly speaking, resemble a memoir on the order of Keller's *The World I Live In*, but neither is this intensely personal novel wholly uninflected by the thoughts, feelings, and experiences of its self-reflective author. *A la recherche du temps perdu* might be approached more usefully as another dimly lighted Proustian interior, inhabited by a narrator frequently mistaken for the author. Through the agency of this narrator also named Marcel, Proust haunts the shadowy corners of his novel in the same manner Hitchcock will later make cameo appearances in his films. In both cases one is never quite sure where the authorial presence is likely to be lurking. To assume that Proust's novel is either all fact or all fiction may miss the point entirely, for Proust's own interest lies precisely in disorganizing the boundary between the two. Continually dissolving and reconstructing the walls between literature and life, not even Proust appears entirely conscious of which interior he occupies—the space of writing or the space of living. During his years at boulevard Haussmann, there never seemed to be very much of a difference.

1

That Proust is a writer of the interior quite nearly goes without saying; we might readily identify this most influential of French modernists in terms Proust himself uses to describe his narrator, a writer who works "from the inside outwards" (I: 94). Walter Benjamin, who declared seven years after Proust's death that *A la recherche* was the "outstanding literary achievement of our time," also claimed that "since the spiritual exercises of Loyola there has hardly been a more radical attempt at self-absorption."[7] Henri Bergson, a cousin of Proust by marriage, was similarly generous in his assessment of *À l'ombre des jeunes filles en fleurs*: "Rarely has introspection been taken so far. It is a direct and continuous vision of interior reality."[8] Hannah Arendt agreed, arguing that through his novel Proust's "inner life, which insisted on transforming all worldly happenings into inner experience, became like a mirror in whose reflection truth might appear." Beginning deep inside his own consciousness, Arendt elaborates, Proust "enlarged this inner experience until it included . . . all members of society."[9] Noting that acts of reading in *A la recherche* always take place in sheltered interiors (in bowers, closets, and rooms), Paul de Man is only one in a long line of philosophically minded critics to declare that, in Proust, "the inner world is unambiguously valorized as preferable to the outside."[10] Inner life is so persistently and favorably opposed to outer life in what Proust called his "novel of introspection" that a small body of criticism has recently emerged to defend the importance of sociality in *A la recherche*, insisting that, in Proust's fiction, the public does not always and inevitably give way to the private.[11]

Proust's embrace of the interior was influenced in part by changes in the urban scene. In an age of unprecedented urban growth, the interior afforded protection from the violent disturbances of a newly modernized Paris. Cultural historians note that as the city increasingly took on the role of a neurasthenic agent, the interior assumed its new cultural function as a soothing anaesthetizer, a place where "the over-stimulated citizen could find refuge . . . from the sensory barrage of the metropolis."[12] This was indeed the case with Proust, who, from 1906 to 1919, sought sanctuary from the sights, sounds, and smells of the city in his second-story apartment on a street not far from the Gare Saint-Lazare. That this apartment is located on a boulevard named Haussmann, in a modern neighborhood constructed on the remnants of old Paris, adds a new layer of meaning to the title of Proust's novel. Not only does Proust's urban boulevard eradicate the signs of the past, it simultaneously functions as a reminder of the national trauma that, for the citizens of Second Empire Paris, effectively stopped time.[13] Haussmann's wide-scale destruction in the 1850s and 1860s of the countless small houses, shops, and marketplaces of Paris, and his concurrent construction of open boulevards with unobstructed vistas, eliminated the most interior spaces of the metropolis. This relentless and aggressive program of exteriorization may well provide a crucial historical context in which to understand the French novel's turn toward interiorization. As if in compensation for everything that has been lost in the urban assault on the interior, the modern novelist moves further inward, searching for the lost object precisely where Proust's narrator finds it, in "the inner walls of his being" (I: 387).

And yet, as other cultural historians point out, Haussmannization, while opening up the enclosed spaces of the city, simultaneously created new urban interiors elsewhere: sidewalks, kiosks, public lavatories. Overturning the common historical view of post-Haussmann Paris as an "extroverted city," Sharon Marcus argues that the metropolis was less a space of spectacle and flânerie than enclosure and privacy. Marcus locates what she calls "the interiorization of Paris" in the historical evolution of architectural perceptions of the apartment house. Whereas before Haussmann the apartment house was understood to be "transparent" and open to the life of the street, after Haussmann the apartment house was viewed as "opaque" and closed to public view.[14] The very openness of Haussmann's new urban plan, it seems, created the need for more hermetic and confined domestic spaces within suddenly fluid and expanding city borders.

102 boulevard Haussmann is, in all respects, a typical Haussmann apartment building, built in the mid-nineteenth century as part of a row of stone structures, with uniform façades distinguished by repetitive plaster moldings and iron grillwork [figure 4.1]. Reacting against the elaborate ornamentation of Louis-Philippe architecture, Second Empire apartment buildings favor regularity over autonomy, employing a design vocabulary of imposing bare walls, modest decorative detail, and clean symmetrical portals. French historian of architecture François Loyer identifies as one of the hallmarks of Haussmannization the re-

Fig. 4.1 102 boulevard Haussmann, shortly after Proust's departure in 1919. In this period drawing, the decorative detail, iron grillwork, and proportional windows of the original building remain intact. Later architectural renovations radically changed the façade, by installing columns, removing ornamentation, and widening windows to make the lower floors below Proust's former apartment look more like a bank.

placement of ternary compositions with binary ones, illustrated in Proust's building by the paired window openings and double doors creating an overall impression of balanced uniformity. Haussmann imposed order on what he saw as a chaotic and incoherent environment, reorganizing the city as if he were tidying up a drawing room. Expanding on the domestic metaphor, Loyer observes that Haussmann's apartment buildings "came to resemble books lined up in a bookcase, or drawers in a piece of furniture."[15] Proust's six-story apartment house, identical in mass and scale to the buildings surrounding it, comprised just one book in Haussmann's extensive urban library. To find the distinctive details in a Haussmann building, one is invited to look on the inside, to move beyond the uniform façade and to enter into the private world behind.

In the building's foyer a front staircase for residents and a back staircase for servants extend the architectural binarism into the interior, with a large entrance hallway linking outer street to inner courtyard. A Haussmann building in fact boasted two façades: a front exterior facing the public zone of the commercial street, and a matching back exterior facing the private zone of the service courtyard. By treating the inner façade as a near-replica of the outer façade,[16] Haussmann's two frontalities further interiorize the chambers within, separating servants from their employers and removing the bourgeois inhabitant from the vital communal transactions of the courtyard, associated in the age of hygiene with the abject and hidden waste products of modern living. Sometime after 1900, an elevator was installed in the center of the stairwell, conveying Proust directly to his second-floor apartment and obviating the need to climb the narrow and dimly lit front stairs.[17] Exiting this central elevator, any visitors to the apartment, standing on the central landing, could be identified by a servant through a bull's eye window [figure 4.2]. With the windows in every room of the apartment except the kitchen and servant's bedroom closed and curtained year-round, and with the apartment telephones all eventually removed, this internal window, together with the numerous service bells also located along the hallway joining kitchen to vestibule, functioned as the dwelling's sensory opening onto the outside world. Because the front rooms were so tightly sealed against the sounds and sights of a busy urban boulevard, the structure's center of surveillance migrated to the back of the apartment, where household staff served as Proust's private sentinels, his surrogate eyes and ears.

Much of what we know about the living quarters at 102 boulevard Haussmann comes from the extraordinary memoir of

F I G . 4.2 *Œil de bœuf* window. With the front windows closed and curtained against the sounds and sights of the boulevard, this small oval window looking onto the second-story landing operated as the apartment's
main eye onto the outside world. *Author photograph.*

Céleste Albaret, Proust's *bonne à tout* or general housekeeper
who, at the age of eighty-two, published her surprisingly detailed
memories of life in the Proust household from 1913 to 1922.
Céleste Albaret has been interpreted as just another "hermetic
seal" for Proust, equivalent to the cork lining on his bedroom
walls.[18] Yet this spirited and opinionated woman was clearly
much more than a buffer; close attention to Albaret's memoir reveals that Proust treated his loyal but independent housekeeper
variously as a servant, a confidante, a mother, a daughter, a scold,
a spy, and (inevitably) a literary model. "We created our own sort

of intimacy,"[19] remarks Albaret, the only woman Proust ever will-
ingly admitted into his bedroom, and one of the few people close
enough to Proust to provide a reliable account of his daily routine
and work habits. At once inside and outside her employer's inner
circle of family and friends, Albaret provides a chronicle of the
Proust household that is as subtly critical as it is openly affectionate.[20] Most notable for my own reading of the literary interior,
Proust's housekeeper brings to her reconstruction of the apartment—its surfaces and apertures, its furniture and design—a documentary eye for particularity. Céleste Albaret narrates in words
what Edmund Engelman captures in images, describing in precise
detail the location and appearance of every object in Proust's bedroom with the same systematic thoroughness Engelman's camera
brings to his visual record of Freud's office.

Albaret's recollection of the apartment layout describes a classic Haussmann interior, with two public drawing rooms and a
main bedroom at the front overlooking the avenue, a kitchen and
children's bedroom at the back overlooking the service courtyard,
and a vestibule, two water-closets, dining room, and extra chamber
in between [figure 4.3]. In the Proust family's previous apartments
at 9 boulevard Malesherbes and 45 rue de Courcelles, Proust and
his brother Robert occupied the two bedrooms closest to the
kitchen; at 102 boulevard Haussmann, Proust moved to the front
bedroom on the boulevard, symbolically assuming the spatial position of power once held by his parents.[21] Proust used the chamber
behind his bedroom, when not occupied by one of his male secretaries, as a dressing room, and even considered moving his own
bedroom to this smaller back room, a space insulated from the
boulevard and easier to heat. But he remained in the front bedroom
for the duration of his thirteen-year stay, evidently preferring the
din of the street to the stench of the courtyard. Considerable distance also separated Proust's chamber from Céleste Albaret's bedroom located next to the kitchen and between the two stairwells, a
room Albaret calls a "combined cockpit and listening post com-
manding the whole apartment" (188). Tellingly, Albaret sees even

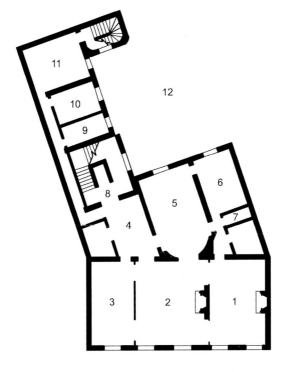

Key:
1 - Proust's Bedroom
2 - Large Salon
3 - Small Salon
4 - Vestibule
5 - Dining Room
6 - Dressing Room
7 - W.C.
8 - Landing
9 - Bath
10 - Albaret's Bedroom
11 - Kitchen
12 - Courtyard

FIG. 4.3 Floor Plan of apartment. The noisiest bedroom in the house, Proust's front chamber nonetheless had the singular virtue of standing at the farthest remove from both courtyard and kitchen, implying that Proust's sensitivity to strong smells ultimately outweighed his aversion to loud sounds.

her command center as, in reality, no more than a thoroughfare, "a brief halt on the way to the bedroom." Proust's entire apartment, she writes, "was really a desert surrounding his room" (317).[22]

Only by closing himself off spatially could Proust occupy fully the expanding world of his novel, a narrative space as intimate as it is capacious. In the confines of his bedroom Proust did to the traditional novel what Haussmann did to medieval Paris, removing old structural boundaries to create new visual perspectives. By lengthening sentences, expanding chapters, and unfurling syntax, Proust performed on the novel a kind of literary Haussmannization, recasting novelistic space in a way as controversial for literature as Haussmann's urban renewal project was for architecture.[23] Like Haussmann's model apartment, Proust's consummate novel has been routinely taken to task for its massive size and its repetitive motifs. With *A la recherche du temps perdu*, Proust cut a wide swath through the familiar and cramped quarters of literary history, brazenly reorganizing space and time in a way Haussmann would have admired and may even have inspired. At once a final articulation of classical order and an early expression of modern interiority, Proust's seven-volume novel simulates his seven-room apartment in both outline and scale. Proust's fiction, no less than Haussmann's architecture, represents, in every sense of the word, a *monumental* achievement.

2

The apartment at 102 boulevard Haussmann was, from the beginning, a family monument. After his mother's death in the apartment at rue de Courcelles, an inconsolable Proust, at the age of thirty-five, sent friends to investigate other living quarters so that he might escape from a place made hazardous by memory. Although Proust instructed his emissaries to avoid houses that were too dusty, loud, or uncomfortable, he ultimately settled on an apartment that was all these things. Of his decision to move to a busy boulevard with a tramway, Proust admitted that his new home, with "the dust of the *quartier*, the incessant noise, and the trees leaning right up against the window, of course falls well short of the apartment I was looking for." Entirely unsuitable for his purposes, the apartment on boulevard Haussmann attracted Proust for sentimental reasons; it was the home of his great uncle Louis Weil, a familiar apartment where mother and son watched Weil die in the very room Proust later selected for his own.[24] Proust, it appears, left one place of mourning only to occupy another. Unable to relinquish completely the object of his deepest affections, Proust left the family apartment but refused to part with his parents' furniture. Resisting his brother Robert's suggestion that the family heirlooms be put up for sale, Proust transported as much furniture to boulevard Haussmann as the smaller apartment could hold, putting another three roomfuls in storage. The goal for Proust in retaining these painful reminders of life at rue de Courcelles was to reconstitute the very place he initially sought to escape, "the place where Mama rests."[25]

Biographers are of one mind in their assessment of the large and heavy Proust family furniture: "fussy" observes William Sansom, "shabby" declares Edmund White, "inferior" pronounces George Painter.[26] As harsh as these epithets may seem, they pale in comparison to the response of Oscar Wilde, who, invited by Proust to dine at the family apartment, reportedly exclaimed to Proust's parents: "How ugly your house is!"[27] Even Proust's mentor, Comte Robert de Montesquiou, was compelled to lament to the young aesthete, "How unfortunate that you should not like objects!"[28] Proust never denied that the family furniture he brought to 102 boulevard Haussmann was unattractive; indeed, he may have viewed his uncle's apartment, which he proclaims a "triumph of bourgeois bad taste,"[29] as a quite suitable setting for his own drab middle-class furnishings. On the subject of interior design, Proust and his narrator speak as one: "I had never sought . . . to furnish for aesthetic effect, to arrange rooms artistically. I was too lazy for that, too indifferent to the things that I was in the habit of seeing everyday" (V: 174). When Proust did buy expensive objects, he gave them away. A gift giver rather than an art collector, Proust was a veritable anti-Swann. Other French novelists like Zola and Balzac carefully displayed in their homes (and exhaustively catalogued in their writings) every valuable possession they owned.[30] Proust, by contrast, stored most of his furniture out of sight in his dining room, an unused chamber described by Albaret as a "repository crammed to the ceiling" (317).

Contrary to Montesquiou's belief, Proust did in fact like objects; he simply prized his possessions more for their affective than their aesthetic value. In Proust's life as in his fiction, pieces of furniture operated as personal vehicles of memory rather than as social harbingers of taste. Objects are talismanic subjects for Proust, fetishistic signs of the simultaneous absence and presence of the dead: "In this cult of grief for our own dead, we pay an idolatrous worship to the things that they loved" (IV: 797). This "idolatrous worship" constitutes a form not of passive melancholia but of active resistance, a steadfast refusal of time's relentless forward movement toward an irreversible future. "Our obscure attachments to the dimensions, to the atmosphere of a bedroom," Proust's narrator clarifies, constitutes "a secret, partial, tangible and true aspect of our resistance to death, of the long, desperate, daily resistance to the fragmentary and continuous death that insinuates itself throughout the whole course of our life" (II: 722). A bedroom, and all the familiar things in it, can forestall death because the past lies hidden in material objects. Proustian object-love operates, in short, as the antidote to lost time.

Proust's passionate attachment to the somber and seemingly lifeless furniture of his parents can be attributed, in great measure, to his belief in the power of objects to embody the subjects to whom they belong. Like the personified furniture at the Hotel in Doncières, "an assembly of rooms as real as a colony of people" (III: 80), or the Verdurin's brocade-covered cardtable "raised to the dignity of the person since, like a person, it had a past, a memory" (V: 287), the ponderous furniture in Proust's bedroom, memorial pieces that at first appear to encrypt Proust, in fact release him from a solitary confinement precisely by reanimating the very figures whom he mourns. Proust was hardly alone in his bedroom, surrounded as he was by the subjective lives of inanimate objects, those "obstinately mute witnesses" and "scrupulous confidants" (II: 994) that bear faithful testimony to the presence of the past.

From his brass bed in the most protected corner of the bedroom, Proust could take in at a glance both his father's velvet library armchair, angled inwards to face the bed, and his mother's grand piano immediately behind it, occupying the structural center of the room [figure 4.4]. Proust's private chamber appears as an amalgamation of Swann's library and Odette's dressing room, both places associated by the narrator with privacy and intimacy. This bourgeois bedroom combines two highly gendered spaces into one, displaying together the desk and books of a man's study with the screen and mirrors of a woman's boudoir. By mixing masculine and feminine design styles, Proust clearly intended to resurrect both his deceased parents. And yet the gender polarity defining Proust's bedroom subtly favors maternal heirlooms over paternal ones, with the grand piano dwarfing the library armchair, and a copy of a Boulle worktable inscribed with Jeanne Proust's initials physically obstructing two revolving bookcases most likely imported from Adrien Proust's study.

This tension between masculine and feminine interior décor accentuates an even stronger opposition in the bedroom between Occident and Orient, between the room's matching French rosewood chest, wardrobe, and mirrors and its more colorful Ceylonese cabinet, Chinese screen, and Oriental rug. Heavy Second Empire furniture invoking the militarism of the Napoleonic West provides ballast to more delicate Oriental furniture connoting the exoticism of the Far East. The Eastern accents in Proust's bed-

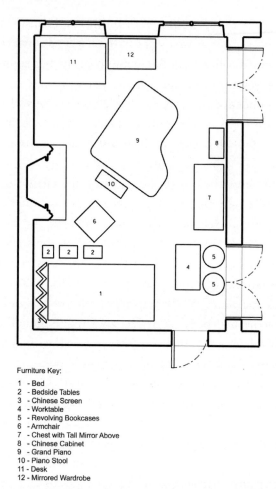

Furniture Key:

1 - Bed
2 - Bedside Tables
3 - Chinese Screen
4 - Worktable
5 - Revolving Bookcases
6 - Armchair
7 - Chest with Tall Mirror Above
8 - Chinese Cabinet
9 - Grand Piano
10 - Piano Stool
11 - Desk
12 - Mirrored Wardrobe

FIG. 4.4 Bedroom diagram, with furniture. Proust's cluttered bedroom left little room for maneuvering, with his mother's worktable blocking easy access to the bookcases and her grand piano pushed so close to the mirrored wardrobe that the latter was never opened. From the fortified corner of his bed set on diagonal to the bedroom's main entrance, Proust could monitor all three of the room's entranceways as well as its two windows, assuming a position of defense against both threshold and aperture.

room immediately bring to mind the only fully outfitted Orientalist interior in *A la recherche*, Odette's courtesan apartment before her marriage to Swann. Odette de Crecy's Oriental draperies,

Turkish beads, Japanese lanterns, and Chinese porcelain, ornaments, and screens all represent a distinctly Western fantasy of the
Orient as a feminized space, a place of sensual gratification and
timeless mystery.[31] The imposing five-panel Chinese screen behind
Proust's own bed, together with the large Oriental bedside rug,
isolates the bed itself as the room's center of exoticism. Significantly, it is here that Proust, fulfilling his narrator's dream, writes
a modern version of *Thousand and One Nights*. And it is here
that Proust discovers the "Open Sesame" (VII: 888) that unlocks
the past, coming to the gradual realization that his novel is the
open door he has been seeking.

At a time when Jews in France were viewed as foreign and exotic, Proust's lovers and friends were forever orientalizing Proust,
comparing his "huge Oriental eyes" (Daniel Halévy) to "Japanese
lacquer" (Antoine de Bibesco).[32] If, in Proust's world, things become persons, persons also convert into things; Léon Daudet
thought of the ivory-skinned Proust as a "Chinese trinket," while
Laure Hayman dubbed him a "little porcelain psychologist."[33] Orientalism connoted objectification, with Proust himself, like so many
other educated Jews of the period, becoming one more fashionable
artifact in the salons and bedrooms of the Faubourg Saint-Ger-
main.[34] Proust himself played up his oriental appearance by dressing in a Japanese housecoat and slippers. Wearing colorful eastern
garb and reclining indolently on his bed, the sedentary but regal
Proust reminded Albaret of "a young Oriental prince" (150), a sul-
tan holding court. The choice to write like the Comtesse de Noailles
semi-recumbent in bed, rather than upright at his uncle's desk, thus
not only feminized Proust, it also exoticized him, revealing the
depths of self-pleasuring implicit in the act of nocturnal writing.

But did Proust do more than simply *write* in bed? Was the bed
merely a site of sublimation, of sexual energy translated into literary production, or did the recesses of Proust's bed offer up the illicit pleasures promised by those tales of *Thousand and One
Nights* that so scandalize the narrator's mother in *A la recherche*?

Proust's infatuation with younger men is indisputable, and his voyeurism well known, but did Proust use his bedroom at boulevard Haussmann for sexual assignations? Céleste Albaret vigorously denies it, while nevertheless confirming rumors of Proust's visits to male brothels—adventures, Albaret quickly adds, pursued strictly in the interest of novelistic research (196–7). It is entirely possible that Proust had sex in his bedroom, if not with other men, then with himself. Here, too, the loyal Albaret is anxious to counter rumors of Proust's onanism, insisting that, "apart from eating, washing, dressing, and using his notebooks and pen, he seldom did anything with his hands" (195). Albaret's very defensiveness on the subject of her employer's bodily desires suggests that Proust, who as an adolescent was routinely sent by his father to bordellos to cure his "bad habit," and who later as a writer made a religion out of his childhood visits to the orris-scented closet, was not without ready recourse to sexual stimulation and release. Certainly the proximity of several live-in male chauffeurs and secretaries, though their stays in Proust's household were invariably brief, provided both temptation and opportunity for Proust to fulfill his sexual fantasies, whatever his housekeeper may remember to the contrary.[35]

And yet, the representation of Proust's bedroom as literary cloister is not altogether an untenable one. Clearly visible from Proust's bed, on the white marble top of the rosewood chest, stands the most peculiar curio in Proust's bedroom, a small white statue of the infant Jesus wearing a crown of grapes. The only devotional figure in a room otherwise devoid of religious iconography, Proust's kitschy Christian relic replicates the picture of the Virgin Mary on a little table altar that stood in his Aunt Élisabeth Amiot's sickroom at Illiers. Continuing the family tradition of cloistered invalidism, the irreligious Proust places his icon on the same chest that holds his thirty-two black-leather notebooks for *A la recherche*, effectively conferring reverential status on the novel in its infancy. Proust's Aunt Élisabeth (the model for Aunt Léonie) bequeathed to her nephew several pieces of furniture, including the green half-length *chaise-longue* upon which the young Proust, like his narrative counterpart, "tasted for the first time the delights of love" (II: 622).[36] Proust later gave this sofa, along with some of his aunt's chairs and curtains, to Albert Le Cuziat, the former footman turned proprietor of a male brothel that Proust occasionally visited, a brothel conveniently located on rue de l'Arcade, close by boulevard Haussmann.[37] In *A la recherche* the Narrator describes these old pieces in their new surroundings as unhappy supplicants, "appealing to me like those apparently inanimate objects in a Persian fairy-tale" (II: 622). Whether or not the increasingly reclusive Proust felt genuine remorse in subjecting these living family heirlooms to public defilement, this dramatic act of property divestiture suggests that, by the time he had begun to conceive of *Sodome et Gomorrhe*, Proust may well have decided to throw the sex out with the sofa.

After the sofa's unceremonious banishment, all of Proust's sexual ventures—including his alleged predilections for sadomasochistic voyeurism and for rat torture—take place outside the bedroom and, in these particular instances, inside Le Cuziat's brothel, the new home for the seat of Proust's sexual experiments. Julia Kristeva reads Le Cuziat's brothel, and its scenes of profanation and debauchery, as "the antithesis of the writing laboratory of which Céleste is the vestal virgin."[38] While Proust's bedroom is not without its own sensual appeal, it does seem clear that, at boulevard Haussmann, Proust's exploration of interiority became increasingly focused on literary rather than physical acts of discovery. To see the more tantalizing tales of *Thousand and One Nights* enacted before him (VI: 862), Proust, like his narrator, had to leave his cell. At the same time, the presence of Proust's family furniture in Le Cuziat's establishment may, in fact, have extended the bounds of Proust's interiority, furnishing an unknown public place with all the comforts of home. Proust found solace and pleasure in his periodic visits to the brothel because his gift of furniture had already transformed a foreign and friendless space into a familiar and familial one. This extension of the domestic interior into the public realm, however, did not carry the physical act of writing along with it. Indeed, by separating the space of sex from the space of writing, Proust may have been trying to erect a *cordon sanitaire* between his physical desires and his literary ambitions. A highly sexualized interior where little actual sex seems to have taken place, Proust's isolated bedroom provides a fitting habitation for this writer of romantic obsession and sexual frustration. Edmund White puts the contradiction best: Proust was, within the confines of his bedroom walls, "a playboy monk" (93).

3

The approach to Proust's *sanctum sanctorum* is a highly mediated one, requiring the visitor to pass through four closed doors within the apartment before finally arriving at the bedroom. The difficulty in accessing the writer's bedroom is compounded by a further system of barriers constructed around the doors themselves. Although the bedroom wall adjoining the main salon contained two large sets of double doors, the set closest to Proust's bed was kept permanently shut, while the set furthest from the bed allowed public admittance through only one door, additionally fortified by a heavy curtain to guard against drafts. A third smaller single door, located at the foot of Proust's bed, provided entry from a back hallway that also led to a dressing room. Used only by Proust, and occasionally by Albaret, this private back door opened onto a world of bodily functions that Proust preferred to screen off entirely from the space of the bedroom proper. The revolving bookcases and Boulle worktable, strategically placed immediately in front of the closed double doors, structurally brace the corner where these two walls of publicity and privacy meet, providing extra reinforcement to a boundary that, in Proust's world, must be vigilantly policed. Positioning his bed at the farthest remove from the bedroom's many apertures, Proust could carefully monitor all three entranceways, suggesting that it is the threshold that marks for Proust the room's greatest stress point, its site of maximum structural tension.

In one sense, all of *A la recherche* might be read as a long series of ever-receding doors, with each new threshold symbolizing a new stage in the narrator's gradual social ascent. To the narrator, a doorway represents possibility, pleasure, and progress. Proust's narrator repeatedly plots to gain entry to the exclusive salons of the social and cultural aristocracy of France. Crossing the thresholds of the Swann, the Verdurin, or the Guermantes households constitutes one of the narrator's chief preoccupations, an obsession as strong as his desire for Albertine, and a good deal more consistent than his passion for writing. At the same time that Proust's narrator concentrates his energies on discovering the secret password that will permit doors to open magically before him, all of Proust's own efforts are devoted to keeping doors closed and household traffic at an absolute minimum. To Proust, a threshold represents a site of sudden penetration, a source of ready contagion, and a means of necessary separation. Completely inverting George Simmel's privileging of doors that speak over walls that remain mute, Proust values the "dead geometry" proffered by the wall over the "permanent interchange" offered by the door.[39] At 102 boulevard Haussmann, everyone was expected to close doors, and no one was allowed to slam them. The only person who regularly violated Proust's mandate was Reynaldo Hahn, a lifelong friend and one-time lover who, decades later, is principally remembered by Proust's housekeeper as the man who would "leave a draft behind" (Albaret 230).

Windows are no less dangerous openings to Proust, vulnerable orifices that must be aggressively safeguarded against the ever-present threat of external penetration. Even more than the figure of the threshold, the window haunts Proust's artistic imagination. It is through windows that Proust's narrator observes the secrets of sex, whether he is spying through a country house window on

Mlle Vinteuil and her friend engaged in lesbian foreplay, or peering through a bull's eye window on Charlus and the butcher boy engaged in sadomasochistic whipping. Because a window can conduct both sight and sound, it retains its crucial epistemological importance even when the narrator cannot see through it; by means of a closed fanlight window the narrator fears to open, Jupien and Charlus's sexual encounter in the tailor shop is more overheard than observed, reminding us that every primal scene is as much auditory as it is visual. Yet, despite his own strong voyeuristic impulses, Proust chose to write about these sexual spectacles in a space notable for its extreme hostility to the window. Blocked on the outside by closed wooden shutters and on the inside by drawn velvet-lined curtains, these sealed windows further partition the sexual from the literary, emphatically precluding any opportunity for the voyeuristic or exhibitionistic sexual pleasures normally offered by the transparent glass of a bedroom window. Proust creates an interior for himself that is the very opposite of the Montjouvain house, the male brothel, or the tailor shop; he fashions a self-contained, impenetrable space that permits him to closet his voyeurism while writing about it. Voyeurism and exhibitionism, however, were not banished altogether from the bedroom. They were simply redirected and internalized, as Proust confronted his own deepest desires through the transparent medium of the novel itself, the closest this intensely private writer ever came to an act of public exhibitionism.

Sleeping during the day and writing at night, Proust maintained his nocturnal schedule by physically blocking out the invading rays of light that "anaesthetized" his creativity (V: 437).[40] Because it was such a dark and solemn space, it is tempting to read Proust's bedroom in the same manner I have suggested that we read Freud's office, as a mausoleum in which it is ultimately himself whom the writer entombs. But Proust's bedroom, nearly devoid of collections of any kind, presents a very different sort of space than the museum-like interior of Freud's office, filled with its thousands of funerary objects. The inside-out logic that gov-

erns Proust's sense of an interior inverts the common association
of light with life and darkness with death, as the lyrical concluding lines of *A l'ombre des jeunes filles en fleurs* make clear. Proust
ends this book with the opening of a window curtain that floods
the narrator's hotel bedroom with light. Surprisingly, the dazzling
light reveals a lifeless exterior, a summer day "as immemorially
ancient as a sumptuously attired dynastic mummy" (II: 1018).
Proust compares the opening of the bedroom curtains to the un-
wrapping of an embalmed corpse, where the dead subject is not
the waking body inside the room but the dawning day outside it.
The window dressings in this scene cloak an exterior rather than
an interior space, with the curtains functioning as a shroud for a
dead outside world, preserved as carefully as the royal bodies of
antiquity. This extraordinary image of the mummified exterior is
as illuminating as it is startling, providing one possible explana-
tion for Proust's well-known aversion to light and affinity for
darkness. For Proust, life is what is lived on the inside. To see
what is natural or real, the mind's eye must turn inwards, away
from the distractions of an already ossified external world.

The curtained and shuttered casements at boulevard Haussmann operate more like mirrors than windows, redirecting the eye
back into the interior. Proust's bedroom contained two mirrors,
the wardrobe mirror occupying the entire space between the two
windows, and the large hanging mirror filling much of the upper
wall space between the two double doors. Situated squarely between the bedroom's two sets of blocked portals, rather than over
the fireplace mantel as was the fashion, it is the mirrors that open
up the bedroom by providing an impression of exterior depth.
The exterior they reveal, however, is a reflected interior; mirrors
draw the eye outward only to return the gaze inward in a closed
circuit of vision. To the degree that its opaque surface participates
in the erasure of externality while simultaneously providing the illusion of an outside world, the mirror would appear to offer
Proust the perfect metaphor for the spatial and temporal disloca-
tions effected by the work of involuntary memory. A mirror pro-

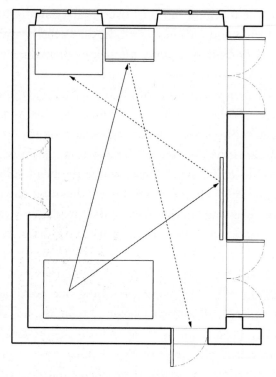

FIG. 4.5 Plan diagram of two mirrors. The placement of mirrors between the bedroom's windows and doors prevented Proust from seeing his own self-reflection but provided him with a second means of surveillance for monitoring the room's most vulnerable points: the window closest to the head of his bed and the door closest to its foot.

vides us with a view of our self occupying a space where we are not. A mirror allows us to see our self outside of our self. A mirror permits our self to verify itself, to find itself, over and over again, in sudden acts of self-reflection. The figure of the looking-glass is such an important symbol of self-contemplation for Proust that he even considered titling his novel *The Mirrors of Dream*.[41]

And yet, Proust places his bedroom mirrors in two locations that make any literal act of self-reflection impossible [figure 4.5]. The angles of both mirrors, each situated in the middle of a wall, prevent Proust in his corner from seeing himself as he writes in bed while at the same time providing an added sense of physical security. When he looked at the wardrobe mirror between the windows, Proust saw a reflection of the door to the back hallway, offering him a second means of surveillance for monitoring one of the bedroom's most private portals. When he looked at the large ceiling-height mirror between the bedroom doors, Proust saw a reflection of his uncle's desk in front of the window, piled high with books, a double layer of fortification against the outside world. By leaning to his left, Proust could also see reflected, in the same mirror, the white marble fireplace mantelpiece, with its pair of blue-globed candelabra and matching bronze clock in between. The sole freestanding clock in the room,[42] this timepiece, facing in the same direction as Proust, could be viewed from the bed only through the mediation of the mirror, as if to emphasize Proust's philosophy that one can only approach time obliquely, through the agency of reflection.

Neither of the bedroom's two mirrors capture Proust's own reflection, unlike the reflective surfaces that keep his narrator awake, "tormented by the presence of some little bookcases with glass fronts" and "a large cheval-glass" (II: 717). The location of the looking-glasses in Proust's bedroom protect him from what his narrative double fears most: the mirror's lethal ability to turn subjects into objects by capturing and immobilizing their images. Whereas Freud allowed his visage to be petrified in order to become a mirror to his patients, Proust's aim was first to become a mirror to himself before offering up his novel as a mirror to his readers. The best writer, he concludes in *A la recherche*, is "the one who knows how to become a mirror and in this way can reflect his life" (VII: 742). Only by clearly reflecting his own life can the writer simultaneously provide readers with an unclouded glass in which to see themselves: "In reality every reader is, while he is reading, the reader of his own self. The writer's work is merely a kind of optical instrument which he offers to the reader to enable

him to discern what, without this book, he would perhaps never
have perceived in himself" (VII: 949). The novel is the true mirror
in Proust's bedroom, and involuntary memory the reflective mechanism by which to reencounter lost selves, much in the same way
Proust's narrator comes face to face with his dead grandmother
"as in a mirror" (IV: 785). Because "the dead exist only in us" (IV:
786), the mediation of the novel-as-mirror allows Proust to resus-
citate the dead without himself ever passing through the looking
glass. The surface of the Proustian mirror remains opaque, suggesting that, even where the aperture of the self is concerned,
Proust was not above erecting protective defenses around the al-
luring but dangerous practice of radical introspection.

4

The bedroom's most prominent defensive barrier may finally be
not the shuttered windows or the obstructed doors but the cork
sheets lining both the room's four walls and its nearly twelve-foot-
high ceiling. While Freud chose baize to soundproof the doors of
his consulting room, Proust selected the more popular and effective cork for his bedroom insulation, intending eventually to disguise the tan panels with wallpaper.[43] Proust never did wallpaper
the cork, allowing the bedroom walls to turn black over time, further darkening an already dim room. If the little patch of yellow
wall in Vermeer's *View of Delft* creates the illusion of spatial
depth,[44] Proust's blackened cork walls produce the opposite impression of spatial constriction. The placement of the cork—originally the same color as the parquet floor—on both ceiling and
walls removes the line of demarcation between horizontal and
vertical planes, in effect dematerializing boundaries and creating a
spatial void. The homogeneous color of walls, ceiling, and floor
visually shrink the bedroom, transforming an open and lofty inte-

rior into a more concentrated and inward space. Moreover, the cork, by providing a further layer of insulation between the bedroom and the rest of the apartment, physically separates Proust from the life of the household and from the people on the other side of the wall who labor to serve him.

Proust was certainly not unaware of the curious capacity of a wall to establish human intimacy. *La Prisonnière* begins with the narrator and Albertine performing their ablutions in adjoining bathrooms, talking to each other, "in double privacy," across a thin partition (V: 3). This affectionate scene echoes an earlier and more famous one in which the narrator summons his grandmother from an adjacent hotel bedroom at Balbec by knocking three times on the wall (in imitation, perhaps, of the three knocks that traditionally open French theater). The narrator compares this partition to a musical instrument, with a surface as responsive as a "violin" and vibrations as sensitive as a "piano" (IV: 790). At the Grand Hotel at Cabourg, Proust would send signals to Céleste Albaret in the exact same manner, using a shared party wall as his instrumental messenger. Communication by gesture or word across a physical boundary emerges as a recurrent spatial theme in *A la recherche* and operates as a telling figure for Proust's own mediated relation to the outside world. Like Dickinson who preferred to address her interlocutors through a door ajar, Proust understood the intense pleasures of conversation across a spatial divide. A partition not only enhances interpersonal intimacy, it makes such tender exchanges possible. Proust generally preferred sending letters to his friends over paying them visits, revealing a deep-seated suspicion that the best way to sustain a relationship was to stay audible but out of sight. Invisibility had the desirable effect of heightening the attention paid to Proust's words, permitting the writer to efface himself in favor of his writing. For Proust, the most significant communications take place not despite physical barriers but by way of them.

Yet after the entry of technology into the modern interior, the architectural plane of the wall ceases to function as a ready instrument of communication. In Proust's own bedroom, the transmitting wall is literally muffled, giving way to the more modern electric bell and home telephone, both installed within easy reach of the bed. Proust kept a telephone in his bedroom at boulevard Haussmann for over seven years, before finally removing it toward the end of 1914. At the dawn of a world war, in which Proust was to lose a number of his friends, the telephone had become too painful a reminder of exactly what it had always been: a disembodied voice carrying messages from the dead. The narrator's telephone conversation with his grandmother, during which he receives a "premonition of an eternal separation" (III: 135), is one of several telephone scenes in Proust's writings based on an actual phone call from his mother many months after the death of her father. Proust's description of his mother's grief-stricken voice stops the heart: "suddenly over the telephone came to me her poor broken, bruised voice, changed forever from the one I had always known, now full of cracks and fissures; and it was on gathering from the receiver those bleeding, broken pieces that for the first time I had the dreadful sensation of what had broken forever within her."[45] The telephone can finally make audible to Proust the depths of his mother's loss because the telephone is the very medium of death and mourning, the technological vocalization of the absence at the heart of all subjectivity. Indeed, Proust's phantom telephone provides perhaps the most memorable description in twentieth-century literature of modern subjectivity as the possibility of disconnectability.[46] What unnerves Proust most about the telephone, that "supernatural instrument" (V: 24), is the potential for the phone line to go dead, leaving him a bereft "Orpheus" speaking into the void (III: 137). The only new technology Proust ever explicitly repudiated, the telephone was ultimately removed from the bedroom, not merely because it posed a distraction to his work, but because it symbolized for the writer of *A la recherche du temps perdu* the sorrows of time passing, rather than the joys of time regained.

Proust's rejection of the telephone evidently extended to the théâtrophone, a second bedroom phone which, for a monthly fee, permitted Proust to listen to live operas and concerts simply by holding a receiver to his ear. The théâtrophone brought music into the interior, converting the bedroom into a concert chamber: "Now I can be visited in my bed by the brook and the birds of the *Symphonie pastorale*, which poor Beethoven enjoyed no more directly than I since he was completely deaf."[47] The simultaneous disconnection of all of the apartment's telephone lines silenced the théâtrophone as well, removing Proust's chief form of entertainment and effectively turning the bedroom into what Benjamin has called, in another context, "an ear that has lost the power of hearing."[48]

After the loss of the théâtrophone, Proust, on at least one occasion, invited into his home a chamber music group to play for him Beethoven's Thirteenth Quartet and, more importantly, César Franck's Quartet, the inspiration for the fictional Vinteuil's violin sonata. Two of the musicians, Gaston Poulet and Amable Massis, recall several concerts held around 1916 in the bedroom at boulevard Haussmann, with Proust lying motionless and apparently asleep on a green divan. Céleste Albaret remembers only one such concert, in 1920, in the salon at rue Hamelin, with Proust resting on a long reclining green velvet chair she identifies as borrowed for the occasion from the boudoir.[49] A careful consideration of the actual space of the bedroom at boulevard Haussmann may help resolve this long-standing mystery, since the various historical sources on Proust's apartment nowhere mention the presence in the bedroom of a green divan. Nor would there have been adequate space, in the extremely cluttered confines of the bedroom, for a four-man quartet with two violins, a cello, and a viola, even without the addition of extra chairs for the musicians and a sofa for Proust. Moreover, there is no more unfriendly sound conductor than cork, a porous oak wood which, as Proust would well have known, created the worst possible acoustical conditions for a live concert. More likely these private performances did indeed take place at boulevard Haussmann, but in the large drawing room rather than in the bedroom. The argument that the concerts could only have been staged in the bedroom because of the location there of the piano offers somewhat less than compelling evidence when one recalls that Gaston Poulet's ensemble was a *string* quartet.

Whatever the true story behind these private home concerts, music played an instrumental role in the physical composition of Proust's bedroom interior, with his mother's grand piano clearly occupying the room's center of gravity. The most obtrusive object in the room, this piano dominated Proust's subconscious life, its ivory keys simulating his mother's voice more powerfully than any telephone line. Both the composer Reynaldo Hahn and (on rare occasion) Proust himself played the bedroom piano (Albaret 55); yet even this musical monument to the artistry of Jeanne Proust, like all the other sound instruments in the room, was eventually rendered silent. The piano, along with the telephone and the théâtrophone, may have appeared as rivals to Proust, struggling to achieve through his novel-writing a similar "isolation of the voice" (III: 136). Proust was learning in his bedroom workshop to channel his own voices, which is perhaps why, in *A la recherche*, he dismissively describes the piano as "an inanimate object . . . capable of a power of exasperation to which no human being will ever attain" (IV: 817). In his efforts to give voice to literature, Proust over time came to view the piano in the same way he once responded to the telephone, as a "lifeless piece of wood [that] began to squeak" (III: 135).

Because the organ of the ear remains perpetually open, even in sleep, sound strikes Proust as the most violent of human sensations, an external assault upon a defenseless interior. Only "the withdrawal of sound, its dilution," he hypothesizes, can "rob it of all its aggressive power" (III: 73). When Proust has Robert Saint-Loup draw attention to the narrator's "auditory hyperaesthesia" (III: 69), he betrays his own keen sensitivity to noise, a problem Proust tried to address through the use of Quiès earplugs.[50] Proust saw deafness as the very precondition for writing. Twice in *Le Côté de Guermantes* he isolates the image of deaf ears as the model for human creativity. In his story of an invalid with stopped ears, Proust demonstrates that it is only by artificially deadening sound that one can experience its rebirth: "take away for a moment from the sick man the cotton-wool that has been stopping his ears and in a flash the broad daylight, the dazzling sun of sound dawns afresh, blinding him." Elaborating on his synaesthetic metaphor, Proust adds that, with the dawning of sound, we are present "at the resurrection of the voice" (III: 74). In a second related tale of a "stone-deaf man," Proust again dreams of a world without sound, "an Eden, in which sound has not yet been created." This prelapsarian fantasy presents silence as "chastity" and noise as "vulgarity" (III: 75). Notably, both parables attribute to their hearing-impaired subjects divine creative powers. Speaking perhaps self-referentially, Proust notes that "in the bedroom itself the sick man has created, not, like Prometheus, fire, but the sound of fire" (III: 74). Out of silence, a world, indeed a word, is created. These parables of sound together suggest that what Proust creates out of the auditory sensory void that is his bedroom is nothing less than voice, literary voice. The principle for Proust as a writer is simple: if "incessant noise in our ears" describes "in a continuous narrative" all that is happening in the world (III: 73), then he will suspend this other narrative in favor of inventing his own.

The idea of a mind creating *ex nihilo* owes much to René Descartes—another writer, Proust happily observes, who wrote from his bed.[51] Descartes bases his *cogito ergo sum* on the total suppression of the senses. "I shall now close my eyes, I shall stop my ears, I shall call away all my senses," he writes in the *Meditations*, proposing that the only way to achieve thought is to numb sensation.[52] Like Descartes, Proust is as likely to speak in his work of sense *deception* as sense *perception*. Of all the five senses, the two so-called "higher senses," vision and hearing, are the least trustworthy to Proust. Because "sounds have no position in space" and often disguise their point of origin, acoustic experience is really "acoustic error" (III: 72 and 96). Vision can be even more fallible. In one of dozens of narrative passages on the unreliability of sight, Proust cautions that "one's vision is always clouded" and that one's every first sight is really an optical illusion (II: 903–4). In his study and consulting room, Freud grapples with the distortions of sight and sound by spatially bifurcating them; in his bedroom, Proust simply excludes them both. Such sensory hermeticism may at first strike a reader of *A la recherche* as exceedingly curious: are not the senses the very vehicles of Proustian memory, the physical stimulus for the sudden retrieval of the past? Paradoxically, Proust found it necessary to suspend the senses in order to write about them. To *think* the experience of involuntary memory, Proust had to stop *doing* it, if only for the time it took to convert sensory impression into literary language.

Proust's distrust of vision accounts for the paucity of artworks in the bedroom at boulevard Haussmann, a space so devoid of artistic embellishment it made Proust's room at rue de Courcelles look like a museum by comparison. On the walls of Proust's previous bedroom hung at least four pictures: a watercolor of trees (presented to him as a gift by the sculptor Marie Nordlinger), a photograph of Leonardo Da Vinci's *Mona Lisa*, a photograph of the cathedral at Amiens, and a photograph of Whistler's *Carlyle*. In this latter 1873 painting [figure 4.6], Thomas Carlyle, famous for his verbal rather than visual portraits of contemporaries, sits in left profile in front of two indistinct paintings, looking away from them with an air of

FIG. 4.6 James McNeill Whistler's *arrangement in grey and black, no. 2: Portrait of Thomas Carlyle* (1872–73). A photographic copy of Whistler's oil painting of the famous Victorian social critic hung on Proust's bedroom wall at 45 rue de Courcelles. By the time Proust moved to 102 boulevard Haussmann, he had rejected the design convention of hanging visual artwork in the bedroom, a move perhaps presaged by his earlier attraction to the Whistler portrait in which Carlyle turns out of profile and away from the wall paintings beside him. *Courtesy of Glasgow Museums: Art Gallery and Museum, Kelvingrove.*

melancholic distraction. None of these pictures at rue de Courcelles, the place where Proust translated Ruskin, hangs on the bedroom walls at boulevard Haussmann, suggesting that Proust may have taken a page out of Carlyle's book and elected in the end to turn away altogether from the lure of representational art. Stripping the art from his walls, Proust instead infused all of his passionate aesthetic sensibilities into the interior of his autobiographically inflected novel, constructing a narrative display of hundreds of individual portraits and places, "as though one's life were a picture gallery" (I: 21).

With its bare walls and muted lighting, Proust's quiet bedroom interior comprises an intimate devotional space, a private tabernacle of ecumenical design. The bedroom's refusal of representational art and preservation of literary manuscripts calls to mind a Jewish synagogue, with its ban on graven images and its veneration of the sacred text. At the same time, Proust's statue of the infant Jesus resting next to the manuscripts on the altar-like rosewood chest (the same chest that contained Proust's rosary) conjures up a Christian church, a miniature version of the windowless Madeleine located only a few streets away.[53] Although the dark brown woods of the furniture and the discolored cork of the walls and ceiling drain the bedroom of much of its color, the room's many shiny surfaces—the bronze clock and candelabra, the bronze bed frame, the parquet floors, the lacquered black piano, and even the dark blue curtains—all reflect glimmers of light cast by the bedside lamp. The bedroom's dominant color scheme, gold on black, merely enhances the shrine-like atmosphere of the room. If there is a memorable devotional figure in the bedroom of boulevard Haussmann, it is surely Proust himself, framed in bed by the cross-pattern of the headboard, which is in turn framed by the five-paneled Chinese screen, its stenciled gold figures on a black background depicting, in imitation of windows, an exterior scene. A hybrid of synagogue and church, Proust's bedroom décor reconciles his mother's Judaism with his father's Catholicism, while adding the writer's own brand of eastern exoticism.[54]

Despite or perhaps because of his deceased parents' pervasive influence on the design and tone of the bedroom, Proust chose to hang both a portrait of his father and a portrait of his mother in the large drawing room, accessible to viewing but safely out of sight from the bedroom. Proust was particularly concerned that the 1880 portrait of his mother, which he believed corresponded to her actual image only when she was "so incredibly rejuvenated

FIG. 4.7 1893 oil portrait of Proust by Jacques-Emile Blanche. The painter emphasizes in this portrait his twenty-year old subject's oriental features, or what Blanche later called "the pure oval face of a young Assyrian." *Courtesy of Réunion des Musées Nationaux/Art Resource, NY and © 2003 Artists Rights Society (ARS), New York/ADAGP, Paris.*

by death," would be deeply painful to him.[55] Only in death, Proust believed, do we resemble our artistic likeness, a sentiment prompting the inevitable comparison of Proust's own portrait by Jacques-Emile Blanche to Wilde's picture of Dorian Gray.[56] Blanche's oil portrait, which Proust would contemplate "as if seeing himself in a mirror" (Albaret 150), started as a full-length likeness but was returned to Proust by the temperamental artist with the lower half of the body removed [figure 4.7]. Showing only the upper torso and head, Blanche paints an idealized image of what the ailing Proust might have hoped to see had one of the bedroom mirrors been positioned opposite to the foot of his bed—namely, a dark-eyed, beardless, youthful man, wearing a layer of jackets and a yellow camellia. Interestingly, Proust placed the Blanche portrait in the small rather than the large drawing room, suggesting that he did not wish even his artistic double to be distracted by the images of his dead parents. It is likely, given the location of doors, windows, and bookcases in the two adjoining drawing rooms, that Proust's portrait in the small salon hung on the opposite side of the very same wall that displayed one or both of his parents' portraits in the large salon. Facing in opposite directions, the images of Proust's parents looked expectantly in death, as they often did in life, toward the closed doors of their son's bedroom, while Proust's own doppelganger continued to elude the unblinking gaze of his vigilant guardians. Wherever these family portraits were placed in the two salons, Proust, by relocating all figurative art from the private space of the bedroom to the public realm of the drawing rooms, defuses the threat posed by the visual arts as effectively as he manages the competing demands of sound technology. While the sight of a painting or a photograph ultimately strikes Proust as less intrusive than the sound of a piano or a ringing telephone, a work of visual art nonetheless draws the eye outward, deflecting the concentration of a more inward, and more properly literary, gaze.

So far I have identified a series of discrete tensions that, like the binary architecture defining the apartment building itself, organizes the interior of Proust's bedroom: feminine and masculine, east and west, church and synagogue, soul and body, aperture and wall, sound and sight. I now want to bring all these components together to explore the space of the bedroom as a whole, revealing the different roles this familiar room played in Proust's life and literature. One might well wonder why Proust felt it necessary to restrict his living quarters to a single chamber within a generously apportioned apartment. But to live a multitudinous life, Proust did not need to occupy more than one room, for the simple reason that the bedroom was already a shifting stage set. Like the bedroom at Illiers, its walls and furniture transfigured by the revolving images of a magic lantern, the bedroom at boulevard Haussmann functioned as many different rooms at once, colored by the projections of a writer's restless imagination. The following pages address four of the most prominent backdrops suggested by Proust's immediate surroundings: the bedroom as study, sickroom, darkroom, and theater. I conclude with a discussion of Proust's last days at a new apartment on rue Hamelin, the place where all four settings converge in a painful denouement.

5

The bedroom at boulevard Haussmann was, first and foremost, a place for writing. Mark Wigley identifies the man's study as the first truly private sphere within the home. Described by Wigley as "an intellectual space beyond that of sexuality," the study was the place where a man was "free to 'marry literature' in secret."[57] Unlike the typical bourgeois bedroom, which publicizes the act of conjugal relations by placing an imposing marriage bed in the center of the room, Proust's bedroom-study privatizes the act of writing by pushing its simple brass bed into the farthest corner of the room, creating a sequestered niche for Proust to consummate his union with language. Albaret notes a dramatic contrast between the ostentatiously large and elaborately decorated furniture filling most of the bedroom and the much smaller and plainer furniture comprising Proust's writing corner (56). The Proustian space of writing is, if not entirely artless, then nonetheless minimalist. The very particular arrangement of simple pieces of furniture around the brass bed suggests that writing, for Proust, is an unassuming act supported by all the ordinary accoutrements of everyday life.

Arranged lengthwise next to the upper section of the bed were three small tables, all within arm's reach. A carved bamboo table closest to the Chinese screen held books, handkerchiefs, and hot water bottles. An enclosed rosewood table in the middle contained not only a small bedside lamp but also, within its open doors, all of the equipment for writing: pens, penholders, inkwell, watch, manuscripts, notebooks, and (in Proust's last years) spectacles. A third walnut table at the end accommodated a coffee tray during the day and a bottle of Evian water at night.[58] The precise sequencing of these three bedside tables exhibits the warring tensions that buffeted Proust's daily life. The two outside tables, dedicated almost exclusively to the care and upkeep of the body, structurally bracket the central table devoted to the stimulation and health of the mind, the physical at once supporting the intellectual while at the same time threatening to overwhelm it. At first conveying an appearance of clutter, the three bedside tables are in fact highly organized; together they neatly circumscribe thought with sensation in an apparent demonstration of Proust's theory of writing from the senses.

The bedside tables partly serve the function of a desk for the bedridden writer. Proust had his choice of desks upon moving into boulevard Haussmann, including "the fine desk" from his father's own study and a smaller desk his mother had inherited from her grandparents. Choosing neither of these parental cenotaphs, Proust elected to retain his great Uncle Weil's huge oak desk in its original place in front of the window, reasoning that this sturdy family marker could stand as a symbol of the "imagination, the only setting in which places remain the same."[59] Even as a much younger writer, Proust opted to write at the dining room table rather than to sit at his parents' desks, revealing his strong desire for a self-defined writing space, free of familial influence. Proust never used his uncle's desk other than to stockpile books; indeed, Albaret notes that she "never saw him write even the shortest note standing up" (270). Instead Proust wrote from a semi-recumbent position, suspended mid-way between the realms of sleeping and waking, using his knees as a desk. One might say that Proust had found a better purpose for his legs than walking, converting his limbs into a prosthetic support for his writing.

In keeping with the unpretentious décor surrounding the bed, Proust's writing materials were similarly commonplace, even elementary. Abjuring the more modern and more popular fountain pens, Proust remained faithful to Sergeant-Major nibs, the simple ink pens schoolchildren used along with the square glass inkwells with stoppers that Proust also favored. To write about the events of the past, Proust clearly preferred to utilize period implements, although, in a declaration of anti-fetishism rare amongst writers, Proust claimed not to care what kind of pen he used (Albaret 271). For paper this prolific writer chose school exercise books purchased in bulk, and for his famous "paperoles" (small sheets used for manuscript notations) Proust availed himself of whatever stray bits of paper were at hand, including scraps, envelopes, and magazine covers. There was no shortage of paper at boulevard Haussmann; in fact, Proust had paper to burn, using the same small pads of square paper both to write messages to his housekeeper and to light his fumigation powders. To Proust, the stuff of writing was incendiary. His walls and ceiling insulated with the same material used to make paper, Proust was aware that if a German bomb were to hit boulevard Haussmann, his rooms "would go up like torches" (Albaret 95). During the war Proust stoked his own miniature conflagration, instructing Albaret to incinerate all thirty-two of his black-leather notebooks in the kitchen stove. Inverting the roles of kitchen and bedroom, Proust created a household in which food was served in the bedroom and manuscripts were burned in the kitchen. The apartment at boulevard Haussmann was, in Albaret's oft-stated opinion, truly an "upside down" world (7, 49, and 333).

When he was feeling well, Proust would invite Albaret into his bedroom for late night conversations. Perched on the end of his bed "like a policeman on duty," he would question his cooperative "captive" on life outside the bedroom walls (117). In the morning, Proust at the head of his bed nearly always communicated with Albaret by silent gesture or by scribbled notes; in the evening, Proust at the foot of his bed occasionally engaged his housekeeper in all night talking vigils. In Proust's bedroom-study, writing and speech occupy two completely different temporal and spatial orders, the one dependent upon the careful retention of breath, the other upon its exhalation. The space of Proust's bed encompassed both extremes, mapping a spectrum from silence to sound. The bed, like the tables beside it, operates as another microcosm, with writing and speech, privacy and publicity, reflection and interrogation, stillness and animation, solitude and companionship, illness and health all defining the polarities of Proust's telescoped world. Yet what the bed ultimately demonstrates is that such lived oppositions are never stable ones. The writing bed was also, simultaneously, the sickbed. As much as the bedroom was a study, it was also a sickroom, the place where Proust spent nearly as many hours burning paper as he did inscribing it.

6

As an invalid, Proust, like his aunt before him, wielded a considerable amount of power from his bed, a point not lost on the beleaguered Albaret, who writes in her memoir that even when she was in town she could feel Proust directing her actions from his sickroom (11). In many ways Albaret was as much a nurse as a maid, allocating most of her daily labor to warming the bed linens, changing the hot water bottles, supervising the fires, preparing the footbaths, and, above all, encouraging her undernourished charge to eat and to drink. As a neophyte nurse, Albaret had much to contend with during her ten-year service to an employer whose accumulating ailments included not just asthma but emphysema, laryngitis, bronchitis, aphasia, rheumatism, uremia, migraines, fatigue, nausea, insomnia, and cardiac palpitations. The son and brother of two respected doctors, Proust occasionally sought medical treatment but generally chose to rely on his own experience, declaring confidently to Lucien Daudet, "I shall be Doctor Proust."[60]

To André Gide, Proust explains: "an asthmatic never knows if he will be able to breathe, and he can be certain of nearly suffocating in a new home."[61] When Proust moved into boulevard Haussmann, he suffered an asthma attack that lasted almost fifty hours, a crisis he had hoped to avoid when he expressed the desire to Madame Catusse that his new apartment be just "like a hospital."[62] In his attempt to model his bedroom on a hospital room, Proust may have been influenced by his father, France's inspector general of sanitary services and a specialist in hygiene and infectious diseases. But the dark and stuffy apartment at boulevard Haussmann actually presents the very antithesis of Adrien Proust's prescription for the hygienic house, an interior "'flooded with light and air which are the two most powerful tonics and antiseptics we know.'"[63] Adrien Proust may have halted the spread of cholera in France, but he never succeeded in curing his son's asthma, which may be why, as an adult, Proust disregarded all received medical wisdom and pursued his own therapeutic remedies.

Proust's self-medications included daily fumigations of Legras powder so strong his neighbors complained of the stench, and at least two bowls of *café au lait* a day. Both the smoke from the fumigations and the caffeine from the coffee had the desired effect of clearing Proust's bronchial tubes, but, as Ronald Hayman points out, the chemicals they contained may have directly contributed to Proust's palpitations, blurred vision, headaches, and sleeplessness (253–4). His success as a doctor clearly a qualified one, Proust was willing to endure severe side effects so that he might minister to the site of his earliest physical trauma: his nose. A fall at the age of nine in the Champs-Élysées broke Proust's nose, and may have induced the asthma that began immediately after this childhood accident. Forty years later, just a year before his death, Proust calculated that he had withstood over the years as many as one hundred and ten nasal cauterizations to treat his worsening asthma.[64] Surprisingly, these nose operations did not impair Proust's sense of smell, a power of olfaction so responsive to odors that the entire household was organized around it. Acutely sensitive to scents of all kinds, Proust banned from the apartment flowers, perfumes, and even floor polishes. Candles were lit in the kitchen to distance Proust from the faint smell of sulfur, while the small amount of food he consumed was ordered from local restaurants like the Ritz to avoid the irritation of cooking aromas several rooms away.

"Taste and smell alone," the narrator comments in *Du côté de chez Swann*, "bear unflinchingly, in the tiny and almost impalpable drop of their essence, the vast structure of recollection" (I: 50–1). More than vision, hearing, or touch, smell (and by association taste) is physiologically the sense most directly linked to the brain, and thus most likely to induce the sudden jubilation of an involuntary memory. Yet for the highly allergic Proust, taste and smell possess a far more sinister side; they bear not just "the vast structure of recollection" but also, and more seriously, the continual threat of suffocation. Upon moving into boulevard Haussmann, Proust was so concerned about traces of his mother's perfumes and powders adhering to the family heirlooms that he considered disinfecting all his bedroom furniture if he could only tolerate the smell.[65] Involuntary memory, it turns out, carries certain risks; Proust believed that recollecting his mother through smell could kill him, in more than a figural sense. Later in his life Proust harbored similar anxieties about the letters he received, going so far as to devise a special box for disinfecting all incoming correspondence with formol. It seems that Proust considered even paper, the raw material of his writing, as a potential contaminant that could be toxic to his health.

Proust's sensitive nose also explains why the apartment's central heating system, which dried out his delicate nasal tissues, was never turned on. Feeling "literally asphyxiated" by the water-heater's dry air,[66] Proust only allowed wood fires—in the kitchen to warm his household staff and in the bedroom to dispel powder fumes. Far from a center of domestic affection and communal amity, the fireplace represented to Proust merely the bedroom's sole means of ventilation and a dangerous source of drafts.[67] For physical warmth, Proust relied principally on woolen clothes, pyjama jackets, pullover sweaters, hot water bottles, and a woolen blanket and quilt. The bedroom's sole armchair piled high with pullovers, Proust would ring for a new sweater whenever one slipped from his shoulders; in similar fashion, he would reach for a new handkerchief from the bamboo table, dropping each piece of linen on the floor after a single use. Proust's immobility no doubt exacerbated his continual chill, turning his whole body into an "animated barometer" (V: 73), capable of detecting even the slightest atmospheric changes. Proust knew better than anyone that we are only aware of our bodies when something is wrong. As early as 1897 Proust identified himself as an invalid reduced to living through his senses, "indifferent to other people, to life, to everything outside my own wretched body."[68]

This intense suffering of the invalid body—what Proust, in Dickinsonian fashion, called "my Calvary"[69]—was not unproductive; indeed, Proust's painful physical condition was quite nearly reproductive. The enclosed room at boulevard Haussmann, with its stacks of clean towels, its bed sheets changed daily, its draught-curtains covering both windows and entry, and its hot water at the ready both day and night, resembles nothing so much as a lying-in room. The comparison of Proust's bedroom to a birthing room is more than fanciful. In *Le Temps retrouvé*, the narrator describes his efforts to create a novel in explicitly reproductive terms: "I felt myself enhanced by this work which I bore within me as by something fragile and precious which had been entrusted to me to which I should have liked to deliver" (VII: 1093). Expounding on his "book's incubation" (VII: 1095) and "labour of construction" (VII: 1099), the narrator clarifies: "the idea of my work was inside my head, always the same, perpetually in process of becoming. But even my work had become for me a tiresome obligation, like a son for a dying mother" (VII: 1100). Proust understood his ill health and physical immobility as the inevitable consequence of gestating and nurturing a fully formed novel. Wayne Koestenbaum has noted that the emergence of a women's literary tradition in the nineteenth century made it common for men at the *fin de siècle* to imagine their literary labors as a form of female procreation.[70] At the same time the figuration of writing as maternity was also used to caricature men of leisure like Proust, who appeared to at least one fellow writer to have taken the metaphor too far. In a highly critical review of *Pleasures and Days*, the novelist Jean Lorrain, with whom Proust would later fight a duel, dismissed the languid and sickly Proust as "'one of those pretty little society boys who've managed to get themselves pregnant with literature.'"[71]

To rescue the image of Proust writing in bed from the dangers of feminization, Walter Benjamin offers to posterity the more manly analogy of Michelangelo painting the ceiling of the Sistine Chapel.[72] Whichever model of creation best suits Proust's curious art of writing on his back, the novel that is the end result of his considerable exertions bears the telltale marks of its author's travails. Specifically, the unnaturally elongated sentences and odd grammatical pauses in *A la recherche* mimic the breathing of an asthmatic. Benjamin links Proust's literary style directly to his physical condition: "asthma became part of his art—if indeed his art did not create it. Proust's syntax rhythmically and step by step reproduces his fear of suffocating" (214). Illness infects not just text but reader. Anatole France privately objected that Proust crafted "'sentences interminable enough to make you consumptive.'"[73] Proust's corporeal style alienated readers who were not fully prepared to take to their beds in order to nurse an admittedly demanding novel. For Proust, however, a sickbed was the natural place for literature, and illness the inevitable penalty for writing. "We must constantly choose between health and sanity on the one hand, and spiritual pleasures on the other," observes the narrator of *A la recherche* (V: 121). In the end, Proust chose spiritual over physical well being, electing, like his fictional writer Bergotte, to lead "the vegetative life of a convalescent, of a woman after child-birth" (III: 340).

7

Eyes ever sensitive to sunlight, the bed-ridden Proust composed the entirety of *A la recherche* in semi-darkness. Although the bedroom at boulevard Haussmann possessed a large electric chandelier and at least two candelabra, Proust used only the small green-shaded bedside lamp to illuminate the pages of his writing while his face remained in shadow (Albaret 54). The image of Proust enveloped in darkness calls to mind the nineteenth-century portrait photographer, his head and often his whole body concealed by the drapes of the camera, capturing images of his subjects while remaining himself unseen. In some ways, the curtained bedroom appears to operate as the original version of a *camera obscura*, an actual enclosed room, its apertures entirely covered save for a single small opening that permits a ray of sunlight to imprint on the opposite wall an inverted image of the external world. The figuration of the bedroom as a camera exposes Proust's own method of writing as a form of camerawork, adapting from photography a series of important stylistic techniques, including framing, focusing, zooming, contrasting, and flattening.[74] Proust's novelistic penchant for the illuminating detail also shares an affinity with photography—the practice of "luminous

writing"—as does his near-photographic memory. Albaret, recall-
ing an incident in which Proust spied on his neighbors' private
dinner from the kitchen window at rue Hamelin, praises her employer's rapid powers of observation as more accurate than a
camera: "in thirty seconds everything was recorded, and better
than a camera could do it, because behind the image itself there
was often a whole character analysis based on a single detail"
(252).

But thinking of the bedroom as a camera combines what for
Proust were two very different actions: the act of taking a mental
picture and the act of putting that image into words. Significantly,
the scene of voyeurism that Albaret describes takes place in the
kitchen, not in Proust's bedroom. Proust records his visual impressions outside the space of writing, only later returning to his bedroom workshop to imprint them onto the page. In point of fact,
the bedroom, lacking any opening for natural light, fails to operate
as a true *camera obscura*. Dimly illuminated by the artificial green
glow of the bedside lamp, the sealed bedroom more closely resembles not a camera but a darkroom, the interior place where Proust
takes his externally recorded images and patiently develops them.

The reading of the interior as a darkroom is a theme developed at some length in *A la recherche*, which repeatedly analogizes the work of memory to the art of photography: "What we
take, in the presence of the beloved object, is merely a negative,
which we develop later, when we are back at home, and have once
again found at our disposal that inner darkroom the entrance to
which is barred to us so long as we are with other people" (II:
932). A memory, like a photograph, possesses two temporalities:
the time of the actual event, and the time of its belated understanding. Proust's bedroom functions as the darkroom where the
"negative" taken by memory is gradually brought into view:
"Our memory is like one of those shops in the window of which is
exposed now one, now another photograph of the same person"
(II: 951). Memory, obeying the same fetishistic logic as photogra-

phy, is profoundly anti-narrative: "memory begins at once to record photographs independent of one another, eliminates every
link, every kind of sequence" (II: 936). Proust's task, however, is
not to insert these disjointed memories into narrative sequence as
a cinematographer might do, but rather to resist the narrative
flow of his own novelistic medium and to recapture instead the
fixed images in their original pristine state. In Proust's eyes, film
offers an entirely inappropriate analogue for the novel: "Some
critics now liked to regard the novel as a sort of procession of
things upon the screen of the cinematograph. This comparison
was absurd. Nothing is further from what we have really perceived than the vision that the cinematograph presents" (VII:
917). Proust preferred to imagine the novel as a kind of linguistic
photo album,[75] a collection of disparate portraits and images that,
in their relative fixity, work against the temporal flow of the cinema. More than film, a photograph stops time. A photograph
fragments space. A photograph exactly reproduces itself. A photograph, in short, simulates the work of involuntary memory (the
retrieval of "a fragment of time in a pure state") better than the
continuous, fast-moving medium of film ever could.

Given Proust's deep-seated distrust of vision, it is at first surprising that he would select for his dominant metaphor of involuntary memory the visual art of photography. But it is precisely
the deceptive power of the mechanical eye that makes this analogy
work, for involuntary memory operates as an "optical illusion"
that conflates the past with the present (VII: 906). Involuntary
memory is a photographic superimposition, a confusion of sensory perception. Proust saw that the truth of an involuntary memory resides in its very artifice, though few know how to read such
mental artifacts: "their past is like a photographic darkroom en-
cumbered with innumerable negatives which remain useless because the intellect has not developed them" (VII: 931). Dedicating
his life and his art to the development of these innumerable negatives, Proust concentrates on exposing under his bedroom lamp

one image in particular: himself. "One feels like a negative which shows only blackness," his narrator admits, "until one has placed it near a special lamp and . . . looked at [it] in reverse" (VII: 933). This "special lamp" is literature, which the narrator compares in the same passage to a mirror, "rendering visible to ourselves that life of ours which cannot effectually observe itself" (VII: 932).

Exactly how much of Proust's literary act of self-development is reflection and how much is invention? In *The Mirror and the Lamp*, M. H. Abrams distinguishes between two philosophical models of literary creativity: the mirror that passively reflects reality and the lamp that actively creates it.[76] Proust draws on both models to describe his work of self-development, suggesting that every mirror requires a lamp to be seen. The device of the camera, which requires both an external source of light and an internal reflex mirror, combines Abrams's two metaphors into one, making it ultimately impossible to distinguish between a "real" self and an "artificial" self. Photographs were originally identified both as "mirrors of nature," mimetically reflecting the external world, and as "magic lanterns," imaginatively creating that world. Echoing the earliest understanding of this new creative medium, the Proustian photograph of memory is at once mirror and lamp, exposing every act of reflection as a work of invention, and every labor of invention as a product of reflection.

This conflation of reflection and invention frames one of the most memorable images in *A la recherche*: the grandmother's photograph. Unaware that his dying grandmother wishes to bequeath to him a picture of herself in the guise of better health, the narrator mocks her foolish affectation in front of the camera. Only long after his grandmother has died does the narrator understand the nature of this kindly act of pretension and finally detect in his grandmother's photographic countenance the very real signs of her terminal illness. Initially what the narrator objects to in the photograph is the artificiality of both the medium and its subject.

Because of the human penchant for posturing and posing, people are already simulations, already "snapshots of themselves" (VII: 984). Later the narrator recoils not from the photograph's fabrication but from its realism, its uncanny foreshadowing of the death of its subject. "Whether or not the subject is already dead, every photograph is this catastrophe," Roland Barthes writes in *Camera Lucida*, comparing his own mother's Winter Garden snapshot to the grandmother's photograph in *A la recherche*.[77] What Barthes's theory of photography takes away from Proust's novel is the realization that a photograph is both dead and alive, both an index of reality and a repository of fantasy. The truth of a photograph lies somewhere in between these two realms, which is why Barthes ultimately concludes that "in order to see a photograph well, it is best to look away or close your eyes" (53).

Motivated by exactly this logic, Proust stored his personal photographs out of sight in the bedroom's rosewood chest of drawers. The only collection Proust ever permitted himself, this cache of images included photographs of actresses, friends, and family. Proust even retained pictures of distant relations because, in his words, "I want my grandparents and even their parents, whom I did not know, but whom Mama loved, to be near me."[78] Each photograph was, for Proust, a keepsake, a souvenir, a fetish. Photographs were also, importantly, incitements to writing. According to the French photographer Brassaï, Proust's private photograph collection functioned as "a prodigious reservoir he could draw from to compose his characters" (27). Yet, Proust was careful not to look too long or too closely. To Simone de Caillavet, whose own photograph Proust was zealously pursuing, he explains: "my memory, fatigued by drugs, is so faulty that photographs are very precious to me. I keep them as reinforcements and do not look at them too often so as not to exhaust their powers."[79]

No picture was to Proust more powerful than the photograph of his mother taken a few days before her death in 1905. This

poignant image, the model for the grandmother's photograph in *A
la recherche*, was Jeanne Proust's last gift to her son. As Proust reminded Madame Catusse who took the memorial photograph, his
mother both "wanted and did not want to be photographed, out
of a desire to leave me a last image and out of fear that she would
look too sad."[80] Proust was no less ambivalent than his mother
about this *dernière image*, both wanting and not wanting to view
it. On one occasion Proust had Albaret place the photograph of his
mother on the corner of the mantelpiece so he could see it from
bed, but just two days later had it removed. "Habit," he reasoned,
"stops one from really remembering people and objects" (Albaret
143).[81] As much as a photograph is an aid to memory, it is also an
obstruction; a photograph impedes memory if the image is overex-
posed. Photographs constantly displayed before us quickly lose
their aura and become completely and irretrievably banal.

Proust's fear of domesticating the technological image apparently did not extend to living family members. The only photographs not hidden from sight were pictures of Proust and his
brother Robert as children, prominently displayed on top of the
Chinese cabinet within direct view of the bed [figures 4.8 and 4.9].
What did Proust see in these images of childhood and fraternity
that made them less threatening, or perhaps more intriguing?
What secret did these particular photographs hold for Proust, who
might contemplate them as frequently and as long as he wished?
These rather ordinary studio photographs are already banal, cast
in the conventional codes of Victorian portrait photography. In the
photograph of the two identically dressed brothers together, both
face directly into the camera, with Marcel's hands resting protec-
tively on his younger brother's thigh. In the photograph of Marcel
alone, dubbed the "young Prince" by Albaret, a prepubescent
Proust dressed in velvet pantaloons, a ruffled shirt, and a large silk
bowtie perches on a banister against an ornate interior backdrop,
holding a cane across his lap. Did Proust detect, in these stylized
photographs of early childhood, signs of an emerging sexual iden-

FIG. 4.8 The sole visual images displayed openly in Proust's bedroom were photographs of Marcel and Robert Proust as children. Robert Proust, so conspicuously absent from Proust's novel, occupies a particularly prominent place in the bedroom, while portraits of Proust's deceased parents, who make important cameo appearances in the book, are relegated to the salon. *Courtesy of Bibliothèque nationale de France.*

tity, visual evidence of a "latent" homosexuality? One might recall that the photographer of the grandmother's picture in *A la recherche* is none other than Robert Saint-Loup, and that the mystery of the darkroom in which Saint-Loup seduces the lift boy is the secret of homosexuality. Early twentieth-century sexology and psychoanalysis both characterize homosexuality through the language of photography, borrowing heavily from its scientific rhetoric of fixation, inversion, exposure, and development. Could it be that what Proust was slowly bringing to light in his literary darkroom was a portrait of the artist as a young gay man? What-

FIG. 4.9 Photograph of Marcel Proust as a young adolescent. Proust believed that only pictures of ourselves in childhood reveal to us our true likeness. This particular image, also displayed in the bedroom, may have represented to Proust a snapshot of his sexual persona in its earliest stage of development. *Courtesy of Bibliothèque nationale de France.*

ever private fascination these photographs exerted over the writer, their prominent display in the bedroom bears further testimony to the larger insight that only a picture of childhood can reveal to us our true likeness, an image of a self that we never really knew and only gradually come to recognize.

8

In his persistent exploration of the power of involuntary memory, Proust is drawn to photography chiefly for its splitting of time.

However, the photograph that possesses two temporalities also manifests just two spatial dimensions. All surface and no depth, a photograph "is completely lacking in subjectivity."[82] In many ways, the three-dimensional space of the theater offers a far better artistic metaphor for a novel of introspection, countering the bounded flatness of the photograph with the receding depths of the stage. Many of the photographs Proust collected, like the portraits of actresses also accumulated by his great uncle Weil, were images of the theater. Proust's lifelong enthusiasm for the theater directly influences not only the structure of *A la recherche*, with its various narrative intermissions,[83] but its literary content as well. One enterprising critic has identified in the novel, in addition to Proust's use of nearly five hundred theatrical metaphors, literary allusions to twenty-five actors, fifty plays, and thirty dramatists.[84] These strands of dramatic material might in and of themselves constitute a novel, so pervasive are the narrative's references to the theater. Might the private act of writing an introspective novel itself be considered something of a public performance, a self-conscious staging of the elusive drama of interiority?

In his 1896 essay, "*Le tragique quotidien*," Belgian dramatist Maurice Maeterlinck advocates a new kind of stage drama based upon interior reflection. Maeterlinck's theater of inner life imagines "an old man sitting in his armchair, simply waiting by his lamp, listening unconsciously to all the eternal laws that reign round his house." This "motionless old man," he adds, "lives in reality a deeper, more human and more universal life than the lover who strangles his mistress, the captain who wins a victory, or the 'husband who avenges his honor'."[85] Maeterlinck's new armchair theater, with its solitary figure sitting attentively by a lamp, comes eerily close to describing Proust's own *tragique quotidien* at boulevard Haussmann. The contemplative Proust was not merely the central actor in this domestic drama, he was also its author, director, and stage manager, controlling every element in the bedroom from the lighting, setting, and dialogue to the timing of all entrances and exits. At the same historical moment actors were learning to perform on stage "as if at home,"[86] Proust was learning at home how to perform as if on stage.

Proust's distinctive mannerisms, his curious attire, and his studied poses all struck acquaintances as highly theatrical. Whether in bed wearing gloves or standing in his *cabinet de toilette* eating noodles, Proust cut a dramatic, even comic figure. "In order to understand the atmosphere at Proust's, go to the *Comédie Française*," Jean Cocteau writes in *Opium*, comparing Proust's cluttered apartment to the back stage of France's premier theater, full of dramatic props, dust sheets, and musical instruments.[87] Albaret's description of her first meeting with her mysterious employer also emphasizes the staginess of Proust's interior chamber:

> I reached the fourth door, opened it without knocking, pushed aside the heavy curtain on the other side . . . and went in. The smoke was so thick you could have cut it with a knife. . . . All I could see of M. Proust was a white shirt under a thick sweater, and the upper part of his body propped against two pillows. His face was hidden in the shadows and the smoke from the fumigation, completely invisible except for the eyes looking at me—and I felt rather than saw them. . . . I bowed toward the invisible face and put the saucer with the croissant down on the tray. He gave a wave of the hand, presumably to thank me, but didn't say a word. Then I left. (16)

In Albaret's description, Proust enacts in his bedroom not the high classical drama of the *Comédie Française* but the low music hall theater of magic and pantomime. Wreathed in smoke and speaking not a word, he performs in front of Albaret's very eyes an act of self-vanishing.[88] For Proust, the ability to make oneself disappear marks the sign of a true writer. Like a great stage actor or a virtuoso pianist, the gifted writer can become transparent: "he is simply a window opening upon a great work of art" (III: 44). Elsewhere in *A la recherche* the narrator confesses that "he should have liked to be a character in those *Arabian Nights*" in which there appears a genie "invisible to everyone else" (V: 250). Or yet again, Proust's narrator pictures his bedroom as a palace where, quoting directly from Racine's *Esther*, "'a dread majesty contrives to render me invisible to my subjects'" (V: 419). The desire to be invisible was a profound one for the voyeuristic Proust, who in social gatherings preferred to remain part of the background, as much a spectator as an actor.

The bedroom theater at boulevard Haussmann did not always feature a dumb show. Albaret recounts numerous instances of late-night monologues, with Proust sitting on the end of his bed and reenacting memorable scenes from his evening. An excellent mimic, Proust brought home to his lonely housekeeper "a salon full of people," prompting Albaret to claim years later that she was "the privileged spectator of the most beautiful theater in the world" (127). And yet even during these nocturnal performances, Proust was capable of "a strange faculty of vanishing, while his lips went on speaking" (128). Cocteau goes even further than Albaret, suggesting that Proust's soft but harmonious voice issued from some place outside his body, as if he were a "ventriloquist."[89] In making his voice and even his person disappear, Proust could privately play both actor and director while publically occupying the less visible role of spectator. Whenever Proust summoned a friend to his room for a public audience, more often than not it was he who assumed the role of onlooker, placing his visitor in the uncomfortable role of performer. This subterfuge worked well for the inquisitive Proust, allowing him to draw out his friends without giving very much of himself away.

In the nineteenth and early twentieth centuries, private home theaters were proliferating all over France; all one needed was a stage set and a curtain.[90] Proust, of course, had both. In Proust's bedroom theater, visitors were given key roles and encouraged to take center stage, while their host watched from the sidelines. Only on these social occasions was the overhead chandelier ever lighted, irradiating the visitor seated in the armchair while leaving Proust characteristically in shadow. Though the bedroom was his stage, Proust himself was rarely seen entering or exiting the room. Even Albaret, who herself played such a major supporting role in Proust's domestic drama, complained about Proust's unnerving ability to soundlessly appear in a room, and just as quietly vanish. Visitors, in contrast, were summoned by Proust to appear at boulevard Haussmann at a prearranged time, and were often asked to wait patiently in the wings, like "actors who are next to appear on stage" (II: 354). Once on stage, they were invited to entertain their host by gossiping, storytelling, reminiscing, or (in the case of Reynaldo Hahn) occasionally playing the piano. When his visitors left, a curtain literally closed behind them, leaving Proust to ponder the meaning of the drama that had just unfolded.

Of course, the real drama of the bedroom takes place without any other people present. The central action of the bedroom, one can imagine Proust insisting, is "the theatre and drama of my going to bed there" (I: 48). Sleeping and waking provide the dramatic material for neither a realist nor a naturalist theater but a surrealist one. In describing how the bedroom of the present mysteriously morphs into all the bedrooms of the past, Proust draws specifically on the language and the technology of the modern stage. Adolphe Appia, a Proust contemporary and a proponent of symbolist theater, argued that the structural supports of the stage itself (walls, ceiling, and even floors) should be movable elements of the performance.[91] Proust evidently agreed, for with each return to the past in the narrator's bedroom, "the wall would slide away in another direction" (I: 7). Interiority, in Proust's view, operates like a surrealist stage set. In the theater of the unconscious, walls can move, people can transform, places can merge, and times can coincide. Only as the mind comes to full consciousness and its "scene shifters" finally stabilize is a "drop lowered right at the front of the stage," separating once again our view of the present from our glimpse of the past (II: 878). Armchair and bed—the stage vehicles that carry Proust's narrator "at full speed through time and space" (I: 5)—always and inevitably, in the production of time past, return to the present. In truth, neither lost time nor lost space is ever completely regained.[92] Fugitive moments "rise up like a stage set" before us (I: 51), but the individual scenes they present never finally cohere into a dramatic whole. In this respect, too, Proust's theater of memory is more surrealist than realist, with time and space themselves emerging as the main protagonists of a modern drama preoccupied with what lies behind the curtain of tangible experience.

Thus, in both the literal space of the bedroom and the figurative space of the novel, Proust insists on placing the spectator center stage, making the act of observation as significant as its object. It is important to note that when Proust utilizes the theatrical metaphor of the "fourth wall" in *A la recherche*, he does so to describe not the space behind the proscenium arch at the Opéra, where the narrator has gone to watch Berma perform in *Phèdre*, but the auditorium's balconies and viewing stalls, lyrically described as "so many little suspended drawing-rooms, the fourth walls of which had been removed" (III: 35). This spatial figure offers an apt metaphor for understanding the structure of the novel itself, made up of juxtaposed interior spaces that bring us directly into the mind of the viewer. In the novel of introspection, the stage that counts most is the plane of private perception and internal reflection. Proust, through the device of a narrator named Marcel, inserts himself into the very spectacle that he analyzes. In the modern novel as Proust understood it, where nothing is more stage-worthy than the writer's own cognitive drama, an author finds far fewer places to hide. The genius of *A la recherche* is that it removes the fourth wall of the nineteenth-century novel and, in doing so, eliminates the border between a fictional inside and a nonfictional outside. One never quite knows *where* one is in the

Proustian novel, an experience of disorientation directly akin to the confusion suffered by the narrator who awakes at the beginning of the book not knowing where, or even who, he is. Moving through the transparent fourth wall of *A la recherche* is like journeying through "an inward Lethe" (IV: 787), where the play of memory and forgetting characterize the very experience of reading, and where not even the audience is exempt from the search for lost time.

9

When Proust was forced to leave boulevard Haussmann in May 1919,[93] he sought temporary refuge in a furnished fourth floor apartment on rue Laurent-Pichat that belonged to the stage actress Réjane, the model for the fictional Berma. This thin-walled, noisy apartment offered one attractive compensation: it doubled as a theater stall, providing a clear view into an apartment across the courtyard where the actor Le Bargy, of the *Comédie Française*, could be seen and heard fighting with his wife, going to his bathroom, and declaiming his lines. In October of the same year Proust moved to a fifth floor apartment on rue Hamelin, a somewhat smaller space than the quarters at boulevard Haussmann, but nonetheless large enough to accommodate at one point a staff of five, including a second maid, a chauffeur, a typist, and a secretary.[94] As Proust's health deteriorated, his household grew proportionately. Proust died at rue Hamelin surrounded by people and burdened by the responsibilities of managing an increasingly large domestic staff, a curious and ironic fate for a self-proclaimed recluse.

Like Freud after him, Proust did what he could to reconstitute in unfamiliar surroundings the very place from which he had been exiled. Again selecting for his bedroom a room at the farthest end of the apartment, Proust placed in storage the piano, the mirrored wardrobe, and the matching chest that once held his statue and notebooks.[95] He retained, however, all of the furniture that together created his intimate writing corner, arranging the brass bed, Chinese screen, three tables, and velvet armchair in the exact same positions they occupied at boulevard Haussmann. Before leaving this apartment Proust had already sold some of the family furniture at auction. One senses in Proust, in these last years of his life, considerably less ambivalence towards his dead parents, a change confirmed by Proust's decision to display in the small salon at rue Hamelin, for the first time, his parents' portraits side by side with his own (Albaret 325). Proust's placement of his own likeness in the company of his departed parents might also signal a deeper and more disturbing awareness, a growing conviction that he himself was already dead, already no more than a memorial image of himself.

Proust's late correspondence is replete with references to his corpse-like state. He informs Jacques Boulenger that he has, in effect, "been dead for a long time," and he identifies himself to Rosny aîné as "one who is no longer any better than a corpse."[96] Albaret maintains that even at boulevard Haussmann Proust resembled a cadaver; with his eyes so often closed and his body pale and rigid, "anyone coming in his room might have taken him for dead" (70). Proust, who as an invalid claimed to find it tedious to "die more than once,"[97] played a corpse long before he actually became one. In *A la recherche* Proust's narrator acknowledges that it is difficult to picture one's death: "When we try to consider what will happen to us after our own death, is it not still our living self which we mistakenly project at that moment?" (VI: 530) Proust's words uncannily echo Freud's insight that it is impossible to imagine our own death, because "whenever we attempt to do so we can perceive that we are in fact still present as spectators."[98] Yet Proust goes further than Freud, concluding that a conscious awareness of death is entirely beside the point: "the death of oneself is neither impossible nor extraordinary; it is effected without our knowledge, sometimes against our will, every day of our lives" (VI: 494). Every time sleep overtakes us, we journey, like Orpheus, through the underworld. More appropriately, we each become sleeping Albertines—bodies with the "rigidity of stone" wrapped in sheets "like a shroud," our heads alone "emerging from the tomb" (V: 366).

The image of the sleeper-corpse precisely describes Proust himself in his final months at rue Hamelin. Confined to his bed by dizzy spells, racked by rheumatism, weakened by malnutrition, sickened by pneumonia, and tormented by hallucinations, the dying Proust blanketed himself up to the neck, at the height of summer, under seven layers of wool and a fur coat. Exhausted by a regime of "morphine, aspirin, adrenaline, euvalpine, sparteine" and "every other drug" one can imagine, a despondent Proust writes to Émile Mâle that "I have just spent long years actually in the tomb, where I still am."[99] For Proust's numerous death re-hearsals, the bed conveniently doubled as a bier. Eventually Proust was laid out in the same place where he composed his novel, and in the exact same position,[100] prompting one to wonder whether the act of writing may have represented all along to the asthmatic Proust a form of self-bereavement, and whether the novel Proust completes in his bedroom-bier may in fact constitute the writer's self-obituary.

In his last days Proust was remarkably lucid, "watching him-self die" in Albaret's words (349), and dictating additions to the episode of Bergotte's death staged in front of Vermeer's *View Of Delft*. On one of his final outings Proust had experienced a dizzy spell of his own at an exhibition of Dutch paintings. Prostrated by the power of the image, the writer himself became the spectacle, subject to the curious looks of others. Proust never believed the critical commonplace that a dead artist achieves immortality through the art that survives him. His fainting spell in the museum confirmed his deepest suspicions that the artist is instead just an-

FIG. 4.10 Postmortem portrait of Proust by André Dunoyer de Segonzac.
In addition to Man Ray's well-known black and white photograph of
Proust, Paul César Helleu executed a *dernier portrait* in metal point that
took nearly ten hours, while Dunoyer de Segonzac produced two more wash
drawings, also in ink. At least one sculptor, Robert Wlérick, attempted to
immortalize Proust's visage in three-dimensional form. *Courtesy of Réunion
des Musées Nationaux/Art Resource, NY and © 2003 Artists Rights Society
(ARS), New York/ADAGP, Paris.*

other decomposing piece of art, a work of sculpture hardened and
diminished over time until he becomes a "finished effigy" (III:
335). After Proust's death on November 18, 1922, the bedroom at
rue Hamelin briefly became an art studio, with no less than four
artists attempting to capture Proust's effigy [figure 4.10].[101] The
excellent condition of Proust's body, which appeared to be natu-
rally embalmed (Albaret 361), prompted Robert Proust to extend
his brother's formal viewing, allowing not only professional
artists but close friends and distant acquaintances to enter
Proust's private bedchamber to take their own mental picture of
the acclaimed writer who, three years earlier, had won French literature's *Prix Goncourt*. In the four days after his death at rue

Hamelin and before his burial at Père-Lachaise cemetery, Proust became for others an *objet d'art*, inciting amongst his mourners both shared personal reminiscence and unembarrassed idolatrous worship. He became, in the end, a relic of time past, the very photograph of memory his own work so lovingly memorializes.

Proust's tomb at Père Lachaise cemetery in Paris, where he was buried in the same plot as his parents. The names of Adrien and Jeanne Proust are inscribed on the side of the black marble tombstone, literally cast into shadow by their more famous son. *Author photograph.*

Coda

TO ENTER INTO THESE LITERARY CHAMBERS is to enter into conversation with the dead. It is also to arrive at the place where the writers themselves talked to the dead, constructing private home theaters of loss and memory. All four writers I discuss in this book fashioned their writing space as a memorial space. All four drew on their physical surroundings to confront their own fears of mortality. And all four died where they wrote. Proust may not have been alone in viewing his writing space as a transitional space; Dickinson, Freud, and Keller also regarded the most interior chamber of their personal life as the portal to a next life—an "afterlife" conceived, in truth, not so much as a life after death as a life after writing. Of the rituals of mourning that so powerfully define the literary workspace, the most profound may be a silent lament for the fading of the writer's own creativity, for the loss of language itself.

There is no evidence that any of the four authors I address in this book personally knew or even read each other (indeed, only Keller had a passing knowledge of the other three). And yet, their stories overlap in ways both large and small. Each writer discovered, in the deepest recesses of the domestic interior, expansive intellectual lives. Each encountered in modern technology a way of understanding the secrets of their own human interiority. Each endowed certain of their personal possessions with subjective lives, drawing both sustenance and sorrow from the objects they gathered close around them. Each exhibited a particularly vexed relation to mirrors, which were either banished from the actual space of writing or placed strategically nearby to capture a particular reflection. And most strikingly, each embodied a reflective surface for others, becoming, as they grew older, a curious if familiar icon, an *objet d'art*.

The recurrent interplay of subject and object in the space of writing reminds us that if the writer's interior is a memorial chamber, it is also a living archive. While writers' homes are furnished with the often comforting, sometimes painful, and always poignant reminders of the dead, they also take their character from the activities and preoccupations of the living. For every sign of literary eccentricity found in these interiors (a favorite pen, a beloved portrait), one encounters many more testaments to quotidian living (a tarnished comb, a linen handkerchief). Profound objects collide with banal objects. If there is one central insight all four of these writers share, it may be the recognition that, in a modern world filled with totemic objects, the banal *is* profound. Finding inspiration in their immediate surroundings, these four writers of the interior recognize what so many of their contemporaries overlooked—namely, that even things as seemingly inconsequential as an open door, a broken relic, a warm hand, or a crumbly teacake can be the stuff of great literature.

Writers' lairs, private though they may be, are nonetheless places where lives unfold, relationships evolve, and imaginations ignite. To maintain deep personal ties while writing about them, each writer cultivated what I would call a social solitude, a way of being fully present in the world while still achieving a knowing distance from it. The great paradox in encountering these very introspective writers is how their public visibility grew in direct proportion to their need for privacy. Each semi-reclusive figure mastered the art of securing attention for his or her writing by disappearing from public view, whether the exile was self-imposed and prolonged (Dickinson and Proust), or involuntary and periodic (Keller and Freud). Perhaps these prolific writers intuited that the best way to be heard is not to be seen, an insight that indeed has contributed to the mythologization of all four authors, both during their lifetimes and since.

The preceding chapters can be read in many ways: as literary criticism, as architectural history, or as cultural theory. In my mind, the chapters work best as miniature biographies—narratives of not just person but place. In presenting these cultural and literary biographies, I have attempted to show how the place where writing emerges is not an empty or impoverished space but a full and dynamic one. The intensely private act of putting thoughts into words takes place in an environment enlivened by the sights and sounds, the textures and smells, and even occasionally the tastes of a fully embodied life. When all is said and done, what I have most wanted to convey in these pages is the way in which interiors shape imagination. This book pays tribute to the place where writing happens, in the modest hope that detouring through someone else's sense of an interior might bring us, in prodigal fashion, more confidently back to our own.

Notes

Introduction

1. Virginia Woolf, "The Leaning Tower" (1940), in *The Moment, and Other Essays* (New York: Harcourt, Brace, and Company, 1948), 128.

2. Mark Girouard, *Life in the English Country House: A Social and Architectural History* (New Haven and London: Yale UP, 1978) and *Life in the French Country House* (London: Cassell and Company, 2000); Gwendolyn Wright, *Building the Dream: A Social History of Housing in America* (Cambridge, Mass.: The MIT P, 1981); Dolores Hayden, *The Grand Domestic Revolution* (Cambridge, Mass.: The MIT P, 1981); Alice T. Friedman, *Women and the Making of the Modern House: A Social and Architectural History* (New York: Harry N. Abrams, Inc, 1998).

3. Judith Fryer, *Felicitous Space: The Imaginative Structures of Edith Wharton and Willa Cather* (Chapel Hill and London: U of North Carolina P, 1986), xiv; Marilyn Chandler, *Dwelling in the Text: Houses in American Fiction* (Berkeley: U of California P, 1991), 17–20; Ellen Eve Frank, *Literary Architecture: Essays Toward a Tradition* (Berkeley: U of California P, 1979), 3, 4, 7, and esp. 2–22.

4. Martin Heidegger, "Poetically Man Dwells," in *Rethinking Architecture*, ed. Neil Leach (New York and London: Routledge, 1997), 112 and 118; Gaston Bachelard, *The Poetics of Space* (Boston: Beacon P, 1994, orig. pub. 1958), 6.

5. Heidegger, 110.

6. Emily Dickinson, *The Complete Poems of Emily Dickinson*, ed. Thomas H. Johnson (Boston: Little, Brown and Company, 1955), Poem 1182.

7. Sigmund Freud, *Introductory Lectures on Psycho-Analysis* (1917), *The Standard Edition of the Complete Psychological Works of Sigmund*

Freud, trans. and ed. James Strachey, 24 vols. (London: The Hogarth Press, 1953–74), 16: 295.

8. Marcel Proust, *Remembrance of Things Past*, trans. C. K. Moncrieff and Terence Kilmartin, vol. 3 (New York: Vintage, 1982), 1089.

9. Proust, 504, 554.

10. In "Touching Words: Helen Keller, Plagiarism, Authorship," Jim Swan observes that "the blind woman's walk through the world is an intensely *narrative* activity," adding that "blindness means a continuous exercise of memory and prediction." In Martha Woodmansee and Peter Jaszi, eds., *The Construction of Authorship: Textual Appropriation in Law and Literature* (Durham and London: Duke UP, 1994), 63.

11. See, for example, Edgar de Noailles Mayhew, *A Documentary History of American Interiors: From the Colonial Era to 1915* (New York: Scribner, 1980); John Cornforth, *English Interiors 1790–1848: The Quest for Comfort* (London: Barrie & Jenkins, 1978); William Seale, *The Tasteful Interlude: American Interiors through the Camera's Eye, 1860–1917*, 2nd ed. (Nashville, Tenn.: American Association for State and Local History, 1981); Gail Caskey Winkler and Roger W. Moss, *Victorian Interior Decoration: American Interiors, 1830–1900* (New York: Henry Holt, 1986); and Lisa Lovatt-Smith, *Paris Interiors* (Cologne: Taschen, 1994). For a more critical view of the ideology of the domestic interior, see *Domestic Space: Reading the Nineteenth-Century Interior*, ed. Inga Bryden and Janet Floyd (Manchester: Manchester UP, 1999).

12. Walter Benjamin, *The Arcades Project*, trans. Howard Eiland and Kevin McLaughlin (Cambridge, Mass.: The Belknap P of Harvard UP, 1999), 220.

13. Benjamin, 216. Benjamin's contention that the twentieth century has destroyed this form of bounded dwelling—"today this world has disappeared entirely, and dwelling has diminished" (221)—strikes me as a highly contestable one even in Benjamin's own time. While some versions of twentieth-century architecture may indeed be more open and transparent than the more enclosed and opaque structures of the nineteenth century, the general association of dwelling with encasement has by no means disappeared, and in some ways may have only taken deeper root in a culture still preoccupied with privacy and protection.

14. For a concise narrative of the historical emergence of the domestic interior, see Witold Rybczynski, *Home: A Short History of an Idea* (New York: Penguin Books, 1986), esp. 41–48.

15. As labor became more centralized, the domestic interior came to symbolize a place of rest, relaxation, and renewal, a cultural refuge from the political world of commerce, competition, and corruption. Yet for women and servants, the harsh realities of domestic work made the interior no less a hazardous space than the exterior world it was said to oppose. For more on domesticity in the nineteenth century, see Glenna Matthews, *"Just a Housewife": The Rise and Fall of Domesticity in America* (Oxford: Oxford UP, 1987), Phyllis M. Palmer, *Domesticity and Dirt: Housewives and Domestic Servants in the Unites States, 1920–1945* (Philadelphia.: Temple UP, 1989), Mary P. Ryan, *The Empire of the Mother: American Writing about Domesticity, 1830–1860* (New York: Institute for Research in History and the Haworth P, 1982), and Mary Kelley, *Private Woman, Public Stage: Literary Domesticity in Nineteenth-Century America* (Oxford: Oxford UP, 1984).

16. Michelle Perrot notes that in the nineteenth century, "literature, long silent about décor, suddenly began to describe interiors in minute detail, reflecting a change in the way people looked at places and things." *A History of Private Life*, eds. Philippe Ariès and Georges Duby, vol. 4 (Cambridge, Mass.: Harvard UP, 1990), 356.

17. Didier Maleuvre, *Museum Memories: History, Technology, Art* (Stanford: Stanford UP, 1999), 137. In *Literature and Material Culture from Balzac to Proust* (Cambridge: Cambridge UP, 1999), Janell Watson adds that, in the nineteenth-century novel, "alterations in classic plot structure correlate closely to alterations in traditional configurations of household furnishings" (4). Maleuvre and Watson, who both seek to understand the bourgeois interior from a literary point of view, also both interestingly take the bibelot as a central object of study.

18. Edmond de Goncourt, *La Maison d'un artiste* (Paris: Charpentier, 1881), 7. For a more detailed reading of de Goncourt's fetishization of the interior, see Maleuvre, 151–54.

19. William James, *Principles of Psychology*, vol. 2 (New York: Dover Publications, Inc., 1950, orig. pub. 1890), 43.

20. French novelist Édouard Dujardin, in his 1887 novel *Les Lauriers sont coupés*, was the first writer to employ the technique of *monologue intérieur*, a phrase coined later by another French novelist, Paul Bourget, and cited extensively by French critics after the publication of James Joyce's *Ulysses* in 1922. Although often used synonymously to denote the free flow of inner experience, "stream of consciousness" and "interior monologue" sometimes vary in critical usage. In brief, "stream of

consciousness" retains a sense of the author's presence in the depiction of a character's interior life, while "interior monologue" presents the flow of a character's thoughts without authorial interruption. Leon Edel's *The Modern Psychological Novel* (New York: Grosset and Dunlap, 1964) remains the classic reference text on stream of consciousness and the interior monologue.

21. *The Art of the Novel: Critical Prefaces by Henry James* (New York: Scribner's, 1937), 46–47.
22. Benjamin, 14.
23. Benjamin, 19.
24. Theodor W. Adorno, *Kierkegaard: Construction of the Aesthetic*, trans. Robert Hullot-Kentor (Minneapolis: U of Minnesota P, 1989), 42, 46. Benjamin includes, in a section on mirrors, a lengthy citation from this book by Adorno (542), suggesting that the window mirror framed Benjamin's own analysis of interior reflection in *The Arcades Project*. Adorno, in turn, borrows the window mirror from Kierkegaard, who posits it as modernity's chief symbol of interiority.
25. The metaphor belongs to Adorno: "The *intérieur* is the incarnate imago of Kierkegaard's philosophical 'point': everything truly external has shrunken to the point" (44).
26. Benjamin, 21, 17.
27. Susan Buck-Morss, *The Dialectics of Seeing: Walter Benjamin and the Arcades Project* (Cambridge, Mass.: The MIT P, 1989), 81.
28. Adorno, 41.
29. See Jonathan Goldberg, *Writing Matter: From the Hands of the English Renaissance* (Stanford, Calif.: Stanford UP, 1990); Tamara Plakins Thornton, *Handwriting in America: A Cultural History* (New Haven and London: Yale UP, 1996); Jeffrey Masten, Peter Stallybrass, and Nancy J. Vickers, eds. *Language Machines: Technologies of Literary and Cultural Production* (New York and London: Routledge, 1997); Lisa Gitelman, *Scripts, Grooves, and Writing Machines: Representing Technology in the Edison Age* (Stanford, Calif.: Stanford UP, 1999); and Friedrich A. Kittler, *Gramophone, Film, Typewriter*, trans. Geoffrey Winthrop-Young and Michael Wutz (Stanford, Calif.: Stanford UP, 1999).
30. Margreta de Grazia, Maureen Quilligan, and Peter Stallybrass, eds., *Subject and Object in Renaissance Culture* (Cambridge: Cambridge UP, 1996), 3. The editors provide an excellent summary of subject/object relations in the Renaissance, demonstrating how the reciprocal ex-

changes of people and things in the early modern period in truth denaturalizes the assumed sovereignty of subjects over objects.

31. Among the most influential of these design books were Charles L. Eastlake's *Hints on Household Taste in Furniture, Upholstery and other Details*, ed. Charles C. Perkins (Boston: J. R. Osgood and Company, 1872); Clarence Cook's *The House Beautiful: Essays on Beds and Tables, Stools and Candlesticks* (New York: Charles Scribner's Sons, 1881); Robert William Edis's *Decoration & Furnishing of Town Houses* (New York: Scribner and Welford, 1881), Mary Eliza Joy Haweis's *Beautiful Houses* (New York: Scribner and Welford, 1882); Rosamund Marriott Watson's *The Art of the House* (London: G. Bell and Sons, 1897); and Edith Wharton and Ogden Codman Jr.'s *The Decoration of Houses* (New York: C. Scribner's Sons, 1902). Basing his history of domestic design on these and other popular and professional guidebooks, Adrian Forty observes that "the nineteenth-century bourgeoisie turned the home into a palace of illusions, which encouraged total dissociation from the world immediately outside." See Forty's *Objects of Desire: Design and Society Since 1750* (London: Thames and Hudson, 2000), 101.

32. John Lukacs, "The Bourgeois Interior," *American Scholar* 39:4 (Autumn 1970), 623.

33. The mouth appears to be the organ least involved in the human perception of interiority, but as I suggest in my final chapter on "Proust's nose," the association of taste with smell implicates even the seemingly marginal mouth in a narrative of temporal and spatial memory.

34. *Correspondance de Marcel Proust*, ed. Philip Kolb, 21 vols. (Paris: Plon, 1970–93). Letter to Camille Vettard, around March 1922 (21: 77). In a similar vein, the contemporary author Gish Jen remarks of her self-imposed withdrawal from writing, "I felt as though I had lost one of my senses." See Gish Jen's "Inventing Life Steals Time; Living Life Begs it Back," *The New York Times*, Monday December 4, 2000, E2.

Chapter 1

1. John Cody, *After Great Pain: The Inner Life of Emily Dickinson* (Cambridge, Mass.: Harvard UP, 1971), and Maryanne M. Garbowsky, *The House without the Door: A Study of Emily Dickinson and the Illness of Agoraphobia* (London: Associated UP, 1989). Cody updates his earlier thesis on Dickinson's neurotic personality in his foreword to Garbowsky's more recent study of Dickinson's agoraphobia. I might note

here, in response to the popular perception of Emily Dickinson as "agoraphobic," that the term "agoraphobia" was not coined until 1871, by the German neurologist Alexander Karl Otto Westphal. Not until after Dickinson's death in 1886 can the clinical concept of a pathological fear of open spaces (initially understood as exclusively a male disorder) properly be said to arrive in America.

2. See Wendy Martin, *An American Triptypch: Anne Bradsteet, Emily Dickinson, Adrienne Rich* (Chapel Hill: U of North Carolina P, 1984), and Adrienne Rich, "Vesuvius at Home: The Power of Emily Dickinson," in *On Lies, Secrets, and Silence: Selected Prose 1966–1978* (New York: W.W. Norton and Company, 1979), 157–83.

3. Judith Farr, *The Passion of Emily Dickinson* (Cambridge, Mass.: Harvard UP, 1992), 24–5; Cynthia Griffin Wolff, *Emily Dickinson* (Reading, Mass.: Addison Wesley, 1988), 167.

4. Thomas H. Johnson, *Emily Dickinson: An Interpretive Biography* (Cambridge, Mass.: Harvard UP, 1955), 81; Jean McClure Mudge, *Emily Dickinson and the Image of Home* (Amherst, Mass.: U of Massachusetts P, 1975), 6; and Jane Donahue Eberwein, *Dickinson: Strategies of Limitation* (Amherst, Mass.: U of Massachusetts P, 1985), 38. Eberwein refers here to the lines from Dickinson's Poem 1601: "Immured the whole of Life / Within a magic Prison." *The Complete Poems of Emily Dickinson*, ed. Thomas H. Johnson (Boston: Little, Brown and Company, 1955). Henceforth all poems will be cited by number in the text.

5. On the social and political history of the private/public distinction, see Jeff Weintraub and Krishan Kumar, eds., *Public and Private in Thought and Practice: Perspectives on a Grand Dichotomy* (Chicago: U of Chicago P, 1997).

6. Jay Leyda, *The Years and Hours of Emily Dickinson* (New Haven: Yale UP, 1960), vol. 1, xxi, and Sharon Cameron, *Lyric Time: Dickinson and the Limits of Genre* (Baltimore and London: The Johns Hopkins UP, 1979), 18.

7. Charles Anderson, *Emily Dickinson's Poetry: Stairway of Surprise* (New York: Holt, Rinehart and Winston, 1960), 55.

8. The Homestead legally passed out of Dickinson ownership as early as March 1833, when the mortgage was foreclosed and the house was sold to General David Mack. While Samuel Fowler Dickinson relocated to Ohio with his wife and youngest daughter, Edward Dickinson and his young family remained as tenants in the Homestead for an-

other seven years. With the General, his wife, their three young children, and (for a time) Edward's younger brother Frederick occupying the east side, conditions in the Homestead remained crowded though apparently comfortable. For a brief description of the Homestead during the Mack years, see Lucius Boltwood's letter of November 5, 1842, which describes a party held there for at least one-hundred and fifty guests (Leyda, *Years* 1: 72).

9. Richard B. Sewall, *The Lyman Letters: New Light on Emily Dickinson and Her Family* (Amherst, Mass.: U of Massachusetts P, 1965), 1.

10. *The Letters of Emily Dickinson*, ed. Thomas H. Johnson (Cambridge, Mass.: The Belknap P of Harvard U, 1958), Letter 182. Henceforth all letters will be cited by number in the text.

11. Clifford Edward Clark, Jr., *The American Family Home, 1800–1960* (Chapel Hill: U. of North Carolina P, 1986), 36.

12. Barton Levi St. Armand, *Emily Dickinson and Her Culture: The Soul's Society* (Cambridge: Cambridge UP, 1984), 308. Austin Dickinson was eventually to have paid his father less than the full value of the house, but Edward Dickinson died before the debt was paid.

13. Andrew Jackson Downing, *The Architecture of Country Houses* (New York: Dover, 1969), 269. It is not entirely clear how directly Austin or Edward Dickinson were influenced by Andrew Jackson Downing, although Austin's wife notes in her essay "Society in Amherst" that her husband "had long studied" Downing's work (qtd. in Mudge 244). Austin Dickinson was particularly well informed about architecture and landscaping. Not only did he own an inscribed volume of Calvert Vaux's *Villas and Cottages*, he also sought advice on the landscaping of the Dickinson property from Frederick Law Olmstead, the designer of New York's Central Park (St. Armand, 20). A Northampton architect, William Fenno Pratt, designed the Evergreens, and while no documents have surfaced to shed light on the designer for the 1855 Homestead renovations, it is possible that the same architect worked on both houses.

14. Martha Dickinson Bianchi, *Emily Dickinson Face to Face: Unpublished Letters with Notes and Reminiscences* (Boston and New York: Houghton Mifflin, 1932), 25.

15. Downing preferred what he saw as the more American-friendly Gothic Revival style of the 1840s to the culturally anachronistic Greek Revival style of the 1820s and 1830s. American houses that imitate Greek temples draw his special ire: "as these buildings have sometimes as much

space devoted to porticoes and colonnades as to rooms, one may well be pardoned for doubting exactly for what purpose they were designed" (32).

16. Mudge, 244.

17. Karen V. Hansen takes this caution as the methodological starting point of her study of working-class men and women in pre-Civil War New England. See *A Very Social Time: Crafting Community in Antebellum New England* (Berkeley: U of California P, 1994), 24.

18. Little was known about the actual design of the kitchen until a 2001 research and restoration project at the Homestead, which uncovered both the room's original 1855 pine floors and its original paint colors. Decidedly muted in tone, the kitchen's gray floors, light brown walls, and faux oak-grained woodwork created a placid, almost neutral space for the family dramas that daily transpired there.

19. Martha Dickinson Bianchi, *The Life and Letters of Emily Dickinson* (Boston and New York: Houghton Mifflin, 1924), 69.

20. For a more thorough accounting of this affair, see Polly Longsworth, *Austin and Mabel* (New York: Farrar, Straus, Giroux, 1984). In her 1897 legal deposition, the Dickinson family servant, Maggie Maher, testified that Austin and Mabel met alone in the Homestead dining room, or sometimes the library, three or four times a week, for three or four hours in the afternoon or forenoon, with the doors shut (413).

21. Alex Preminger and T. V. F. Brogan, eds. *The New Princeton Encyclopedia of Poetry and Poetics* (Princeton: Princeton UP, 1993), 714–15.

22. For two readings attentive to the problem of delimiting the spatial and temporal borders of a Dickinson poem, see Sharon Cameron's *Lyric Time*, and Virginia Jackson's *Dickinson's Misery: A Theory of Lyric Reading* (Princeton: Princeton UP, forthcoming).

23. Eberwein, 53.

24. On the personal associations of the doorstep for Dickinson, see the more detailed reading in Mudge, 49–52.

25. The literal doorstep Dickinson mentions in this letter refers to the front stoop of the Pleasant Street house; yet, the threshold of the front door remains for Dickinson a powerful symbolic site throughout her life, routinely associated with Sue. In the nineteenth century, back and side entrances were for daily use, while the front door was reserved for important ceremonial occasions, perhaps enhancing the ritual meaning with which Dickinson endowed the figure of the front doorstep.

26. The door ajar also recalls one of nineteenth-century America's most popular novels, Elizabeth Stuart Phelps's *The Gates Ajar*. As Maria Farland notes in a reading of Dickinson's 1862 poem "I cannot live with You" (P 640), this poem's image of lovers reuniting in a home beyond the grave alludes not only to Phelps's bestseller, published six years later, but to many of the other popular sentimental fictions of Dickinson's age, novels in which "friends and family would be reunited in snug, heavenly homes complete with elaborate interior decorations and detailed housekeeping regimes" (371). See Farland's "'That tritest / brightest truth': Emily Dickinson's Anti-Sentimentality," *Nineteenth-Century Literature* 53 (1998): 364–89.

27. Georg Simmel, "Bridge and Door," in *Rethinking Architecture*, ed. Neil Leach (New York and London: Routledge, 1997), 66–9.

28. Leyda, *Years* 1: 301–02. Dickinson, who took both voice and piano lessons as a child, was known to play (in the words of her friend Kate Scott Anthon) "weird & beautiful melodies, all from her own inspiration" (Leyda, *Years* 1: 367).

29. Martha Nell Smith, *Rowing in Eden: Rereading Emily Dickinson* (Austin: U of Texas P, 1992), 248–9.

30. Bianchi, *Emily*, 34.

31. Millicent Todd Bingham, *Ancestor's Brocades: The Literary Debut of Emily Dickinson* (New York and London: Harper & Brothers Publishers, 1945), 12. Martha Dickinson Bianchi's memory of meeting Dickinson when Martha was a young girl again places the meeting in a dimly lighted space, specifically the "Northwest Passage." Dickinson received her niece in the "little back hall that connected with the kitchen. It was dimly lighted. She asked if I would have a glass of wine or a rose." See *Emily*, 25–6.

32. Qtd. in Willis Buckingham, ed. *Emily Dickinson's Reception in the 1890s: A Documentary History* (Pittsburgh: U of Pittsburgh P, 1989), 208–9. Higginson's first trip to the Homestead was in 1870. For an alternate description of Higginson's first encounter with Dickinson, see L342a.

33. Qtd. in Richard Sewall, *The Life of Emily Dickinson* (Cambridge, Mass.: Harvard UP, 1974), 425.

34. Farr, 35–42. Farr explains that since the 1830s in America, portraits of postulants in their wedding gowns were common. By the 1860s, pre-Raphaelite art had been introduced in America, fueling the fascination with Madonna art in general and nuns in particular.

35. In "What is Poetry?" (1833), John Stuart Mill writes: "Eloquence is *heard*, poetry is *overheard*." *Essays on Poetry*, ed. F. Parvin Sharpless (Columbia, S. C.: U of South Carolina P, 1976), 12. For an excellent reading of Mill's definition of lyric for subsequent poetry, see Herbert F. Tucker's "Dramatic Monologue and the Overhearing of Lyric," in *Lyric Poetry: Beyond New Criticism*, ed. Chaviva Hošek and Patricia Parker (Ithaca: Cornell UP, 1985), 226–43.
36. Mary Loeffelholz, *Dickinson and the Boundaries of Feminist Theory* (Urbana and Chicago: U of Illinois P, 1991), 131.
37. For an account of Dickinson's medical history, including her visual impairment, see Norbert Hirschhorn and Polly Longsworth, "'Medicine Posthumous': A New Look at Emily Dickinson's Medical Conditions," *The New England Quarterly* 69.2 (1996): 299–316.
38. Jonathan Crary, *Techniques of the Observer: On Vision and Modernity in the Nineteenth Century* (Cambridge, Mass.: MIT, 1990), 129.
39. Murray Baumgarten reprints Carlyle's 1852 "Manuscript on Creeds," published in truncated form by Froude under the title "Spiritual Optics," in his essay "Carlyle and 'Spiritual Optics'." *Victorian Studies* 11.4 (1968): 514.
40. Leyda, *Years* 2: 76.
41. Sewall, *Life*, 52. See also Elizabeth Phillips, *Emily Dickinson: Personae and Performance* (University Park, Pa.: Pennsylvania State UP, 1988), 22–3.
42. Sewall, *Life*, 415.
43. For more on class in Emily Dickinson's life and poetry, see Jay Leyda's "Miss Emily's Maggie," *New World Writing: Third Mentor Selection* (New York: New American Library, 1953), 255–67, and Betsy Erkkila, "Emily Dickinson and Class," *American Literary History* 4.1 (1992): 1–27. Thomas Foster has recently argued that Dickinson's retreat to her bedroom, her internal exile within the home, neither reinscribes the ideology of separate spheres nor transcends it. Rather, Dickinson's "homelessness at home" (P 1573) clears a space for poetic production by refining, from the inside, a white middle-class woman's relation to domesticity and the private sphere. See Foster's *Transformations of Domesticity in Modern Women's Writing: Homelessness at Home* (New York: Palgrave Macmillan, 2002).
44. Bingham, *Home*, 413.
45. Bingham, *Home*, 414.

46. Mabel Loomis Todd's autobiographical sketch, "Scurrilous but True," is cited in its entirety in Sewall, *Life*, 275–92. On the subject of Austin's understanding of his sister's withdrawal, Todd continues: "He told me about her girlhood and normal blossoming and gradual retirement, and her few love affairs; her life was perfectly natural. All the village gossip merely amused him" (282).

47. Lavinia's strongest defense of Emily's reclusive nature comes in a response to the growing public mythology surrounding her sister's character. To a reviewer of Dickinson's *Letters* (1894), Lavinia wrote in January 1895: "Emily's so called 'withdrawal from general society', for which she never cared, was only a happen. Our mother had a period of invalidism, and one of her daughters must be constantly at home; Emily chose this part and, finding the life with her books and nature so congenial, continued to live it, always seeing her chosen friends and doing her part for the happiness of the home" (qtd. in Sewall, *Life*, 153).

48. Sandra Gilbert and Susan Gubar, *The Madwoman in the Attic: The Woman Writer and the Nineteenth-Century Literary Imagination* (New Haven and London: Yale UP, 1979), 583.

49. Mudge, 147 and 102, and Daneen Wardrop, *Emily Dickinson's Gothic: Goblin with a Gauge* (Iowa City: U of Iowa P, 1996), 23.

50. Sewall, *Life*, 400 and 603.

51. In this poem's first posthumous publication in 1891, Mabel Todd substituted for "timid" the antonym "mighty," implying that the poet's bedroom was a more imaginatively expansive space than Dickinson herself would acknowledge. Yet, for Dickinson, "timid" and "mighty" were never oppositional to begin with, but were always interchangeable terms. Typically in Dickinson's poetry, the unimposing are invincible and the invincible are unimposing (P 796).

52. Tucker, 236.

53. Bianchi, *Emily*, 65–66.

54. Clark, 25.

55. There is no documentation clarifying how frequently the cupola was used, by Emily or any of the Dickinson family members. The proximity of the attic staircase to the poet's bedroom, and the opportunity the cupola afforded for the kind of expansive views Dickinson describes so memorably in both her poetry and her letters, make it unlikely that she never visited the cupola.

56. On the history of the evolving design of the American cemetery, see David Charles Sloane, *The Last Great Necessity: Cemeteries in American History* (Baltimore: The Johns Hopkins UP, 1991).

57. Wolff, 70 and 340.

58. Leyda, *Years* 2: 474. Whereas Dickinson's own physician, Dr. Orvis Furman Bigelow, attributed Dickinson's death to Bright's disease (a degenerative illness caused by kidney failure), recent assessments of Dickinson's health identify the most likely cause as heart failure due to severe primary hypertension. See Hirschhorn and Longsworth, 309–16.

59. Leyda, *Years* 2: 471.

60. Gary Laderman, *The Sacred Remains: American Attitudes Towards Death, 1799–1883* (New Haven: Yale UP, 1996), 9.

61. Leyda, *Years* 2: 475. Higginson's diary entry further describes the Homestead itself as "a more saintly & elevated 'House of Usher'."

62. St. Armand, 74–76; Farr, 1–13; Leyda, *Years* 2: 470 ff.

63. *Called Back* was the title of another popular sentimental novel of the period by the writer Hugh Conway, which Dickinson found to be a "haunting story" (L 856). This 1883 novel was staged as a melodrama at the Springfield Opera House just a month before Dickinson's death.

Chapter 2

1. See Edmund Engelman's "A Memoir," which follows the published English language version of the photographs, *Berggasse 19: Sigmund Freud's Home and Offices, Vienna 1938* (New York: Basic Books, 1976), 134. Rita Ransohoff's photographic captions visually orient the reader, while Peter Gay's preface to the volume, "Freud: For the Marble Tablet," provides an eloquent historical and biographical introduction. Readers might also wish to consult the more recent German edition of Engelman's photographs, *Sigmund Freud: Wien IX. Berggasse 19* (Vienna: Verlag Christian Brandstätter, 1993), which includes an introduction by Inge Scholz-Strasser, General Secretary of the Freud Haus.

2. Edmund Engelman, personal interview, September 14, 1995. Of these one hundred photographs, fifty-six have been published in the English-language version of *Berggasse 19*.

3. An exception is Beatriz Colomina's important analysis of spectatorship in the architectural interiors of Adolf Loos and Le Corbusier in her *Privacy and Publicity: Modern Architecture as Mass Media* (Cambridge, Mass.: MIT P, 1994).

4. Freud, Letter to his son Ernst, May 12, 1938. In *Sigmund Freud, Briefe 1873–1939*, ed. Ernst L. Freud (Frankfurt-am-Main: S. Fischer, 1960), 435.

5. Engelman, "A Memoir," 136.

6. Susan Suleiman, "Bataille in the Street: The Search for Virility in the 1930s," *Critical Inquiry* 21 (Autumn 1994): 62.

7. Hannah S. Decker, *Freud, Dora, and Vienna, 1900* (New York: The Free Press, 1991), 24. Bruno Bettelheim has speculated that Freud's choice to settle on this respectable but undistinguished street was motivated by a deep cultural ambivalence, as Freud sought to reconcile loyalty to his Jewish beginnings with competing desires for assimilationist respectability. See Bettelheim's *Freud's Vienna & Other Essays* (New York: Vintage, 1991), 20. Bettelheim argues in this review of Engelman's photographs that "studying the psychoanalytic couch in detail does not necessarily give any inkling of what psychoanalysis is all about, nor does viewing the settings in which it all happened explain the man, or his work" (19). Yet Berggasse 19 suggests that just the opposite is the case: Engelman's photographs and the space of the office provide important clues not only to Freud's role as clinician but also to the historical development of psychoanalysis, a practice that evolved in response to the changing social, political, and cultural spaces it inhabited.

8. On the street as a site of "accident and incident," see Peter Jukes's introduction to *A Shout in the Street: An Excursion into the Modern City* (Berkeley and Los Angeles: U of California P, 1990).

9. Edmund Engelman recollects the experience of visiting Freud's cluttered office as similar to being "inside the storage room of an antique dealer." Interview, September 14, 1995.

10. As early as 1901, only five years after beginning his collection, Freud writes of the shortage of space in his office study, already filled with pottery and other antiquities, and of his visitors' anxieties that he might eventually break something. See Freud's *Psychopathology of Everyday Life*, in *The Standard Edition of the Complete Psychological Works of Sigmund Freud*, trans. and ed. James Strachey, 24 vols. (London: The Hogarth Press, 1953–74), 6: 167. All citations from the *Standard Edition* hereafter cited in the text by volume and page number.

11. Letter to Fliess, April 19, 1894, in *The Complete Letters of Sigmund Freud to Wilhelm Fliess: 1887–1904*, trans. and ed. Jeffrey Moussaieff Masson (Cambridge, Mass.: Harvard UP, 1985).

12. Letter to Fliess, June 22, 1894.

13. Letter to Fliess, October 26, 1896.

14. Freud possessed many representations of Osiris, king of the underworld and god of resurrection. Osiris, in some accounts the first Egyptian mummy, was locked into a coffin and set adrift on the Nile. Three different bronze statues of Osiris—two complete figures and a head fragment—adorn Freud's desk, testifying to the importance Freud accorded this particular Egyptian deity.

15. For a more complete discussion of Freud's antiquities, see the essays and selected catalogue in *Sigmund Freud and Art: His Personal Collection of Antiquities*, eds. Lynn Gamwell and Richard Wells (London: Thames and Hudson, 1989). John Forrester provides an especially fascinating reading of Freud's antiquities in his essay "'Mille e tre': Freud and Collecting," in *The Cultures of Collecting*, eds. John Elsner and Roger Cardinal (Cambridge, Mass.: Harvard UP, 1994), 224–51.

16. Theodor Adorno, "Valéry Proust Museum," in *Prisms*, trans. Samuel and Shierry Weber (Cambridge, Mass.: MIT P, 1981), 175. Freud's office bears striking similarities to the house-museum of Sir John Soane in London. For a discussion of the museum as a place of entombment, see John Elsner's "A Collector's Model of Desire: The House and Museum of Sir John Soane," in *The Cultures of Collecting*, 155–76. See also Douglas Crimp, *On the Museum's Ruins* (Cambridge, Mass.: MIT P, 1993).

17. For fuller accounts of the *Kaiserliches Stiftungshaus*, Freud's first home and office, see Ernest Jones's *The Life and Work of Sigmund Freud*, 2 vols. (New York: Basic Books, 1953), 1: 149, and Bettelheim, *Freud's Vienna*, 11–12.

18. Jacques Lacan, *Seminar I: Freud's Papers on Technique*, ed. Jacques-Alain Miller, trans. John Forrester (New York: Norton, 1988), 141.

19. For an excellent discussion of challenges to the traditional humanism of the architectural window, see Thomas Keenan, "Windows: of vulnerability," in *The Phantom Public Sphere*, ed. Bruce Robbins (Minneapolis: U of Minnesota P, 1994), 121–41. See also Colomina, *Privacy and Publicity*, esp. 80–82, 234–38, and 283 ff. An earlier discussion of windows and mirrors can be found in Diana Agrest, "Architecture of Mirror/Mirror of Architecture," in *Architecture from Without: Theoretical Framings for a Critical Practice* (Cambridge, Mass.: MIT P, 1991), 139–155.

20. Lacan, *Seminar I*, 215. See also 78.

21. Jacques Lacan, "The Mirror Stage as Formative of the Function of the I as Revealed in Psychoanalytic Experience," in *Écrits*, trans. Alan Sheridan (New York: Norton, 1977), 2.

22. Mikkel Borch-Jacobsen, *Lacan: The Absolute Master*, trans. Douglas Brick (Stanford: Stanford UP, 1991), 59.

23. *The Wolf Man, by the Wolf Man*, ed. Muriel Gardiner (New York: Noonday, 1991), 139. Sergei Pankeiev also takes note, as all Freud's patients did, of the many objects in the room: "Here were all kinds of statuettes and other unusual objects, which even the layman recognized as archeological finds from ancient Egypt. Here and there on the walls were stone plaques representing various scenes of long-vanished epochs. . . . Freud himself explained his love for archeology in that the psychoanalyst, like the archeologist in his excavations, must uncover layer after layer of the patient's psyche, before coming to the deepest, most valuable treasures" (139). For more on the dominance of the archeological metaphor in Freud's work, see Donald Kuspit, "A Mighty Metaphor: The Analogy of Archaeology and Psychoanalysis," in *Sigmund Freud and Art*, 133–51.

24. H.D., *Tribute to Freud* (New York: McGraw-Hill, 1975), 132. Hereafter, abbreviated "TF" and cited in the text. H.D.'s autobiographical account of her psychoanalytic sessions with Freud provides us with the most complete recollection we have, from the point of view of a patient, of Freud's consulting room. Her memoir offers a narrative counterpart to Engelman's photographs, describing, in surprisingly rich detail, the view from the couch and the sounds, smells, and objects around her.

25. Max Schur, *Freud: Living and Dying* (New York: International UP, 1972), 246.

26. Friedrich Spuhler, *Oriental Carpets in the Museum of Islamic Art, Berlin*, trans. Robert Pinner (London: Faber and Faber, 1988), 10. See also David Sylvester, "On Western Attitudes to Eastern Carpets," in *Islamic Carpets from the Joseph V. McMullan Collection* (London: Arts Council of Great Britain, 1972); Kurt Erdmann, *Seven Hundred Years of Oriental Carpets*, ed. Hanna Erdmann, trans. May H. Beattie and Hildegard Herzog (London: Faber and Faber, 1970); and John Mills, "The Coming of the Carpet to the West," in *The Eastern Carpet in the Western World, from the 15th to the 17th Century*, ed. Donald King and David Sylvester (London: Arts Council of Great Britain, 1983).

For a more detailed treatment of orientalism in the context of Western architecture and interior design, see John M. MacKenzie's *Orientalism: History, Theory and the Arts* (Manchester: Manchester UP, 1995). While many of the older carpets on display in the Vienna exhibition came from mosques, Freud's newer carpets were woven in Northwest Persia, most likely in court workshops.

27. Freud's first office in Berggasse 19 was located on the building's ground floor, beneath the family apartment, in three rooms formerly occupied by Victor Adler. Freud conducted his practice here from 1891 to 1907, when he moved his offices into the back rooms of the apartment immediately adjacent to the family residence.

28. Freud admits toward the end of *Papers on Technique* that "a particularly large number of patients object to being asked to lie down, while the doctor sits out of sight behind them" (12: 139).

29. Luce Irigaray, "The Gesture in Psychoanalysis," in *Between Feminism and Psychoanalysis*, ed. Teresa Brennan (New York and London: Routledge, 1989), 129.

30. Irigaray, 128.

31. Freud's own practice was to take notes from memory after all his sessions that day had been completed. For particularly important dream texts, the patient was asked to repeat the dream until Freud had committed its details to memory (12: 113–14).

32. It is difficult to imagine Freud as entirely a listening ear, the completely passive receptacle of his patients' uncensored speech. Freud's own case histories—from *Dora* (7: 1–122) to "The Psychogenesis of a Case of Homosexuality in a Woman" (18: 145–72)—reveal that, in the therapeutic encounter, he communicated in a more interactive way than this metaphor of doctor as telephone receiver would imply, often challenging and redirecting patients' ostensibly "free" associations.

33. Peter Gay, *Freud: A Life for Our Time* (New York: Anchor Books, 1988), 427.

34. Neil Hertz, "Dora's Secrets, Freud's Techniques," in *In Dora's Case: Freud, Hysteria, Feminism*, eds. Charles Bernheimer and Claire Kahane (New York: Columbia UP, 1985), 229, 234.

35. Avital Ronell, *The Telephone Book: Technology, Schizophrenia, Electric Speech* (Lincoln: U of Nebraska P, 1989), 84. See also 88–96.

36. Psychoanalysis generally reads the space of the doorway in Proustian fashion, as a symbol of change and transition, but in at least one instance the doorway became for Freud a powerful image of arrested

movement. In a letter to his sister-in-law Minna Bernays dated May 20, 1938, written as he anxiously awaited permission to emigrate, Freud compares the experience of impending exile to "standing in the doorway like someone who wants to leave a room but finds that his coat is jammed." Cited in *The Diary of Sigmund Freud, 1929–1939*, trans. Michael Molnar (New York: Charles Scribner's Sons, 1992), 236.

37. Letter to Fliess, June 30, 1896.

38. Jacques Derrida, *Memoirs of the Blind: The Self-Portrait and Other Ruins*, trans. Pascale-Anne Brault and Michael Naas (Chicago and London: U of Chicago P, 1993), 30. Derrida traces a tradition of prints and drawings depicting figures of blindness, including three of the visionary blind men alluded to here: Oedipus, Tiresias, and Tobit.

39. Freud recounts this dream both in the letter to Fliess cited here, dated November 2, 1896, and later, in slightly altered form, in *The Interpretation of Dreams* (4: 317–18). See also Freud's analysis of another deathbed dream, "Father on his death-bed like Garibaldi" (5: 427–29).

40. Didier Anzieu, *Freud's Self-Analysis*, trans. Peter Graham (Madison, Conn.: International UP, 1986), 172.

41. Freud discontinued the practice in 1904. See Anzieu, 64.

42. Lynn Gamwell has noted that "almost every object Freud acquired is a figure whose gaze creates a conscious presence." See her "The Origins of Freud's Antiquities Collection," in *Sigmund Freud and Art*, 27.

43. Engelman, "A Memoir," 137.

44. H.D. saw immediately the significance of Freud's reliquary objects, their mirror relation to the patients who came to Freud every day to be "skillfully pieced together like the exquisite Greek tear-jars and iridescent glass bowls and vases that gleamed in the dusk from the cabinet" (TF, 14).

45. C. Nicholas Reeves identifies this particular piece of ancient cartonnage as a frontal leg covering from the mummy of a woman. This ancient cartonnage, situated at eye level immediately to the left of the consulting room chair, offered Freud ample opportunity to reflect on the meaning of death and resurrection, emblematized by the two lower panels which once again depict Osiris, king of the underworld. For a fuller description of this Egyptian mummy covering and its hieroglyphics, see *Sigmund Freud and Art*, 75.

46. Gamwell, in *Sigmund Freud and Art*, 28.

47. Letter to Jung, April 16, 1909, in *The Freud/Jung Letters*, ed. William McGuire, trans. Ralph Manheim and R.F.C. Hull (Cambridge, Mass.:

Harvard UP, 1988), 218. This story of the haunted steles appears in the same letter in which Freud analyzes yet another episode of his recurrent death deliria (this time, the superstition that he will die between the ages of 61 and 62) and in which he makes reference to what he identifies as "the specifically Jewish nature of my mysticism" (220).

48. On the subject of a patient's transference onto the doctor through the medium of objects, see also Freud's *Papers on Technique*: "[the patient] had been occupied with the picture of the room in which he was, or he could not help thinking of the objects in the consulting room and of the fact that he was lying here on a sofa . . . . [E]verything connected with the present situation represents a transference to the doctor, which proves suitable to serve as a first resistance" (12: 138).

49. Jean Baudrillard, "The System of Collecting," in *The Cultures of Collecting*, 12.

50. Eduardo Cadava, "Words of Light: Theses on the Photography of History," in *Fugitive Images: From Photography to Video*, ed. Patrice Petro (Bloomington and Indianapolis: Indiana UP, 1995), 223 and 224.

51. Roland Barthes, *Camera Lucida: Reflections on Photography*, trans. Richard Howard (New York: Farrar, 1981), 14.

52. Sandor Ferenczi, "Introjection and Transference," in *Sex in Psychoanalysis* (New York: Basic Books, 1950), 41.

Chapter 3

1. Helen Keller, *Midstream: My Later Life* (Garden City, NY: Doubleday, 1929), 184. Hereafter cited in the text as *M*.

2. Helen Keller, *The Story of My Life* (NY: Penguin, 1988), xiii. Orig. pub. 1902. Hereafter cited in the text as *S*.

3. Michael Anagnos, *Helen Keller: A Second Laura Bridgman*, 56th Annual Report of the Perkins Institution and Massachusetts School for the Blind, 1888, 10–14. Cited in Dorothy Herrmann, *Helen Keller: A Life* (New York: Alfred A. Knopf, 1998), 64. Keller's unusual life has produced a host of biographies, most of which advance the myth of Keller as a modern-day saint. The two notable exceptions to this trend are Joseph P. Lash's impressively detailed *Helen and Teacher: The Story of Helen Keller and Anne Sullivan Macy* (Reading, Mass.: Addison-Wesley, 1980) and Dorothy Herrmann's lively and informed *Helen Keller: A Life*, cited above. While much of the same material appears in both biographies, I have chosen, for ease of reference, to cite the more current Herrmann biography wherever there is overlap.

4. Georgette Leblanc, *The Girl Who Found the Bluebird* (New York: Dodd and Mead, 1914), 40.

5. Helen Keller, *Teacher* (Garden City, New York: Doubleday and Company, Inc., 1955), 99, 37, and 66. Hereafter cited in the text as *T*.

6. Books as different as Martin Jay's compendious *Downcast Eyes: The Denigration of Vision in Twentieth-Century French Thought*, Moshe Barasch's breezy *Blindness: The History of a Mental Image in Western Thought*, and Jacques Derrida's elegant *Memoirs of the Blind: The Self-Portrait and Other Ruins* all tend to center their philosophical critiques of Western ocularcentrism on the failures or insufficiencies of the eye instead of on the productive powers of the other sense organs. Constance Classen makes a similar point in *The Color of Angels* (New York: Routledge, 1998), where she argues that the deconstruction of ocularcentrism focuses "on the absence of vision, rather than on the presence of non-visual experience." A theorist like Martin Jay, Classen notes, endorses the undoing of modernity's continued fetishism of the eye, but he does so by recommending a "multiplication of a thousand eyes" rather than an epistemological shift to another sensory organ (138). See Jay's *Downcast Eyes: The Denigration of Vision in Twentieth-Century French Thought* (Berkeley: U of California P, 1993), Moshe Barasch's *Blindness: The History of a Mental Image in Western Thought* (New York and London: Routledge, 2001), and Jacques Derrida's *Memoirs of the Blind: The Self-Portrait and Other Ruins*, trans. Pascale-Anne Brault and Michael Naas (Chicago: U of Chicago P, 1990).

7. Keller, too, saw Sullivan as an Orpheus figure in her life, noting in her tribute to Sullivan how touched she was by her teacher's "faith and constancy that reclaimed me, another Eurydice, from the Plutonian shades of dark silence" (*T* 53). The irony, unremarked by Keller, is that Orpheus in fact failed to reclaim Eurydice from the dark silence, sending her, with a single glance, back into the depths of the underworld.

8. See Jacques Lacan's "The Function and Field of Speech and Language in Psychoanalysis," *Écrits: A Selection*, trans. Alan Sheridan (London: Tavistock, 1977), 30–113, and Ferdinand de Saussure's *Course in General Linguistics*, ed. Jonathan Culler, trans. W. Baskin (London: Fontana, 1974).

9. Ellie Ragland-Sullivan, "The Symbolic," in *Feminism and Psychoanalysis*, ed. Elizabeth Wright (Oxford: Basil Blackwell, 1992), 421.

10. Keller had her eyes surgically removed and replaced with prostheses shortly before going on the lecture circuit, in order to make herself

more presentable to a public audience. Not realizing that Keller's eyes were artificial, reporters routinely commented on her "big, wide, open, blue eyes," eyes that "glowed as radiantly as a girl of twenty." DH 181 and 309.

11. Kaja Silverman, *The Acoustic Mirror: The Female Voice in Psycho-analysis and Cinema* (Bloomington and Indianapolis: Indiana UP, 1988). In an earlier book Silverman notes that "the images that figure so centrally in the imaginary register exceed any strictly specular defini-tion," adding that "they can be generated by many other sources." See *The Subject of Semiotics* (Oxford: Oxford UP, 1983), 159. In one of the few scholarly essays on Helen Keller, Jim Swan rightly takes Lacan to task for ignoring the importance of touching, holding, rocking, and other kinesthetic pleasures in the formation of infantile perception and subject formation. See "Touching Words: Helen Keller, Plagiarism, Au-thorship," in *The Construction of Authorship: Textual Appropriation in Law and Literature*, eds. Martha Woodmansee and Peter Jaszi (Durham and London: Duke UP, 1994), 57–100.

12. For more on touch as a sensory system, see Diane Ackerman's *A Nat-ural History of the Senses* (New York: Vintage Books, 1990), 67–123.

13. Maurice Merleau-Ponty, *Phenomenology of Perception*, trans. Colin Smith (London and New York: Routledge, 1962), 316.

14. Merleau-Ponty invokes Keller in his refutation of Specht's theory of the organic unity of the five senses, wondering whether one must agree with the German phenomenologist that "the sonata which I hear is the same one as Helen Keller touches, and the man I see is the same one as the blind painter paints" (*Phenomenology of Perception*, 230).

15. The two genres of autobiography and phenomenology dovetail neatly on the question of experience. In fact, the philosophical practice of phenomenology does not merely sit well with the literary genre of auto-biography; its methodological analysis of experience requires it. What draws Keller to autobiography is the same impulse that draws many of her contemporaries to phenomenology: the opportunity each affords to explore, in Merleau-Ponty's words, "space, time and the world as we 'live' them" (*Phenomenology of Perception*, vii).

16. John Macy, a socialist and literary critic at Harvard, married Annie Sullivan in 1905, having served for several years as an editorial assis-tant to Keller. After living sporadically with Sullivan and Keller in their Wrentham, Massachusetts home, Macy finally left the household for

good nine years later, complaining that the two women had, from the beginning, been in league against him. See DH 178 ff. and Lash 394 ff.

17. Helen Keller, *The World I Live In* (New York: The Century Company, 1908), 64. Hereafter cited in the text as *W*.

18. Maurice Merleau-Ponty, *The Visible and the Invisible* (Evanston: Northwestern UP, 1968), 133–34.

19. Luce Irigaray, *An Ethics of Sexual Difference*, trans. Carolyn Burke and Gillian C. Gill (Ithaca: Cornell UP, 1993), 161, 170.

20. Keller's hands provide a suggestive metaphor for rethinking ethics in the twenty-first century. In place of the Levinasian face based on the remoteness of vision, Keller's hands offer a different model of ethics based on the proximity of touch. How would our understanding of ethics change if we shifted from the distance senses of sight and sound to the contact senses of touch, taste, and smell?

21. Elsewhere Keller comments that "hearing is the deepest, most humanizing, philosophical sense man possesses" (*M* 115).

22. See Annie Sullivan's letter to Sophia Hopkins, March 20, 1887, in which Sullivan describes Keller's transformation from wild "creature" and "savage" into "gentle child," cited in DH 44. Keller deemed her early speech lessons a complete failure. Though she did on occasion attempt to communicate orally, a translator was still required, since most listeners found her speech incomprehensible.

23. Cited in Lash, 77. The report of Keller's cousin, who recalled that to learn the function of the vocal chords it was necessary for Keller frequently to "put her sensitive fingers in Teacher's mouth, sometimes far down her throat, until Teacher would be nauseated" (DH 77), suggests that the labor of learning speech was a far more invasive, and far more intimate, process than the more sanitized story Keller and Sullivan routinely re-enacted on stage for the public.

24. *Helen Keller's Journal: 1936–1937* (Garden City, New York: Doubleday, 1938), 243. Hereafter cited in the text as *J*.

25. See Clifford Edward Clarke Jr., *The American Family Home: 1800–1960* (Chapel Hill and London: The U of North Carolina P, 1986), 132–35, 163–69.

26. American Foundation for the Blind, Press Release, November 8, 1939.

27. Annie Sullivan to Michael Anagnos, March 1889, cited in DH 65.

28. Cameron Clark, Architect, List of Alterations for Arcan Ridge II (January 17, 1947). While most of Clark's commissions were residential

dwellings, he is perhaps better known in New York City for his design of the Harlem and East River Drives Underpass and the redevelopment of the Brooklyn Bridge area.

29. Cameron Clark to Helen Keller, November 20, 1939.

30. Charles A. Riley II, for example, identifies Wright as the most important influence on the contemporary design of barrier-free living. See Riley's *High-Access Home: Design and Decoration for Barrier-Free Living* (NY: Rizzoli, 1999), especially 31–6.

31. In a 1956 memoir about Keller, the writer Van Wyck Brooks provides a thorough inventory of the gifts bestowed on Keller after the fire by friends and admirers in Japan: "The rooms are furnished with inlaid tables, lamos, trays, boxes, chests, Satsuma pieces, ornaments by the greatest ceramist in Japan, carved ivory figures, prints, an imperial picnic kit of lacquer and gold, gifts from a Shinto priest and an incense-burner, inlaid with gold and silver, presented by the Emperor of Japan." *Helen Keller: Sketch for a Portrait* (NY: E.P. Dutton & Co., Inc., 1956), 142–3. Nella Brady, another intimate of the Keller household, insisted that Polly Thompson never recovered from the fire, finding the new furniture and possessions poor replacements for the originals.

32. For more on Keller's friendship with the artist Jo Davidson, see Van Wyck Brooks, 122–32, or Davidson's own memoir, *Between Sittings* (New York: The Dial P, 1951).

33. The French government granted Keller permission to touch the sculptures in the Louvre, where she examined Rodin's "The Thinker," and perhaps "Winged Victory" as well. The Italian government went so far as to erect elaborate scaffolding to permit Keller to explore by hand Michelangelo's *David*. Pictures of Keller "seeing" the most famous statues in the world make up a surprisingly large percentage of the more than two thousand photographs in the American Foundation for the Blind's Helen Keller Archive. One might note here as well Keller's own comment to Alexander Graham Bell on why a man would never wish to marry her: "I should think it would seem like marrying a statue" (*M* 134).

34. Friedrich A. Kittler, *Gramophone, Film, Typewriter*, trans. Geoffrey Winthrop-Young and Michael Wutz (Stanford, CA: Stanford UP, 1999), 16.

35. Walter Benjamin, "The Work of Art in the Age of Mechanical Reproduction" (1936), in *Illuminations*, ed. Hannah Arendt, trans. Harry Zohn (New York: Schocken P, 1969), 223. Because aura, as Benjamin

defines it in this essay, is "a unique phenomenon of a distance" (243), it evaporates on touch. Touch dissolves aura, disintegrating it on contact.

36. *The Story of My Life* is dedicated "To Alexander Graham Bell, who has taught the deaf to speak and enabled the listening ear to hear speech from the Atlantic to the Rockies."

37. Keller's usurpation of the traditional function of the telephone ironically may have saved her from McCarthy's Communist witch-hunts in the fifties. Keller, a socialist and a pacifist who read Marx and Engels in German Braille and even joined the Industrial Workers of the World on the eve of the first World War, was well known for her radical politics but remained beyond the reach of the FBI, which found it too difficult to place her under surveillance. Neither phone tapping nor electronic eavesdropping could break the code of manual spelling, Keller's chief mode of domestic communication. Keller's surviving public addresses, including "Menace of the Militarist Program" (New York City, December 19, 1915), "Strike Against War" (New York City, January 5, 1916), and "Onward, Comrades!" (New York City, December 31, 1920), can be found in Lois J. Einhorn's *Helen Keller, Public Speaker* (Westport, Connecticut: Greenwood P, 1998). For further insight into Keller's socialist politics, see *Helen Keller: Her Socialist Years*, ed. Philip S. Foner (New York: International, 1967).

38. There is no evidence that Arcan Ridge had a television set, even for Polly Thompson who might have found it a welcome form of entertainment. To Keller, television's dialogue and sound effects might well have been jarring to the hand, a confusing cacophony of nonrhythmic vibrations.

39. Rudolf Arnheim, "In Praise of Blindness," in *Radiotext(e)*, ed. Neil Strauss (New York: Semiotext(e), 1993), 22. Gaston Bachelard makes a similar point in *The Right to Dream*, observing that the radio "needs no face" since in radio "the individual cannot be seen and can himself see no one." See Bachelard's "Reverie and Radio" in *Radiotext(e)*, 220, 221.

40. Upton Sinclair, "Mental Radio," in *Radiotext(e)*, 323 and 321. On Keller and Sullivan's interest in clairvoyance and telepathy, see DH 308.

41. See Kittler, 183, 203, ff.

42. Kittler, 208–21.

43. Nella Braddy, *Anne Sullivan Macy: The Story Behind Helen Keller* (Garden City, NY: Doubleday, 1933), 223. In a letter to George Frisbie

Hoar on November 25, 1901, when John Macy was devoting long hours to assisting Keller in the composition of her first memoir, Keller identifies the typewriter, and not Macy, as her "right hand man." See appendix to *S*, 213.

44. Martin Heidegger, *Parmenides*, trans. André Schuwer and Richard Rojcewicz (Bloomington: Indiana UP, 1992), 86.

45. About this same time, a new group of popular jokes emerged, each beginning "How do you drive Helen Keller crazy?" Interestingly, the answers (rearrange the furniture; give her a screen door to read; put the door knobs on the wall) all exploit deeply rooted human fears of the domestic interior as a site of uncanny defamiliarization, spatial disorientation, and bodily injury.

46. In a personal note to an electrical engineer, Keller confided that her greatest fear was entering Polly Thompson's bedroom and finding her housemate dead (Letter to Mr. A. F. Brooks, October 20, 1952). To assuage Keller's anxiety, the engineer invented a device called the "telerapid," a special telephone that would allow Keller to contact an operator in the event of Thompson's sudden injury or demise. When the time came to use the telerapid, which may well have been located on the second floor, Keller was afraid of leaving Thompson, for fear she would be unable to find her way back to her.

47. Gaston Bachelard, *The Poetics of Space* (Boston: Beacon P, 1964), 7. Orig. pub. 1958.

48. Keller insists that, in comparison to the fires of air raids, crematoriums, and atomic bombs, her own "small conflagration" is nothing (*T* 32).

49. Bachelard, 7–8 and 35.

50. Keller's words are recounted by Lilli Palmer in *Change Lobsters, and Dance* (New York: Macmillan, 1975), cited in DH 297.

Chapter 4

1. *Remembrance of Things Past* (New York: Vintage Books, 1982), VII: 905. This chapter follows the Pléiade edition translated by C.K. Scott Moncrieff and later revised by Terence Kilmartin, although, like most scholars, I prefer the translation *In Search of Lost Time* to Moncrieff's *Remembrance of Things Past*. Individual volumes will be designated by their French titles, with internal citations attributed by volume number: *Du côté de chez Swann* (I), *A l'ombre des jeunes filles en fleurs* (II), *Le Côté de Guermantes* (III), *Sodome et Gomorrhe* (IV), *La Prisonnière* (V), *Albertine disparue* (VI), and *Le Temps retrouvé* (VII).

2. Georges Poulet, *Proustian Space*, trans. Elliott Coleman (Baltimore and London: Johns Hopkins UP, 1977), 106, 16. Poulet's argument for the salience of space is particularly noteworthy when one remembers, as Malcolm Bowie does, that "time . . . has seemed to many admirers of the book to be so clearly its main concern that other candidates for this office have scarcely been worth considering." See *Proust among the Stars* (New York: Columbia UP, 1998), 31.

3. The Comtesse de Noailles's preference for cork as the most effective material for sound insulation appears to have inspired Proust to line his own walls with cork. In the Musée Carnavalet, furniture of the Comtesse de Noailles's bedroom is displayed close by Proust's more fa-mous reconstructed bedroom from rue Hamelin, encouraging direct comparisons between the two.

4. Roger Shattuck, *Proust's Way: A Field Guide to In Search of Lost Time* (New York and London: W. W. Norton and Company, 2000), xx; William Sansom, *Proust and His World* (New York: Charles Scribner's and Son, 1973); Jean-Yves Tadié, *Marcel Proust: A Life*, trans. Euan Cameron (New York: Viking, 2000).

5. Richard Bales, Introduction to *The Cambridge Companion to Proust* (Cambridge: Cambridge UP, 2001), 1.

6. George Painter, in his popular two-volume *Marcel Proust: A Biography* (London: Chatto and Windus, 1959 and 1965), relies perhaps the most heavily on Proust's fiction for biographical information, a method Jean-Yves Tadié sternly criticizes in his own biography, which makes far fewer direct analogies between novel and life. Interestingly, Tadié himself quotes a line from Proust's early novel *Jean Santeuil* as the fac-tual basis of his later claim that Proust "could only write about 'what he himself had experienced'" (276). For biographical information, I draw in this chapter mainly, though not exclusively, from the Tadié vol-ume, the most scholarly and complete of the many Proust biographies.

7. Walter Benjamin, *Illuminations*, ed. Hannah Arendt, trans. Harry Zohn (New York: Schocken Books, 1969), 201, 212.

8. *Correspondance de Marcel Proust*, ed. Philip Kolb, 21 vols. (Paris: Plon, 1970–93). Letter from Henri Bergson, September 30, 1920 (19: 492). All translations from the Proust correspondence are my own.

9. Hannah Arendt, *Antisemitism: Part One of The Origins of Totalitari-anism* (New York: Harcourt Brace & Company, 1951), 80.

10. Paul de Man, *Allegories of Reading: Figural Language in Rousseau, Nietzsche, Rilke, and Proust* (New Haven and London: Yale UP, 1979), 59.

11. The most recent case in point is Edward Hughes's "Proust and Social Spaces," which challenges the dominant critical view of the novel as privileging interior memory and private self-reflection over social intercourse and public conversation. In Bales, *The Cambridge Companion to Proust*, 151–67. For Proust's thoughts on *le roman introspectif*, see his Letter to André Lang, October 1921 (20: 497). "What appears to be exterior," Proust writes in this letter, "we discover within ourselves."

12. Deborah L. Silverman, *Art Nouveau in Fin-de-Siècle France: Politics, Psychology, Style* (Berkeley: U of California P, 1989), 79. For more on the modern city as a sensory stimulant, see Walter Benjamin's *The Arcades Project*, trans. Howard Eiland and Kevin McLaughlin (Cambridge, Mass.: The Belknap P of Harvard UP, 1999), and Susan Buck-Morss's *The Dialectics of Seeing* (Cambridge, Mass.: The MIT P, 1989).

13. Shelley Rice, in *Parisian Views* (Cambridge, Mass.: MIT, 2000), argues that "the crisis of Haussmannization," from which the French have still not recovered, not only ruptured the space of the city but suspended time as well (19). It is this spatial and temporal loss that signals the onset of what we now call modernism, and that offers a more historical reading for Proust's search for lost time.

14. Sharon Marcus, *Apartment Stories: City and Home in Nineteenth-Century Paris and London* (Berkeley: U of California P, 1999), 138–40.

15. François Loyer, *Paris: Nineteenth Century Architecture and Urbanism*, trans. Charles Lynn Clark (New York: Abbeville P, 1988), 238, 251.

16. Loyer notes that the inner façade was so closely modeled after the outer façade that it was relatively easy to confuse the front and back of a Haussmann building (261).

17. One late-night visitor to Proust's apartment describes the building's entrance hall as "sordid" and the stairwell as cast "in darkness." See Violet Schiff's "A Night with Proust," in *London Magazine* 9.56, cited in Ronald Hayman, *Proust: A Biography* (New York: HarperCollins, 1990), 445.

18. Julia Kristeva, *Time and Sense: Proust and the Experience of Literature*, trans. Ross Guberman (New York: Columbia UP, 1996), 183.

19. Céleste Albaret, *Monsieur Proust*, ed. Georges Belmont (New York: McGraw-Hill, 1973), 117.

20. For a more sustained reading of the ambiguous position of servants within the bourgeois household, see Michelle Perrot's "Roles and

Characters," in *A History of Private Life*, Vol. 4, ed. Michelle Perrot (Cambridge, Mass.: Belknap P of Harvard UP, 1990), esp. 232–39.

21. The Proust family occupied several apartments in Paris, all in the eighth arrondissement. Born on July 10, 1871 in his uncle Louis Weil's apartment on 96 rue La Fontaine, Proust spent the first two years of his life at 8 rue Roy before moving to 9 boulevard Malesherbes, the family residence from 1873 to 1900. The next six years were spent at 45 rue de Courcelles, where Proust's father died in 1903 and his mother in 1905. One of Proust's motivations for moving to 102 boulevard Haussmann was to remain in the same neighborhood he grew up in, just blocks away from the family apartments on boulevard Malesherbes and rue de Courcelles. Proust's final two apartments, on 8 bis, rue Laurent Pichat and 44 rue Hamelin were both in the sixteenth arrondissement, still within walking distance of Proust's former homes. It should be noted that Proust himself was never much of a walker; he was an anti-flâneur, one who "always traveled about in taxis and never walked except on carpets and parquets" (Albaret 85).

22. Today visitors to the Proust apartment in what is now the *Banque SNVB* will see a very different physical interior. The wall between landing and vestibule has been entirely removed, as have the walls between the vestibule and dining room and between the small and large drawing rooms. The original elevator shaft in the main stairwell remains, while a second elevator has been added to the small courtyard space to the side of the vestibule. The bedroom has also undergone alterations: two new doors on either side of the fireplace connect the room to the building adjoining it, while the two original main doors to the bedroom may have been narrowed. A large mirror has been installed over the fireplace mantel, but the fireplace itself, along with the parquet floor, is original to the building. In a 1996 restoration, the four walls (but not the ceiling) of Proust's bedroom were lined with cork, adding a Proustian touch to a space currently used as a bank reception room.

23. The lengthening of the Proustian line may be read as Haussmannian in theory only. In actuality, the experience of reading Proust's expansive, sometimes meandering prose slows readers down, sends us down blind alleys, and in general impedes our rapid circulation through the narrative by-ways of a text that repeatedly circles back on itself. The shape and tempo of the novel resemble more accurately a combination of old and new Paris, the city of both open boulevards and narrow side streets that defined the eighth arrondissement of Proust's childhood.

24. Letter to Madame Catusse, October 1906 (6: 233). In this same letter Proust writes: "I could not decide to go live without transition in a house that Mama would not have known, and so I have sublet, for this year, my uncle's old apartment in the house at 102 boulevard Haussmann where I sometimes dined with Mama, and where I saw my uncle die in the chamber that will be my own."

25. Letter to Madame Catusse, December 12, 1906 (6: 326).

26. Sansom, 63; White, *Marcel Proust* (New York: Viking, 1999), 23; and Painter, 2: 283.

27. This anecdote is difficult to confirm, based on a story told by the grandsons of Madame Arthur Baignères, as reported to Philippe Jullian. See Jullian's *Oscar Wilde*, trans. Violet Wyndham (NY: Viking, 1969), 241–42. Tadié gives the story some credence (124), while William Carter reads it as apocryphal. See Carter's *Marcel Proust: A Life* (New Haven: Yale UP, 2000), 126.

28. Letter from Robert de Montesquiou, August 1905 (5: 317).

29. Letter to Madame Catusse, December 12, 1906 (6: 325).

30. On the significance of the bibelot for nineteenth-century French writers, see Janell Watson, *Literature and Material Culture from Balzac to Proust* (Cambridge: Cambridge UP, 1999), and Didier Maleuvre, *Museum Memories: History, Technology, Art* (Stanford: Stanford UP, 1999).

31. Odette's changing fortunes are reflected in the novel through her changing taste in furniture. After her marriage to Swann and the suspension of her life as a coquette, Odette replaces her Chinese dragons with Louis XV garlands. "The Far East," the narrator quips, "was retreating more and more before the invading forces of the eighteenth century" (II: 662).

32. White, 9, 28, and 82.

33. Tadié, 314, 83.

34. In *Antisemitism* Hannah Arendt analyzes, through a reading of Proust's novel, the attractiveness of both Jews and homosexuals to a jaded Parisian salon society "constantly on the lookout for the strange, the exotic, the dangerous" (82).

35. Albaret insists that if Proust's live-in male secretaries, or anyone else for that matter, had been secretly entering Proust's bedroom, her acute "sixth sense" would have detected their comings and goings (186). There has never been scholarly consensus on Proust's sexual identity. George Painter's identification of Proust as a "doomed homosexual"

with "a buried heterosexual boy" deep inside him struggling to get out (1: 50) is rightly criticized for its judgmentalism by J. E. Rivers in *Proust and the Art of Love: The Aesthetics of Sexuality in the Life, Times, and Art of Marcel Proust* (New York: Columbia UP, 1980). Rivers, nevertheless, also insists in the end on the importance of Proust's infatuation with women, concluding that Proust was "homosexually oriented" but not "*a* homosexual" (55). While Proust's homosexuality is no longer in serious critical dispute, scholars continue to seek greater clarity on the exact nature of his sexual practices and desires. Tadié, for example, argues that the core of Proust's sexuality favored voyeurism and masturbation over any form of penetration (70). White notes that Proust's sexual object choice changed over the years from an attraction to gay artistic peers to working-class heterosexuals (124). In *Proust's Lesbianism* (Ithaca and London: Cornell UP, 1999), Elisabeth Ladenson demonstrates that, contrary to what one might assume from a reading of *A la recherche*, the group that sexually interested Proust the least was lesbians (133).

36. Tadié identifies Jacques Bizet (whom Madame Proust eventually forbade her son to see) as the young man most likely to have sexually initiated Proust on Élisabeth Amiot's sofa, although he does not rule out the possibility of an unnamed male cousin (671).

37. Proust may even have helped Le Cuziat purchase the Hôtel Marigny at 11 rue de l'Arcade (Tadié 670), suggesting that Proust knew quite well what he was up to when he donated his aunt's furniture to a man who was already the owner of a public bath.

38. Kristeva, 183.

39. Georg Simmel, "Bridge and Door," in *Rethinking Architecture*, ed. Neil Leach (New York: Routledge, 1997), 67, 68. For more on the opposition between wall and door, see Chapter One.

40. Proust saw the move to boulevard Haussmann as an opportunity to experiment with a more normal daytime schedule; however, unable to work during the daylight hours, Proust rapidly fell back into a routine that he maintained until his death, rising generally around 3 or 4 PM and retiring sometime before dawn.

41. Tadié, 566.

42. Proust also possessed a supply of cheap and dispensable watches, which he could store by the side of the bed and consult at his leisure. The actual timepieces in the bedroom, that daily offered Proust the chance to mark time in the present, held surprisingly little interest for

the novelist, perhaps merely confirming Proust's greater preoccupation with "lost" or "wasted" time.

43. Sansom 82; Philippe Michel-Thiriet, *The Book of Proust*, trans. Jan Dalley (London: Chatto and Windus, 1989), 95.

44. Proust not only learned the importance of depth perception from Vermeer's yellow wall, he gained further lessons in perspective from "those interiors by Pieter de Hooch which are deepened by the narrow frame of a half-opened door" (I: 238). The interest amongst Dutch painters in the walls and apertures of the domestic interior provide an artistic model for the intimate interiors of Proust's novel, which has itself been viewed, by Tadié most prominently, as a Dutch painting in prose (394).

45. Letter to Antoine Bibesco, December 4, 1902 (3: 182).

46. See Avital Ronell, *The Telephone Book: Technology, Schizophrenia, Electric Speech* (Lincoln: U of Nebraska P, 1989). J. Hillis Miller, in a close reading of Proust's telephone passages, highlights the profound cultural dislocation introduced by this radically new voice technology: what "disappears with the telephone is the sense of privacy we used to associate with being safe within the home. The telephone brings the outside in, breaks down the inside/outside dichotomy, and endangers the possibility of private communication." *Speech Acts in Literature* (Stanford, Calif.: Stanford UP, 2001), 190.

47. Letter to Madame Straus, mid-March 1913 (12: 110).

48. In "One-Way Street," Benjamin uses the figure of the deaf ear to identify the open gate of a friend's recently vacated home. *Reflections*, ed. Peter Demetz, trans. Edmund Jephcott (New York: Schocken Books, 1978), 66. Proust draws on the metaphor of the telephone primarily to describe feelings of physical isolation and auditory deprivation. For example, he compares the four lonely months he resided in a sanatorium at Versailles to the experience of living "in a telephone booth." Letter to Madame Catusse, December 12, 1906 (6: 326).

49. "Souvenirs de Gaston Poulet et Amable Massis," *Bulletin de la Société des amis de Marcel Proust* 11 (1961): 424–28; Albaret 329–30. Tadié, like most Proust biographers, throws his support behind Poulet's and Massis's version of the story.

50. The Quiès ear-plugs, which Proust once recommended to Bergson, were kept by his bedside, although Albaret recalls that, because they irritated Proust's ears, these earplugs were only occasionally used (66).

51. "Une Grand-Mère," in *Contre Sainte-Beuve, Précédé de Pastiches et mélanges et suivi de Essais et articles*, ed. Pierre Clarac and d'Yves Sandre (Paris: Gallimard, 1971), 547.

52. René Descartes, *Discourse on Method and Meditations on First Philosophy*, ed. David Weissman (New Haven and London: Yale UP, 1996), 70.

53. Much has been made of Proust's 1919 statement that he originally intended to borrow from cathedral architecture to provide his novel with section titles, like "Portal I Stained Glass Windows of the Apse." A belated response to the critical dismissal of *A la recherche* as a novel without a structure, Proust offers the architecture titles only to immediately dismiss them as "too pretentious." See Proust's Letter to Jean de Gaigneron, August 1919 (18: 359). Subsequent critics have returned to the analogy of the cathedral to continue Proust's defense against those who would find fault with the novel's endlessly expanding shape. See, for example, Bruce Lowery's "La Notion architecturale," in his *Marcel Proust et Henry James* (Paris: Plon, 1964), 237–46; J. Theodore Johnson, Jr.'s "Marcel Proust and Architecture: Some Thoughts on the Cathedral-Novel," in *Critical Essays on Marcel Proust*, ed. Barbara J. Bucknall (Boston: G.K. Hall and Company, 1987), 133–61; and Ellen Eve Frank's "'The Stored Consciousness': Marcel Proust," in her *Literary Architecture: Essays Toward a Tradition* (Berkeley: U of California P, 1979), 117–65.

54. Proust's parents were not particularly devout, and they only occasionally practiced their faiths. Yet Adrien and Jeanne Proust had both their sons baptized and confirmed in the Catholic church, perhaps in an attempt to shield them from the rise in anti-Semitism in late nineteenth-century France. Albaret reports Proust's recollection of his mother's last words to him: "whatever you do, remain a Catholic" (142). On the much under-discussed subject of Proust's conflicted religious identity, see Jonathan Freeman's insightful essay, "Coming out of the Jewish Closet with Marcel Proust," *GLQ* 7:4 (2001): 521–51, and Jean Recanti's *Profils juifs de Marcel Proust* (Paris: Buchet/Chatel, 1979).

55. Letter to Madame Catusse, shortly after October 26, 1906 (6: 262). The portrait of Adrien Proust was painted by Madame Brouardel, the portrait of Jeanne Proust by Madame Beauvais (a professional pseudonym for Madame Charles Landelle).

56. Proust may have aged rapidly from his asthma and other ailments, Tadié writes, but "one look at Blanche's work, and Proust could recap-

ture his youth" (141). Proust's youthfulness was invariably associated with his orientalism. Blanche, for example, describes his own portrait of Proust as the depiction of "the pure oval face of a young Assyrian." See Blanche's *Mes modèles* (Paris: Stock, 1928), 112.

57. Mark Wigley, "Untitled: The Housing of Gender," in *Sexuality and Space*, ed. Beatriz Colomina (Princeton: Princeton Architectural P, 1992), 347, 349.

58. The exercise books were of different kinds. At least thirty-two were covered in black-imitation leather and stored on the chest next to the statue of the infant Jesus. Many more exercise books possessed cardboard covers with canvas bindings and were bought from a stationer on boulevard Haussmann. Some of these cardboard exercise books were used for notes; others were used for the actual manuscript and were assigned numbers. Madame Strauss gave Proust a third set of notebooks distinguished from the others by the "dandyish figures" on their covers. All of these latter notebooks were apparently stored in the rosewood table by Proust's bedside. See Albaret 273–5.

59. Letter to Madame Catusse, December 10, 1906 (6: 317).

60. Letter to Lucien Daudet, November 3, 1917 (16: 280).

61. Letter to André Gide, February 20, 1919 (18: 109).

62. Letter to Madame Catusse, December 10, 1906 (6: 317).

63. Tadié, 31.

64. Letter to Léon Daudet, shortly after July 15, 1921 (20: 403). Even at the end of his life Proust was self-conscious about his nose, both because of a small bump incurred from his childhood accident and because of his chronic nasal drip (Albaret 135). There is no direct evidence to suggest that Proust's embarrassment over his nose derived from any desire to conceal his Jewish identity, even at a time when many Jews in Europe were submitting to cosmetic nose surgery to assimilate into high society or to become less visible to anti-Semites. See Sander Gilman's chapter on "The Jewish Nose" in *The Jew's Body* (New York and London: Routledge, 1991), 169–93.

65. Letter to Madame Catusse, beginning of December 1906 (6: 293).

66. Letter to Georges de Lauris, November 8, 1908 (8: 285).

67. A faulty bedroom fireplace at the apartment on rue Hamelin may have contributed to Proust's death. Two months before his death, Proust worried that he might be inhaling large amounts of carbon dioxide escaping from the broken chimney, a theory he perversely discounted as soon as a doctor confirmed it. See Letter to Armand de Guiche, Sep-

tember 4, 1922 (21: 461), and Letter to Ernst Robert Curtius, September 17 or 18, 1922 (21: 479).

68. "La Personne D'Alphonse Daudet," in *Contre Sainte-Beuve*, 400.

69. Letter to George de Lauris, Sept 26, 1909 (9: 191).

70. Wayne Koestenbaum, *Double Talk: The Erotics of Male Literary Collaboration* (New York and London: Routledge, 1989), 6.

71. White, 75.

72. Benjamin, *Illuminations* 215.

73. White, 72.

74. Mieke Bal, *The Mottled Screen: Reading Proust Visually*, trans. Anna-Louise Milne (Stanford, California: Stanford UP, 1997), see especially 183–237.

75. Other critics have identified the important role photography plays in the composition of *A la recherche*. Georges Poulet remarks that "the only images of themselves Proustian personages are permitted to offer us are similar to those photographs of the same person, of which our albums are full" (26), while Brassai refers to Proust's entire novel as a "gigantic photograph." See Brassai's *Proust in the Power of Photography*, trans. Richard Howard (Chicago and London: U of Chicago P, 2001): xii.

76. M.H. Abrams, *The Mirror and the Lamp: Romantic Theory and the Critical Tradition* (NY: Oxford UP, 1977).

77. Roland Barthes, *Camera Lucida*, trans. Richard Howard (New York: Hill and Wang, 1981), 96.

78. Letter to Madame Catusse, November 5, 1906 (6: 278).

79. Letter to Simone de Caillavet, shortly before January 28, 1910 (10: 40).

80. Letter to Madame Catusse, around November 1910 (10: 215).

81. The rumor that Proust invited a butcher boy at Le Cuziat's brothel to spit on his mother's photograph is difficult to confirm. Albaret denies the story, insisting that photographs of Jeanne Proust never left the bedroom's chest of drawers, save for those times when Proust viewed the photographs in her presence. Brassai, for one, dismisses Albaret's account, although he provides no reason for doing so (77).

82. Bal, 236.

83. Shattuck, in summarizing the plot of the novel, identifies two narrative "intermissions": the third person narration of the love affair between Swann and Odette early in the novel, and the recounting of the marriage of Saint-Loup and Gilberte later in the novel (39–44).

84. John Gaywood Linn, *The Theater in the Fiction of Marcel Proust* (Ohio: Ohio State UP, 1966): 4–5.
85. Maurice Maeterlinck, "*Le tragique quotidien,*" in *Le trésor des humbles* (Paris: Société de Mercure de France, 1896), 187, 188.
86. Jean Jullien, *Le théâtre vivant: essai théorique et pratique* (Paris: Charpentier, 1892): 11.
87. Jean Cocteau, *Opium* (London: Peter Owen, 1990), 94, 98.
88. Proust, nicknamed by Albaret "the magician" (8), learned actual conjuring tricks from a servant, Ernest Forssgren, the son of an amateur magician. Although Proust almost immediately regretted hiring Forssgren, he kept him on for a brief period largely because of Forssgren's knowledge of magic tricks.
89. Jean Cocteau, "*La voix de Marcel Proust,*" in *Poésie Critique*, Vol. 1 (Paris: Gallimard, 1959), 127. If Proust was a ventriloquist, Céleste Albaret was often mistaken for his dummy. After Proust gave up the telephone, Albaret became his public voice, instructed to repeat his messages verbatim. "I carried his voice about with me," Albaret reveals, proudly identifying herself as Proust's "tape recorder." Albaret became so proficient at channeling her employer's quiet voice and precise diction that over the telephone she was frequently mistaken for Proust (216).
90. On the popularity of home theaters, which began to die out in France around the time of Proust's own death, see Mark Girouard's "Putting on a Show" in *Life in the French Country House* (London: Cassell and Company, 2000), 197–217.
91. Adolphe Appia develops his philosophy of the modern theater principally in his *La mise en scène du drame wagnérien* (Paris: L. Cahilley, 1895).
92. See Poulet, 68.
93. The loss of the apartment at 102 boulevard Haussmann, which Proust briefly owned shares in, was partly of Proust's own doing. After Louis Weil died in 1896, he left his apartment to his daughter Jeanne Proust and to his son Georges Weil. Proust and his brother Robert inherited quarter shares of the apartment upon the death of their mother, while Proust's aunt Émilie Weil inherited the other half after the death of her husband Georges. Only a year after occupying the apartment at boulevard Haussmann, Proust agreed to put up his shares, along with those of his brother and aunt, for auction. Foregoing the auction in favor of attending a lecture on architecture hosted by his friend Montesquiou,

Proust was unable to prevent his business-savvy aunt from buying up all the shares of the house and becoming sole owner and landlord of 102 boulevard Haussmann. Proust, who had not payed his rent for several years when his aunt decided to sell the building to a banker in 1919, had no recourse but to move to new quarters at a time when he was physically least able to do so.

94. Proust's household staff, something of an extended family operation, included at the end of his life Céleste Albaret (housekeeper), her husband Odilon (chauffeur), her sister Marie (maid), Odilon's niece Yvonne (typist), and Henri Rochat (secretary). For most of the years of her service at boulevard Haussmann, Albaret (her husband either away at war or motoring clients around France) was the only other person living with Proust in the apartment.

95. The fate of the cork is unknown. Removed from the walls and ceiling at boulevard Haussmann in May 1919, these sheets were rumored to have been sold to a company that manufactured bottle corks, although Albaret insists that the cork sheets were in fact simply placed in storage for possible future use (319).

96. Letter to Jacques Boulenger, March 5, 1921 (20: 116), and Letter to Rosny aîné, shortly after March 8, 1921 (20: 130).

97. Letter to Rosny aîné, shortly after March 8, 1921 (20: 130).

98. Sigmund Freud, "Thoughts for the Times on War and Death" (1915), in *The Standard Edition of the Complete Psychological Works of Sigmund Freud*, trans. James Strachey, Vol. 14 (London: The Hogarth P, 1957), 289.

99. Letter to Lionel Hauser, around April 7, 1921 (20: 163), and Letter to Émile Mâle, June 1, 1921 (20: 297).

100. Robert Proust arranged Proust's arms not in the traditional position for a corpse but in the "working" position they were usually in when Proust was writing his novel (Albaret 360).

101. For more on the postmortem images of Proust, see Jérôme Prieur, *Petit Tombeau de Marcel Proust* (Paris: La Pionnière, 2000). On the general art historical tradition of death-bed portraits, see Emmanuelle Héran, ed., *Le Dernier Portrait* (Paris: Éditions de la Réunion des musées nationaux, 2002).

Bibliography

Abrams, M. H. *The Mirror and the Lamp: Romantic Theory and the Critical Tradition*. NY: Oxford UP, 1977.

Ackerman, Diane. *A Natural History of the Senses*. New York: Vintage Books, 1990.

Adorno, Theodor W. *Kierkegaard: Construction of the Aesthetic*, trans. Robert Hullot-Kentor. Minneapolis: U of Minnesota P, 1989.

———. "Valéry Proust Museum." In *Prisms*, trans. Samuel and Shierry Weber. Cambridge, Mass.: MIT P, 1981.

Agrest, Diana I. *Architecture from Without: Theoretical Framings for a Critical Practice*. Cambridge, Mass.: MIT P, 1991.

Albaret, Céleste. *Monsieur Proust*, ed. Georges Belmont. New York: Mc-Graw-Hill, 1973.

Anderson, Charles. *Emily Dickinson's Poetry: Stairway of Surprise*. New York: Rinehart and Winston, 1960.

Anzieu, Didier. *Freud's Self-Analysis*, trans. Peter Graham. Madison, Conn.: International UP, 1986.

Appia, Adolphe. *La mise en scène du drame wagnérien*. Paris: L. Cahilley, 1895.

Arendt, Hannah. *Antisemitism: Part One of The Origins of Totalitarianism*. New York: Harcourt Brace & Company, 1951.

Ariès, Philippe and Georges Duby, eds. *A History of Private Life*. Vol. 4. Cambridge, Mass.: Harvard UP, 1990.

Arnheim, Rudolf. "In Praise of Blindness." In Strauss. 20–5.

Bachelard, Gaston. *The Poetics of Space*, trans. Maria Jolas. Boston: Beacon P, 1994. Orig. pub. 1958.

———. "Reverie and Radio." In Strauss. 218–22.

Bal, Mieke. *The Mottled Screen: Reading Proust Visually*, trans. Anna-Louise Milne. Stanford: Stanford UP, 1997.

Bales, Richard, ed. *The Cambridge Companion to Proust*. Cambridge: Cambridge UP, 2001.

Barasch, Moshe. *Blindness: The History of a Mental Image in Western Thought*. New York and London: Routledge, 2001.

Barthes, Roland. *Camera Lucida: Reflections on Photography*, trans. Richard Howard. New York: Farrar, 1981.

Baudrillard, Jean. "The System of Collecting." In Elsner and Cardinal. 7–24.

Baumgarten, Murray. "Carlyle and 'Spiritual Optics'." *Victorian Studies* 11.4 (1968): 503–22.

Benjamin, Walter. *Illuminations*, ed. Hannah Arendt, trans. Harry Zohn. New York: Schocken P, 1969.

———. *Reflections*, ed. Peter Demetz, trans. Edmund Jephcott. New York: Schocken Books, 1978.

———. *The Arcades Project*, trans. Howard Eiland and Kevin McLaughlin. Cambridge, Mass.: The Belknap P of Harvard UP, 1999.

Bettelheim, Bruno. *Freud's Vienna & Other Essays*. New York: Vintage, 1991.

Bianchi, Martha Dickinson. *Emily Dickinson Face to Face: Unpublished Letters with Notes and Reminiscences*. Boston and New York: Houghton Mifflin, 1932.

———. *The Life and Letters of Emily Dickinson*. Boston and New York: Houghton Mifflin, 1924.

Bingham, Millicent Todd. *Ancestor's Brocades: The Literary Debut of Emily Dickinson*. New York and London: Harper and Brothers P, 1945.

———. *Emily Dickinson's Home*. New York: Harper and Brothers, 1955.

Blanche, Jacques-Émile. *Mes modèles*. Paris: Stock, 1928.

Borch-Jacobsen, Mikkel. *Lacan: The Absolute Master*, trans. Douglas Brick. Stanford: Stanford UP, 1991.

Bowie, Malcolm. *Proust among the Stars*. NY: Columbia UP, 1998.

Braddy, Nella. *Anne Sullivan Macy: The Story Behind Helen Keller*. Garden City, NY: Doubleday, 1933.

Brassai. *Proust in the Power of Photography*, trans. Richard Howard. Chicago and London: U of Chicago P, 2001.

Brooks, Van Wyck. *Helen Keller: Sketch for a Portrait*. NY: E.P. Dutton & Co., Inc., 1956.

Bryden, Inga and Janet Floyd, eds. *Domestic Space: Reading the Nineteenth-Century Interior*. Manchester: Manchester UP, 1999.

Buckingham, Willis, ed. *Emily Dickinson's Reception in the 1890s: A Documentary History*. Pittsburgh: U of Pittsburgh P, 1989.

Buck-Morss, Susan. *The Dialectics of Seeing: Walter Benjamin and the Arcades Project*. Cambridge, Mass.: MIT P, 1989.

Cadava, Eduardo, "Words of Light: Theses on the Photography of History." In Petro. 220–44.

Cameron, Sharon. *Lyric Time: Dickinson and the Limits of Genre*. Baltimore and London: Johns Hopkins UP, 1979.

Carter, William. *Marcel Proust: A Life*. New Haven: Yale UP, 2000.

Chandler, Marilyn. *Dwelling in the Text: Houses in American Fiction*. Berkeley: U of California P, 1991.

Clark, Clifford Edward, Jr. *The American Family Home, 1800–1960*. Chapel Hill and London: U of North Carolina P, 1986.

Classen, Constance. *The Color of Angels*. New York: Routledge, 1998.

Cocteau, Jean. *Poésie Critique*. Vol. 1. Paris: Gallimard, 1959.

————. *Opium*. London: Peter Owen, 1990.

Cody, John. *After Great Pain: The Inner Life of Emily Dickinson*. Cambridge, Mass.: Harvard UP, 1971.

Colomina, Beatriz. *Privacy and Publicity: Modern Architecture as Mass Media*. Cambridge, Mass.: MIT Press, 1994.

Conway, Hugh. *Called Back*. Chicago and New York: Rand, McNally and Company, 1915. Orig pub. 1883.

Cook, Clarence. *The House Beautiful: Essays on Beds and Tables, Stools and Candlesticks*. New York: Charles Scribner's Sons, 1881.

Cornforth, John. *English Interiors 1790–1848: The Quest for Comfort*. London: Barrie & Jenkins, 1978.

Crary, Jonathan. *Techniques of the Observer: On Vision and Modernity in the Nineteenth Century*. Cambridge, Mass.: MIT P, 1990.

Crimp, Douglas. *On the Museum's Ruins*. Cambridge, Mass.: MIT P, 1993.

Davidson, Jo. *Between Sittings*. New York: The Dial P, 1951.

Decker, Hannah S. *Freud, Dora, and Vienna, 1900*. New York: The Free P, 1991.

Derrida, Jacques. *Memoirs of the Blind: The Self-Portrait and Other Ruins*, trans. Pascale-Anne Brault and Michael Naas. Chicago and London: U of Chicago P, 1993.

Descartes, René. *Discourse on Method and Meditations on First Philosophy*, ed. David Weissman. New Haven and London: Yale UP, 1996.

Dickinson, Emily. *The Complete Poems of Emily Dickinson*, ed. Thomas H. Johnson. Boston: Little, Brown and Company, 1955.

————. *The Letters of Emily Dickinson*, ed. Thomas H. Johnson. Cambridge: The Belknap P of Harvard UP, 1958.

Downing, Andrew Jackson. *The Architecture of Country Houses*. New York: Dover, 1969. Orig. pub. 1850.

Eastlake, Charles L. *Hints on Household Taste in Furniture, Upholstery and other Details*, ed. Charles C. Perkins. Boston: J. R. Osgood and Company, 1872.

Eberwein, Jane Donahue. *Dickinson: Strategies of Limitation*. Amherst: U of Massachusetts P, 1985.

Edel, Leon. *The Modern Psychological Novel*. New York: Grosset and Dunlap, 1964.

Edis, Robert William. *Decoration & Furnishing of Town Houses*. New York: Scribner and Welford, 1881.

Einhorn, Lois J. *Helen Keller, Public Speaker*. Westport, Connecticut: Greenwood P, 1998.

Elsner, John and Roger Cardinal, eds. *The Cultures of Collecting*. Cambridge, Mass.: Harvard UP, 1994.

Elsner, John. "A Collector's Model of Desire: The House and Museum of Sir John Soane." In Elsner and Cardinal. 155–76.

Engelman, Edmund. *Berggasse 19: Sigmund Freud's Home and Offices, Vienna 1938*. New York: Basic Books, 1976.

Erdmann, Kurt. *Seven Hundred Years of Oriental Carpets*, ed. Hanna Erdmann, trans. May H. Beattie and Hildegard Herzog. London: Faber and Faber Limited, 1970.

Erkkila, Betsy. "Emily Dickinson and Class." *American Literary History* 4.1 (1992): 1–27.

Farland, Maria Magdalena. "'That tritest/brightest truth': Emily Dickinson's Anti-Sentimentality." *Nineteenth-Century Literature* 53 (1998): 364–89.

Farr, Judith. *The Passion of Emily Dickinson*. Cambridge, Mass.: Harvard UP, 1992.

Ferenczi, Sandor. *Sex in Psychoanalysis*. New York: Basic Books, 1950.

Foner, Philip S., ed. *Helen Keller: Her Socialist Years*. New York: International, 1967.

Forrester, John. "'Mille e tre': Freud and Collecting." In Elsner and Cardinal. 224–51.

Forty, Adrian. *Objects of Desire: Design and Society Since 1750*. London: Thames and Hudson, 2000.

Foster, Thomas. *Transformations of Domesticity in Modern Women's Writing: Homelessness at Home*. New York: Palgrave Macmillan, 2002.

Frank, Ellen Eve. *Literary Architecture: Essays Toward a Tradition*. Berkeley, Calif.: U of California P, 1979.

Freeman, Jonathan. "Coming out of the Jewish Closet with Marcel Proust." *GLQ* 7:4 (2001): 521–51.

Freud, Ernst L., ed. *Sigmund Freud, Briefe 1873–1939*. Frankfurt-am-Main: S. Fischer, 1960.

Freud, Sigmund. *The Standard Edition of the Complete Psychological Works of Sigmund Freud*, trans. and ed. James Strachey. 24 vols. London: The Hogarth P, 1953–74. (Abbreviated to SE).

———. *The Interpretation of Dreams* (1900), SE 4 and 5.

———. *Psychopathology of Everyday Life* (1901), SE 6.

———. *Fragment of an Analysis of a Case of Hysteria* (1905 [1901]), SE 7: 3–122.

———. *Papers on Technique* (1911–1915 [1914]), SE 12: 85–337.

———. "Thoughts for the Times on War and Death" (1915), SE 14: 273–302.

———. *Introductory Lectures on Psycho-Analysis* (1916–17 [1915–1917]), SE 15 and 16.

———. "Psychogenesis of a Case of Homosexuality in a Woman" (1920), SE 18: 145–72.

———. *The Complete Letters of Sigmund Freud to Wilhelm Fliess: 1887–1904*, trans. and ed. Jeffrey Moussaieff Masson. Cambridge, Mass.: Harvard UP, 1985.

———. *The Freud/Jung Letters*, ed. William McGuire, trans. Ralph Manheim and R.F.C. Hull. Cambridge, Mass.: Harvard UP, 1988.

———. *The Diary of Sigmund Freud, 1929–1939*, trans. Michael Molnar. New York: Charles Scribner's Sons, 1992.

Friedman, Alice T. *Women and the Making of the Modern House: A Social and Architectural History.* New York: Harry N. Abrams, Inc, 1998.

Fryer, Judith. *Felicitous Space: The Imaginative Structures of Edith Wharton and Willa Cather.* Chapel Hill and London: U of North Carolina P, 1986.

Gamwell, Lynn and Richard Wells, eds. *Sigmund Freud and Art: His Personal Collection of Antiquities.* London: Thames and Hudson, 1989.

Gamwell, Lynn. "The Origins of Freud's Antiquities Collection." In Gamwell and Wells. 21–32.

Garbowsky, Maryanne M. *The House without the Door: A Study of Emily Dickinson and the Illness of Agoraphobia.* London and Toronto: Associated UP, 1989.

Gardiner, Muriel, ed. *The Wolf Man, by the Wolf Man.* New York: Noonday, 1991.

Gay, Peter. *Freud: A Life for Our Time.* New York: Anchor Books, 1988.

Gilbert, Sandra and Susan Gubar. *The Madwoman in the Attic: The Woman Writer and the Nineteenth-Century Literary Imagination.* New Haven and London: Yale UP, 1979.

Gilman, Sander. *The Jew's Body.* New York and London: Routledge, 1991.

Girouard, Mark. *Life in the English Country House: A Social and Architectural History.* New Haven and London: Yale UP, 1978.

———. *Life in the French Country House.* London: Cassell and Company, 2000.

Gitelman, Lisa. *Scripts, Grooves, and Writing Machines: Representing Technology in the Edison Age.* Stanford: Stanford UP, 1999.

Goldberg, Jonathan. *Writing Matter: From the Hands of the English Renaissance.* Stanford: Stanford UP, 1990.

Goncourt, Edmond de. *La Maison d'un artiste.* Paris: Charpentier, 1881.

Grazia, Margreta de, Maureen Quilligan, and Peter Stallybrass, eds. *Subject and Object in Renaissance Culture.* Cambridge: Cambridge UP, 1996.

Hansen, Karen V. *A Very Social Time: Crafting Community in Antebellum New England.* Berkeley: U of California P, 1994.

Haweis, Mary Eliza Joy. *Beautiful Houses.* New York: Scribner and Welford, 1882.

Hayden, Dolores. *The Grand Domestic Revolution.* Cambridge, Mass.: MIT P, 1981.

Hayman, Ronald. *Proust: A Biography.* New York: HarperCollins, 1990.

H.D. *Tribute to Freud.* New York: McGraw-Hill, 1975.

Heidegger, Martin. *Parmenides*, trans. André Schuwer and Richard Rojcewicz. Bloomington: Indiana UP, 1992.

———. "Poetically Man Dwells." In Leach. 109–19.

Héran, Emmanuelle, ed. *Le Dernier Portrait.* Paris: Éditions de la Réunion des musées nationaux, 2002.

Herrmann, Dorothy. *Helen Keller: A Life.* New York: Alfred A. Knopf, 1998.

Hertz, Neil. "Dora's Secrets, Freud's Techniques." In *In Dora's Case: Freud, Hysteria, Feminism*, eds. Charles Bernheimer and Claire Kahane. New York: Columbia UP, 1985. 221–42.

Hirschhorn, Norbert and Polly Longsworth. "'Medicine Posthumous': A New Look at Emily Dickinson's Medical Conditions." *The New England Quarterly* 69.2 (1996): 299–316.

Hughes, Edward. "Proust and Social Spaces." In Bales. 151–67.

Irigaray, Luce. "The Gesture in Psychoanalysis." In *Between Feminism and Psychoanalysis*, ed. Teresa Brennan. New York and London: Routledge, 1989. 127–38.

———. *An Ethics of Sexual Difference*, trans. Carolyn Burke and Gillian C. Gill. Ithaca: Cornell UP, 1993.

Jackson, Virginia. *Dickinson's Misery: A Theory of Lyric Reading*. Princeton: Princeton UP, forthcoming.

James, Henry. *The Art of the Novel: Critical Prefaces by Henry James*. New York: Scribner's, 1937.

James, William. *Principles of Psychology*. Vol. 2. New York: Dover Publications, Inc., 1950. Orig. pub. 1890.

Jay, Martin. *Downcast Eyes: The Denigration of Vision in Twentieth-Century French Thought*. Berkeley: U of California P, 1993.

Jen, Gish. "Inventing Life Steals Time; Living Life Begs it Back," *The New York Times*. Monday December 4, 2000, E2.

Johnson, J. Theodore, Jr. "Marcel Proust and Architecture: Some Thoughts on the Cathedral-Novel." In *Critical Essays on Marcel Proust*, ed. Barbara J. Bucknall. Boston: G.K. Hall and Company, 1987. 133–61.

Johnson, Thomas H. *Emily Dickinson: An Interpretive Biography*. Cambridge: Harvard UP, 1955.

Jones, Ernest. *The Life and Work of Sigmund Freud*. 2 Vols. New York: Basic Books, 1953.

Jukes, Peter. *A Shout in the Street: An Excursion into the Modern City*. Berkeley and Los Angeles: U of California P, 1990.

Jullian, Philippe. *Oscar Wilde*, trans. Violet Wyndham. NY: Viking, 1969.

Jullien, Jean. *Le théâtre vivant: essai théorique et pratique*. Paris: Charpentier, 1892.

Keenan, Thomas. "Windows: of vulnerability." In *The Phantom Public Sphere*, ed. Bruce Robbins. Minneapolis: U of Minnesota P, 1994. 121–41.

Keller, Helen. *The Story of My Life*. NY: Penguin, 1988. Orig. pub. 1902.

———. *The World I Live In*. New York: Century Company, 1908.

———. *Midstream: My Later Life*. Garden City, NY: Doubleday, 1929.

———. *Helen Keller's Journal: 1936–1937*. Garden City, New York: Doubleday, 1938.

———. *Teacher*. Garden City, New York: Doubleday and Company, Inc., 1955.

Kelley, Mary. *Private Woman, Public Stage: Literary Domesticity in Nineteenth-Century America*. Oxford: Oxford UP, 1984.

Kittler, Friedrich A. *Gramophone, Film, Typewriter*, trans. Geoffrey Winthrop-Young and Michael Wutz. Stanford: Stanford UP, 1999.

Koestenbaum, Wayne. *Double Talk: The Erotics of Male Literary Collaboration*. New York and London: Routledge, 1989.

Kristeva, Julia. *Time and Sense: Proust and the Experience of Literature*, trans. Ross Guberman. New York: Columbia UP, 1996.

Kuspit, Donald. "A Mighty Metaphor: The Analogy of Archaeology and Psychoanalysis." In Gamwell and Wells. 133–51.

Lacan, Jacques. *Écrits*, trans. Alan Sheridan. New York: Norton, 1977.

———. *Seminar I: Freud's Papers on Technique*, ed. Jacques-Alain Miller, trans. John Forrester. New York: Norton, 1988.

Ladenson, Elisabeth. *Proust's Lesbianism*. Ithaca and London: Cornell UP, 1999.

Laderman, Gary. *The Sacred Remains: American Attitudes Toward Death, 1799–1883*. New Haven and London: Yale UP, 1996.

Lash, Joseph P. *Helen and Teacher: The Story of Helen Keller and Anne Sullivan Macy*. Reading, Mass.: Addison-Wesley, 1980.

Leach, Neil, ed. *Rethinking Architecture*. New York and London: Routledge, 1997.

Leblanc, Georgette. *The Girl Who Found the Bluebird*. New York: Dodd and Mead, 1914.

Leyda, Jay. "Miss Emily's Maggie." *New World Writing: Third Mentor Selection*. New York: New American Library, 1953. 255–67.

———. *The Years and Hours of Emily Dickinson*. 2 vols. New Haven: Yale UP, 1960.

Linn, John Gaywood. *The Theater in the Fiction of Marcel Proust*. Ohio: Ohio State UP, 1966.

Loeffelholz, Mary. *Dickinson and the Boundaries of Feminist Theory*. Urbana and Chicago: U of Illinois P, 1991.

Longsworth, Polly. *Austin and Mabel*. New York: Farrar, Straus, Giroux, 1984.

Lovatt-Smith, Lisa. *Paris Interiors*. Cologne: Taschen, 1994.

Lowery, Bruce. *Marcel Proust et Henry James*. Paris: Plon, 1964.

Loyer, François. *Paris: Nineteenth Century Architecture and Urbanism*, trans. Charles Lynn Clark. New York: Abbeville P, 1988.

Lukacs, John. "The Bourgeois Interior." *American Scholar* 39:4 (Autumn 1970).

MacKenzie, John M. *Orientalism: History, Theory and the Arts*. Manchester: Manchester UP, 1995.

Maeterlinck, Maurice. *Le trésor des humbles*. Paris: Société de Mercure de France, 1896.

Maleuvre, Didier. *Museum Memories: History, Technology, Art*. Stanford: Stanford UP, 1999.

Man, Paul de. *Allegories of Reading: Figural Language in Rousseau, Nietzsche, Rilke, and Proust*. New Haven and London: Yale UP, 1979.

Marcus, Sharon. *Apartment Stories: City and Home in Nineteenth-Century Paris and London*. Berkeley: U of California P, 1999.

Martin, Wendy. *An American Triptypch: Anne Bradstreet, Emily Dickinson, Adrienne Rich*. Chapel Hill: U of North Carolina P, 1984.

Masten, Jeffrey, Peter Stallybrass, and Nancy J. Vickers, eds. *Language Machines: Technologies of Literary and Cultural Production*. New York and London: Routledge, 1997.

Matthews, Glenna. *"Just a Housewife": The Rise and Fall of Domesticity in America*. Oxford: Oxford UP, 1987.

Mayhew, Edgar de Noailles. *A Documentary History of American Interiors: From the Colonial Era to 1915*. New York: Scribner, 1980.

Merleau-Ponty, Maurice. *Phenomenology of Perception*, trans. Colin Smith. London and New York: Routledge, 1962.

———. *The Visible and the Invisible*. Evanston: Northwestern UP, 1968.

Michel-Thiriet, Philippe. *The Book of Proust*, trans. Jan Dalley. London: Chatto and Windus, 1989.

Mill, John Stuart. "What is Poetry?" (1833). *Essays on Poetry*, ed. F. Parvin Sharpless. Columbia, South Carolina: U of South Carolina P, 1976. 3–22.

Miller, J. Hillis. *Speech Acts in Literature*. Stanford: Stanford UP, 2001.

Mills, John. "The Coming of the Carpet to the West." In *The Eastern Carpet in the Western World, from the 15th to the 17th Century*, ed. Donald King and David Sylvester. London: Arts Council of Great Britain, 1983.

Mudge, Jean McClure. *Emily Dickinson and the Image of Home*. Amherst: U of Massachusetts P, 1975.

Painter, George. *Marcel Proust: A Biography*. 2 Vols. London: Chatto and Windus, 1959 and 1965.

Palmer, Lilli. *Change Lobsters, and Dance*. New York: Macmillan, 1975.

Palmer, Phyllis M. *Domesticity and Dirt: Housewives and Domestic Servants in the Unites States, 1920–1945*. Philadelphia, Pa.: Temple UP, 1989.

Petro, Patrice, ed. Fugitive Images: *From Photography to Video*. Bloomington and Indianapolis: Indiana UP, 1995.

Phelps, Elizabeth Stuart. *The Gates Ajar*. Boston: Fields, Osgood, and Company, 1870. Orig. pub. 1868.

Phillips, Elizabeth. *Emily Dickinson: Personae and Performance*. University Park: Pennsylvania State UP, 1988.

Poulet, Gaston and Amable Massis. "Souvenirs de Gaston Poulet et Amable Massis." *Bulletin de la Société des amis de Marcel Proust* 11 (1961): 424–8.

Poulet, Georges. *Proustian Space*, trans. Elliott Coleman. Baltimore and London: Johns Hopkins UP, 1977.

Preminger, Alex and T. V. F. Brogan, eds. *The New Princeton Encyclopedia of Poetry and Poetics*. Princeton: Princeton UP, 1993.

Prieur, Jérôme. *Petit Tombeau de Marcel Proust*. Paris: La Pionnière, 2000.

Proust, Marcel. *Correspondance de Marcel Proust*, ed. Philip Kolb. 21 Vols. Paris: Plon, 1970–93.

———. *Contre Sainte-Beuve, Précédé de Pastiches et mélanges et suivi de Essais et articles*, ed. Pierre Clarac and d'Yves Sandre. Paris: Gallimard, 1971.

———. *Remembrance of Things Past*, trans. C. K. Moncrieff and Terence Kilmartin. Vols 1–3. New York: Vintage, 1982.

Ragland-Sullivan, Ellie. "The Symbolic." In *Feminism and Psychoanalysis*, ed. Elizabeth Wright. Oxford: Basil Blackwell, 1992.

Recanti, Jean. *Profils juifs de Marcel Proust*. Paris: Buchet/Chatel, 1979.

Rice, Shelley. *Parisian Views*. Cambridge, Mass.: MIT P, 2000.

Rich, Adrienne. "Vesuvius at Home: The Power of Emily Dickinson." *On Lies, Secrets, and Silence: Selected Prose 1966–1978*. New York: W. W. Norton and Company, 1979. 157–83.

Riley, Charles A. *High-Access Home: Design and Decoration for Barrier-Free Living*. NY: Rizzoli, 1999.

Rivers, J. E. *Proust and the Art of Love: The Aesthetics of Sexuality in the Life, Times, and Art of Marcel Proust*. New York: Columbia UP, 1980.

Ronell, Avital. *The Telephone Book: Technology, Schizophrenia, Electric Speech*. Lincoln: U of Nebraska P, 1989.

Ryan, Mary P. *The Empire of the Mother: American Writing about Domesticity, 1830–1860*. New York: Institute for Research in History and the Haworth P, 1982.

Rybczynski, Witold. *Home: A Short History of an Idea*. New York: Penguin Books, 1986.

Sansom, William. *Proust and His World*. New York: Charles Scribner's and Son, 1973.

Saussure, Ferdinand de. *Course in General Linguistics*, ed. Jonathan Culler, trans. W. Baskin. London: Fontana, 1974.

Schur, Max. *Freud: Living and Dying*. New York: International UP, 1972.

Seale, William. *The Tasteful Interlude: American Interiors through the Camera's Eye, 1860–1917*, 2nd ed. Nashville, Tenn.: American Association for State and Local History, 1981.

Sewall, Richard B. *The Lyman Letters: New Light on Emily Dickinson and Her Family*. Amherst: U of Massachusetts P, 1965.

———. *The Life of Emily Dickinson*. Cambridge: Harvard UP, 1974.

Shattuck, Roger. *Proust's Way: A Field Guide to In Search of Lost Time*. New York and London: W. W. Norton and Company, 2000.

Silverman, Deborah L. *Art Nouveau in Fin-de-Siècle France: Politics, Psychology, Style*. Berkeley: U of California P, 1989.

Silverman, Kaja. *The Subject of Semiotics*. Oxford: Oxford UP, 1983.

———. *The Acoustic Mirror: The Female Voice in Psychoanalysis and Cinema*. Bloomington and Indianapolis: Indiana UP, 1988.

Simmel, Georg. "Bridge and Door." In Leach. 66–9.

Sinclair, Upton. "Mental Radio." In Strauss. 321–4.

Sloane, David Charles. *The Last Great Necessity: Cemeteries in American History*. Baltimore and London: Johns Hopkins UP, 1991.

Smith, Martha Nell. *Rowing in Eden: Rereading Emily Dickinson*. Austin: U of Texas P, 1992.

Spuhler, Friedrich. *Oriental Carpets in the Museum of Islamic Art, Berlin*, trans. Robert Pinner. London: Faber and Faber, 1988.

St. Armand, Barton Levi. *Emily Dickinson and Her Culture: The Soul's Society*. Cambridge: Cambridge UP, 1984.

Strauss, Neil, ed. *Radiotext(e)*. New York: Semiotext(e), 1993.

Suleiman, Susan. "Bataille in the Street: The Search for Virility in the 1930s." *Critical Inquiry* 21 (Autumn 1994): 61–79.

Swan, Jim. "Touching Words: Helen Keller, Plagiarism, Authorship." In *The Construction of Authorship: Textual Appropriation in Law and Literature*, eds. Martha Woodmansee and Peter Jaszi. Durham and London: Duke UP, 1994.

Sylvester, David. "On Western Attitudes to Eastern Carpets." In *Islamic Carpets from the Joseph V. McMullan Collection*. London: Arts Council of Great Britain, 1972.

Tadié, Jean-Yves. *Marcel Proust: A Life*, trans. Euan Cameron. New York: Viking, 2000.

Thornton, Tamara Plakins. *Handwriting in America: A Cultural History*. New Haven and London: Yale UP, 1996.

Tucker, Herbert F. "Dramatic Monologue and the Overhearing of Lyric." *Lyric Poetry: Beyond New Criticism*. eds. Chaviva Hošek and Patricia Parker. Ithaca and London: Cornell UP, 1985. 226–43.

Vaux, Calvert. *Villas and Cottages*. New York: Harper and Brothers, 1857.

Wardrop, Daneen. *Emily Dickinson's Gothic: Goblin with a Gauge*. Iowa City: U of Iowa P, 1996.

Watson, Janell. *Literature and Material Culture from Balzac to Proust*. Cambridge: Cambridge UP, 1999.

Watson, Rosamund Marriott. *The Art of the House*. London: G. Bell and Sons, 1897.

Weintraub, Jeff and Krishan Kumar, eds. *Public and Private in Thought and Practice: Perspectives on a Grand Dichotomy*. Chicago: U of Chicago P, 1997.

Wharton, Edith and Ogden Codman Jr. *The Decoration of Houses*. New York: C. Scribner's Sons, 1902.

White, Edmund. *Marcel Proust*. New York: Viking, 1999.

Wigley, Mark. "Untitled: The Housing of Gender." In *Sexuality and Space*, ed. Beatriz Colomina. Princeton: Princeton Architectural P, 1992. 327–89.

Winkler, Gail Caskey and Roger W. Moss. *Victorian Interior Decoration: American Interiors, 1830–1900*. New York: Henry Holt, 1986.

Wolff, Cynthia Griffin. *Emily Dickinson*. Reading, Mass.: Addison Wesley, 1988.

Woodmansee, Martha, and Peter Jaszi, eds. *The Construction of Authorship: Textual Appropriation in Law and Literature*. Durham and London: Duke UP, 1994.

Woolf, Virginia. *The Moment, and Other Essays*. New York: Harcourt, Brace, and Company, 1948.

Wright, Gwendolyn. *Building the Dream: A Social History of Housing in America*. Cambridge, Mass.: MIT P, 1981.

Index

Simmel, Georg, 43, 171, 245n.39
Sinclair, Upton, 138
sixth sense, 17, 21, 244n.35
Sloane, David Charles, 228n.56
smell, 17, 19–20, 89, 107, 109,
  115–19, 130–31, 145–46, 151,
  153, 155, 160–61, 191–94, 204,
  215, 221n.33, 231n.24, 237n.20,
  248n.64
Smith, Martha Nell, 225n.29
Soane, John, Sir, 230n.16
sound, 17–20, 49–51, 56–57, 62,
  72, 92–94, 96–97, 100–02,
  107–10, 114–17, 122, 128–29,
  134–35, 138–41, 145, 151, 153,
  155, 158–62, 172, 176–77, 182,
  186, 190, 192, 205–06, 208, 215,
  226n.35, 231n.24, 232n.32,
  236n.36, 237n.20, 237n.21,
  239n.38, 241n.3, 246n.48. *See
  also* deafness
Sphinx, 101
spiritualism, 104, 138, 239n.40
Stallybrass, Peter, 220n.30
St. Armand, Barton Levi, 223n.12
statue, 48, 82–83, 87, 97–100, 103,
  132, 135, 168, 184, 209,
  231n.23, 231n.24, 238n.33,
  248n.58. *See also* antiquities; art
subject and object, 14–17, 36, 72,
  76, 78–81, 83, 85, 87, 94, 97,
  102–03, 105, 111–14, 117–21,
  127, 132, 143, 145, 160, 163–64,
  167, 175, 213–14, 220n.30,
  231n.23
Suleiman, Susan, 74
Sullivan, Anne, 107, 109–11, 118,
  121–26, 128, 133, 136, 138,
  140–43, 148–49, 235n.7,
  236n.16, 237n.22, 237n.23,
  239n.40
Swan, Jim, 218n.10, 236n.11

Tadié, Jean-Yves, 152–53, 241n.6,
  244n.27, 245n.35, 245n.36,
  246n.44, 246n.49, 247n.56

taste, 17, 20, 116, 151, 153,
  163–64, 169, 191–92, 215,
  221n.33, 237n.20, 244n.31
technology, 19, 51–52, 93, 98,
  103–04, 107, 128, 134–48, 178,
  186, 200, 206, 213, 246n.46
telegraph, 128
telephone, 18, 93–95, 135–37, 141,
  146, 158, 178–80, 186, 232n.32,
  239n.37, 240n.46, 246n.46,
  246n.48, 250n.89
television, 137–38, 239n.38
temperature, 88–89, 110, 115, 117,
  119, 130, 160, 193
texture, 88–90, 110, 115, 117,
  119, 129–31, 153, 215. *See also*
  touch
theater, 45–47, 68, 100–01, 107,
  141, 143, 177, 186–87, 203–10,
  213, 228n.63, 237n.23, 249n.83,
  250n.90, 250n.91
Thompson, Polly, 126–27, 132, 134,
  145–46, 148–49, 238n.31,
  239n.38, 240n.46
Thoth, 95
Tiresias, 96, 233n.38
Tobit, 96, 233n.38
Todd, Mabel Loomis, 36, 45–46,
  48, 55, 224n.20, 227n.46,
  227n.51
tomb, 24, 45, 55, 65–68, 79, 85, 94,
  103, 108, 128, 172, 210, 212,
  230n.16. *See also* death
touch, 7–8, 17–20, 78, 90, 107–10,
  112, 116–24, 128–32, 135, 141,
  144–45, 151, 192, 236n.11,
  236n.12, 237n.20, 238n.33,
  239n.35. *See also* texture
transference, 72, 75, 81–82, 93–94,
  102–04, 115, 234n.48
Tucker, Herbert F., 226n.35
Twain, Mark, 111
typewriter, 121, 135, 141–45, 208

uncanny, the, 84, 87, 92, 115,
  240n.45